About the Author

Dr. Sarvottam Kumar is an Associate Professor and Head in the Department of Geography, Dr. Shyama Prasad Mukherjee University (DSPMU), Ranchi in Jharkhand. He obtained his M.A., M.Phil. and Ph.D. degrees from Jawaharlal Nehru University (JNU), New Delhi. He was awarded UGC-JRF Fellowship for his doctoral research work. He not only participated in advance training of ISRO, Dehradun but also framed the curriculum of Diploma in GIS & RS in his working institution, which is still running successfully. He has a teaching experience of more than twenty-five years. He took part as member of syllabus committee in Graduate and Post-graduate Programme several times and he had recently been an active member for preparing the guidelines of NEP in the state of Jharkhand. He has already published one book entitled '*Rural Male Out-Migration*' and his three research papers are also published in different Indian and foreign edited books. And, he has also many articles published in various reputed research journals. He has already supervised Ph.D. research work and ongoing research works are also in way. His areas of academic interest are Population Geography, Settlement Geography and Statistical Methods in Geography.

INFANT MORTALITY AMONG PRIMITIVE TRIBAL GROUPS
A Regional Analysis of Jharkhand

Sarvottam Kumar

CONCEPT PUBLISHING COMPANY PVT. LTD.
NEW DELHI - 110 059

ISBN: 978-93-5594-641-6

First Published 2024

Published and Printed by

Concept Since 1974

Concept Publishing Company Pvt. Ltd.
A/15-16, Commercial Block, Mohan Garden
New Delhi-110059 (India)
T: +91-11-41101460
E: publishing@conceptpub.com, *W*: www.conceptpub.com

Cataloging in Publication--Courtesy: D.K. Agencies (P) Ltd. <docinfo@dkagencies.com>

Sarvottam Kumar, author.
Infant mortality among primitive tribal groups : a regional analysis of Jharkhand / Sarvottam Kumar.
pages cm
Includes bibliographical references and index.
ISBN 9789355946416

1. Infants--Mortality--India--Jharkhand. 2. Jharkhand (India)--Scheduled tribes--Health and hygiene. 3. Jharkhand (India)--Scheduled tribes--Economic conditions. 4. Jharkhand (India)--Scheduled tribes--Social conditions. I. Title.

LCC HB1323.I4S27 2024 | DDC 304.640832 23

Dedicated
In Loving Memory to My Revered Mother
Late Urmila Devi

Foreword

The title of book "Infant Mortality among the Primitive Tribal Groups in Jharkhand" is self-expressive of its theme. This is totally research oriented, painstaking and multidimensional exploration into the undeveloped, uneducated, superstitious and dogmas entrapped lives of the tribal people still living in woods, on the hills and rocky places far from the roads, hospitals, markets and schools, which is a big achievement of scholar Dr. Sarvottam fully dedicated to and sincerely involved into the lives of the primitive people. The kind of approach made in the work and the kind of realism shown cannot be possible unless one identifies himself with these people, becoming a part of their lives as a member in their families. The book is the outcome of a Major Research Project on 'Infant Mortality among the Primitive Tribal Groups in Jharkhand' sponsored by the University Grants Commission of India in which the author is the sole Principal Investigator.

The book endeavours to study the relationship of infant deaths with various demographic and socio-economic variables, responsible for unprecedented level of child deaths. It is observed that high levels of infant deaths are caused by extreme level of poverty, widespread childhood diseases, non-utilization of modern medical facilities, dearth of health facilities, malnutrition, illiteracy among mothers, non-scientific use of tribal and indigenous medicine, poor cleanliness and unhygienic situations, prevailing superstitions about child rearing, non-availability of pure drinking water, poor transportation and lack of communication facilities, delayed breastfeeding, prevalence of single parent family, poor housing designs, heavy liquor consumptions by parents, extreme low level of income, low productivity of land and so on and so forth. It examines all eight primitive tribal groups of the state in a holistic approach, which ultimately portrays the inner weaknesses of society.

It analyses the distribution, growth and concentration of PTGs at district levels on the basis of census data. Furthermore, it concentrates on demographic and socio-economic characteristics, availability of medical and other infrastructural facilities, regional assessments and patterns of infant deaths, health, hygiene and sanitation condition, morbidity among the children and determinants of infant deaths among the primitive tribes in the state on the basis of primary data. The information about location of villages with latitude, longitude and elevation have been incorporated with much care through GPS in this valuable study. The homeland of PTGs is full of stunning landscape, majestic mountains, verdant valleys, serpentine rivers, wonderful waterfalls, lush green forest and exotic wildlife. In fact, it presents variegated vistas of man-environment relationships and demonstrates how the PTGs adapt to the changing environmental conditions and makes an inhospitable habitat to their homeland.

This book is systematically organized and takes into consideration of the latest works done in this particular field. The maps, graphs and diagrams used in the book provide a lucid and meaningful exposition of the concepts. Further again, it is a path breaking methodologically and theoretically, in its examination of the relationship between infant deaths and development. If the suggested strategies such as involvement of local PTGs in medical staffs, spread of health and social awareness among the reproductive age group, amelioration in economic prosperity etc. are not introduced for the PTGs in the state, their population will be reduced dramatically and may be wiped out in near future.

The book is a mirror of the whole of Jharkhand and it will be not only useful and informative for the students and research scholars working on the tribes of Jharkhand; but also guide and enlighten the government agencies and research institutions trying to know and understand the lives of the tribes of state for their ameliorations. The book has provided several practical ways how to change their life, their habits and their centuries old down to earth life style to bring them at par with those of the developed areas. The scholar Dr. Sarvottam has done a great yeoman service to the land and people of Jharkhand by writing this highly realistic, informative and practical guide book in his praiseworthy academic pursuits. The book has been written for the students, research scholars, policy makers and the lovers of Jharkhand, who want detailed information about the infant deaths and their reasons and the ways how to stop them.

Prof. Tapan Kumar Shandilya
Vice-Chancellor
Dr. Shyama Prasad Mukherjee University
Ranchi-834008

Preface

The book is the outcome of a Major Research Project on 'Infant Mortality among the Primitive Tribal Groups in Jharkhand' sponsored by the University Grants Commission of India in which the author was the sole Principal Investigator. It endeavours to study the relationship of infant deaths with various demographic and socio-economic variables, responsible for unprecedented level of child deaths. The research focuses on infant health and mortality and identification of the factors leading to unprecedented demise of children, which requires the interventions and actions that must be scaled up to save lives so that their population cannot be eliminated further. Most foetal, neonatal and post-neonatal deaths can be averted through proven interventions including adequate nutrition, improved hygienic practices, antenatal care, skilled health workers assisting at births, emergency obstetric and new-born care and post-natal visits for the new-borns, delivered through a continuum of care linking households and communities to health systems. Even after crossing the deadline of Millennium Development Goals for universal access to health of children by 2015, the challenges for improving the health of neonates among the PTGs are very critical, which need to be addressed through government interventions and social awareness programmes. Few studies of such exhaustiveness have been taken up in state on infant deaths among the PTGs as this one, which becomes particularly important because it deals with the entire state, which has significantly high primitive rural tribes in its setting. The study has also adopted a balanced geographical approach giving due emphasis on physical setting, origin and evolution, land use types in exhausting details as related to the geographical background, population and socio-economic characteristics. Although it is primarily based on the survey of households, yet micro level analysis of their distributions is fundamentally based on secondary sources of data for Jharkhand. It provides crucial information on the reproductive and child health including socio-economic characteristics of the usual members of households, fertility, family planning, hygiene, sanitation and child deaths in the last three years preceding the survey.

Jharkhand has always been described as a melting pot of races, religions, castes and cultures. On the one hand the colourful and the amazing heterogeneous mosaic of economic affairs are demonstrated in urban way of life whereas the monotonous and rudimentary activities in the rural localities of primitive tribal groups and the rural people are the most deprived, weak and vulnerable sections of the society. Despite achieving a remarkable decline in child deaths in the state as a result of improvement in socio-economic, demographic and family health care factors as well as expansions of medical infrastructural facilities, the level of infant mortality still remains very high in the localities of primitive areas. The state of Jharkhand is a home of over 32 tribal communities out of which eight, namely Mal Paharia, SauriaPaharia, Korwa, Parhaiya, Asur, Birhor, Savar and Birjia are considered as the Primitive Tribal Groups (PTGs) and they are also known as Particularly Vulnerable Tribal Groups (PVTGs) and they lead a distinct lifestyle close to nature but they are poor in all indices of human development. They are also enlisted as endangered and marginal tribes on account of their fast-depleting population and they predominately reside in the interior hilly forest areas, where they lead a very tough life and live-in abject poverty. Due to distant habitation, they have maintained their unique characteristics, which are physical as well as social challenges posed by nature leading to their adaptation to environmental demands. All these bring about changes in their physical, morphological and genetic make up, which sometimes also lead to health problems. They were just about 2.92 lakh in number in 2011 Census, which form about 3.4 per cent of the total tribal population. The primary purpose of this study is to explore an analytical framework to understand the determinant of very high infant mortality from data collected at household and village level. The next objective is to identify their habitations and agglomerations in different geographical regions of the state. Finally, another objective is to develop a theoretical structure of their life style, which leads to very high infant deaths.

I express my sincere gratitude to UGC for the same and to its experts, who went through my Major Research Proposal and whose suggestions gave me further insight for probing the present topic. It represents the first attempt to bring together and interpret the evidences on infant mortality available from one hundred primitive tribal villages studies carried out in all areas of the state. As a result, the book is a valuable addition to the extremely limited literature on this vital subject. I hope, that the information given in this book will immensely help policy makers and programme managers in planning focused policies and programmes. It will be of great help to all those who are working in the area of population and reproductive health of the general population. In fact, this will serve the needs of administrators, planners, academicians, researchers and fill the gap in the study of infant mortality of weaker sections in the state.

My sincere thanks are due to the project fellow Ujjwal Mahato for his willing cooperation and hard work who has prepared the consolidated report of all 100 primitive villages together despite many hardships in the field. I would like to record my deep sense of appreciation to him for carrying out his assignments with competence and responsibility. My sincere thanks are to all the students of University Department of Geography, who have contributed a lot in collections of data, maintaining the quality of data and has made it possible to bring out this publication.

This acknowledgement is not complete without expressing my appreciation of the students like Sunny Asur. At the end, a line of special gratitude to all the respondents who have given their valuable time. My gratitude is also due to the people of primitive tribal groups in Jharkhand for the extraordinary warmth, hospitality and cooperation extended to me without any hesitation. For the practical aspects of map drawing by computer, I am indebted to my colleague, Dr. Surjeet Dutta, who gave me a lot of useful tips and spent his valuable time in explaining some of the basic principles of mapping. I record my heartiest sense of gratitude to him for his technical guidance and all sorts of help in preparation of the map. I also like to acknowledge the valuable help rendered by computer analysist of School of Social Science, JNU, New Delhi, Mr. Verghese for computer data analysis through Statistical Package for Social Science. I owe a deep sense of obligation to librarians of JNU and CSRD Documentation Unit for their constant cooperation and help. Besides this, thanks are also due to librarians of various libraries such as Ratan Tata Library of Delhi School of Economics, BHU Library, National Library, Kolkata, Tribal Research Centre Library of Ranchi, who generally placed the desired materials at my disposal for the preparation of the report.

I wish to extend my sincere thanks to Dr. Yamuna Prasad, who devoted many long hours to go through my manuscripts and his comments and criticisms have been included in the final manuscript. I owe special gratitude to our Vice-Chancellor of DSPMU Ranchi, Prof. Tapan Kumar Shandilya for encouraging me to submit the report of Major Research Project. His valuable suggestions and criticisms of the entire manuscript have greatly improved the quality of this study. Finally, I would like to express my sincere thanks to our previous Vice-Chancellor of DSPMU Ranchi, Prof. S. Narayan Munda, who in his personal capacity took keen interest in academic and administrative aspects of the project and gave me very valuable suggestions from time to time.

I would not have even dared to start the work without the emotional support of my parents. Mere words cannot express my gratitude to Daya and Babuji. I owe a lot to them and they helped me to tackle many impasses. Again, the blessings and supports I got from my family members, were constant sources of inspiration. My wife, Piyushbala extended full cooperation and encouragement at every stage without which this work would not have been possible. Last but not the least, I must thank my son, Marshan and daughter, Mrinalini Vats for their ungrudging sacrifice in the travails of this work. At the end, I take full responsibility for the views put forward and the errors that may occur in the book even in advertently.

Sarvottam Kumar

Contents

List of Tables and Figures

TABLES

FIGURES

List of Abbreviations

AHS	:	Annual Health Survey
ANC	:	Antenatal Care
ARC	:	Acute Respiratory Infection
ASHA	:	Accredited Social Health Activists
CHC	:	Community Healthcare Centres
CMR	:	Child Mortality Rate
CSSM	:	Child Survival and Safe Motherhood
DH	:	District Hospitals
ENMR	:	Early Neonatal Mortality Rate
GDP	:	Gross Domestic Product
HSC	:	Health Sub-Centres
ICDS	:	Integrated Child Development Services
IEC	:	Information, Education and Communication
IFA	:	Iron Folic Acid
IMR	:	Infant Mortality Rate
IPHS	:	Indian Public Health Standards
JSY	:	Janani Suraksha Yojana
LBW	:	Low Birth Weight
LNMR	:	Late Neonatal Mortality Rate
MDG	:	Millennium Development Goals
NFHS	:	National Family Health Survey
NHM	:	National Health Mission
NHP	:	National Health Policy
NMR	:	Neonatal Mortality Rate
NRHM	:	National Rural Health Mission
PHC	:	Primary Health Centres

PMR	:	Perinatal Mortality Rate
PNMR	:	Post-Neonatal Mortality Rate
PTG	:	Primitive Tribal Groups
PVTG	:	Particularly Vulnerable Tribal Groups
RCH	:	Reproductive & Child Health
SBR	:	Still Birth Rate
SDH	:	Sub-Divisional Hospitals
TFR	:	Total Fertility Rate
U5MR	:	Under Five Mortality Rate
UIP	:	Universal Immunization Programme
UNICEF	:	United Nations International Children's Emergency Fund
WHO	:	World Health Organization

Glossary

Antenatal Care: It is the care of pregnant woman, which is usually provided by the health professionals.

Binary Logistic Regression Analysis: The binary logistic regression analysis facilitates in eliciting the effects of several predictor variables, which may be quantitative, categorical or mixture of the two on the response variable, which has only two categories.

Child Mortality Rate (CMR): The child mortality rate is the death of babies, which happens between the first and fifth birthdays.

Child-Woman Ratio: Child-woman ratio is a better indicator of fertility, which measures the ratio between the number of children below the age of 5 years and the women aging between 15-49 years per thousand of reproductive age group.

Chuas: Small springs in a tribal dominated area in which the tribal people collect water for drinking purposes.

Colostrum: It is the first form of milk produced by the mother immediately after the delivery of the new-born. It should not be discarded and all babies should invariably receive it because it is rich in energy, protein, protective antibodies and cellular elements.

Early Neonatal Mortality Rate (ENMR): Those baby deaths, which happens within one week for every thousand live births.

Endogenous Factors: They are related to the formation of foetus in the mother's womb and are biological in nature.

Exogenous Factors: Socio-economic, cultural and environmental factors are considered as exogenous factors, which are more responsible for mortality during post-neonatal period.

Health: It involves the complete spectrum of food habit, intake of nutrient, hygiene, sanitation and medical intervention.

Hygiene: It refers to conditions and practices that help to maintain health and prevent the spread of diseases thereby improves the health of an individual human being and focuses on personal cleaning.

Immunization: Immunization is the essential process for good health of child whereby a child is made immune to an infectious disease typically by the administration of a vaccine.

Infant Mortality Rate (IMR): Late Neonatal Mortality Rate (LNMR): LNMR indicates those baby deaths, which occur between 1 and 4 weeks for every thousand live births.

Live Births: The babies born alive after reproduction from their mother's womb and show any sign of life.

Low Birth Weight: When the weight of baby at birth is below than 2 kg factis, he is recognized as low-birth-weight baby, which often reflects both the mother's nutritional status and the gestation period.

Morbidity: It is the state of being unhealthy for a particular disease or situation, which is considered to be outside the realm of normal well-being and it is often used to describe illness, impairment, or degradation of health.

Neonatal Mortality Rate (NMR): Number of deaths of babies within 28 days for every thousand live births.

Occupation : It refers to a set of activities which predominately engage one's time for primary motive of earning livelihood.

Perinatal Mortality Rate (PMR): It measures the number of late foetal or still birth deaths at or after 7 months of gestation and deaths within the first 7 days for every thousand live births and still births.

Post Neonatal Mortality Rate (PNMR): Deaths of babies from 29 days to the end of the first year per 1,000 live births.

Prelacteal Food: It is the first food given to the new-born before initiating breastfeeding.

Primitive Tribal Groups (PTGs): Schedule tribes having pre-agricultural level of technology, low level of literacy and stagnant or diminishing population. They are also known as Particularly Vulnerable Tribal Groups (PVTG).

Sanitation: It refers to do with the waste we produce through public health conditions related to disposal of human excreta, sewage etc.

Sarna: It is one of the important religions of primitive tribes in Jharkhand wherein people worship nature.

Singbonga and Burubonga: The PTGs worship the sun and the mountain as their important deities and call them as Singbonga and Burubonga respectively.

Stepwise Regression Analysis: It is a method of fitting regression models in which the choice of predictive variables is carried out by an automatic procedure. Its procedure is adopted to obtain an optimum set of independent variables which could explain maximum possible variation in the dependent variables. It enables us to assess the extent of impact of each explaining independent variables upon dependent variables.

Still Birth Rate (SBR): Another measure of reproductive deaths, which happens either in the womb of mother after 20 weeks of gestation period or weight over 500 grams or during labour pain and it is also known as foetal mortality rate, which is of two types: antepartum death and intrapartum death.

U5MR: Death of children below five years of age.

Zero Order Correlation Matrix: A set of variables are created to measure the relationship among these variables in a zero-order correlation matrix and the values of correlation coefficients are presented in the matrix.

1
Introduction

Fertility, mortality and migration are the three important fundamental determinants of population growth. Out of these three determinants, mortality is very important as it declines earlier and fertility follows after a lag, whereas the last one is related to the cultural and economic factors. Fertility and mortality are the two important biological fundamental determinants of population growth. Decline in child mortality, mostly under five years of age is one of the major causes for declining fertility worldwide. Under-five mortality (U5MR) is divided into two groups on the basis of age, viz. infant mortality (0 >1 year of age) and child mortality (1 > 5 year of age). The infant mortality rate is commonly used more than any other measure as a general indicator of socio-economic well-being and of general medical and public health conditions in a country (UNICEF, 2006). It is measured by the total number of deaths of children under the age of one year for every 1000 live births. Despite achieving a remarkable decline in the mortality level in the world, as a result of improvements in socio-economic, demographic and family health care particularly mother and child health care factors as well as scientific and technological advancements in the medical field, the level of infant mortality still remains very high in many developing countries like India. India is a major concern because it constitutes about 17 per cent of the world population. So, the number of infant deaths in India constitutes a large proportion of the total infant deaths in the world.

The concept of primitive tribal groups (PTG) came into existence while formulating the strategy of tribal development known as tribal sub-plan was being formulated. The question of tackling the problem of primitive tribal communities had received the attention of various commissions. These commissions observed and marked imbalances in development in the tribes. Some of them were still at the state of food gathering and they needed the utmost consideration by the government. It was decided that special programmes for extremely backward tribal groups known as Primitive Tribal Groups (PTGs) should be taken by the Ministry of Home Affairs through 100 per cent finance. The criteria followed in identification of primitive tribal groups were: (a) pre-agricultural level of technology, (b) low level of literacy, and (c) stagnant or diminishing population. On the basis of these criteria, 75 communities were identified as PTGs in India and nine tribal groups as PTGs, namely Asur, Birhor, Birjia, Hill Kharia, Korwa, Mal Paharia, Parhaiya, Savar and Sauria Paharia in Bihar. After the bifurcation of Bihar, only 8 primitive tribal groups are found in Jharkhand as Savar and Hill Kharia are two names of the same tribe. They are also known as Particularly Vulnerable Tribal Groups (PVTGs). Out of 8.65 million scheduled tribe population living in the State, 3.4 lakhs are the PTGs. The proportional share of the said eight PTGs of the State engulfs around 3.4 per cent of the total tribal population. The Mal Paharia is numerically largest one among them constituting about 46.45 per cent of the PTG population in the State, followed by the Sauria Paharia nearing about 15.81 per cent of the PTG population of the State. The Birjia, the Savar and the Birhor are numerically the smallest PTGs accounting about 2.15 per cent, 3.31 per cent and 3.67 per cent of the PTG population in the State respectively. The other primitive tribes, namely Korwa, Paharia and Asur incorporate around 12.18 per cent, 8.75 per cent and 7.68 per cent of total primitive tribal population of the State.

The term infant mortality refers to the deaths of children under the age of one year. It is measured by the Infant Mortality Rate (IMR), which is the total number of deaths of children under the age of one year for every 1,000 live births. The infant mortality rate is often divided into two components relating to timing of death: neonatal and post-neonatal. The Neonatal Mortality Rate (NMR) refers to the number of deaths of babies within 28 days for every thousand live births. Sometimes, a special type of neonatal mortality is assessed, viz. Early Neonatal Mortality Rate (ENMR) and Late Neonatal Mortality Rate (LNMR). The ENMR denotes those baby deaths, which happen within one week whereas the LNMR indicates those baby deaths, which occur between 1 and 4 weeks for every thousand live births. The Still Birth Rate (SBR) is another measure of reproductive deaths, which happens in the womb of mother after 20 weeks of gestation period and it is also known as foetal mortality rate, which is of two types: antepartum death and intrapartum death. The Perinatal Mortality Rate (PMR) is another component of infant deaths, which measures the number of still birth deaths at or after 20 weeks of gestation and deaths within the first 7 days for every thousand live births and still births. The Child Mortality Rate (CMR) refers to the deaths of babies, which occurs between the first and fifth birthdays. The Post-Neonatal Mortality Rate (PNMR) refers to the deaths of babies from 29 days to the end of the first year per 1,000 live births. The distinction between neonatal and post-neonatal mortality is important because the factors which affect neonatal mortality are mostly endogenous and post-neonatal mortality mostly exogenous in nature. The endogenous factors are related to the formation of foetus in the mother's womb and are biological in nature. These include age of the mother, birth order, period of gaps between births, pre-maturity, and weight of the child at the time of birth and other biological factors. Socio-economic, cultural and environmental factors are considered as exogenous factors, which are more responsible for mortality during post-neonatal period. These include faulty feeding, malnutrition, poor hygiene, crowding and congestion, lack of sunshine, unavailability of fresh air, polluted water and so on and so forth. It has been found that in countries where infant mortality is low, a large proportion of deaths occurs during the neonatal period, because being developed they have successfully eliminated environmental factors responsible for post-neonatal deaths (Raj, 2003).

Origin of the Research Problem

The first round of National Family Health Survey (NFHS-1) in 1992-93 and the second round of National Family Health Survey

(NFHS-2) in 1998-99 showed that infant mortality in Jharkhand is one of the highest among all Indian states. Even in the third report of National Family Health Survey (NFHS-3) in 2005-06, Jharkhand stands at the seventh position. However, the Infant Mortality Rate (IMR) has quite improved in Annual Health Survey of 2010-11, National Family Health Survey-4 of 2015-16, SRS Bulletin of 2013 and SRS Bulletin of 2019. Though Jharkhand holds a good position in various demographic and social indicators like crude birth rate and sex ratio etc.; it stands very poorly in case of infant mortality rate. Due to high infant mortality rate, the crude death rate in Jharkhand is also one of the highest in India. In Jharkhand, the coverage of antenatal services is high compared to the other poor states; yet the level of infant mortality rate has not fallen below in relation to the other poorer states. To know the micro factors which are very important to reduce the infant mortality, we need more research in this regard. In Jharkhand 41 per cent of population belongs to either Scheduled Caste (SC) or Scheduled Tribe (ST). All reports show that the socio-economic and demographic indicators are poorer in SC and ST population than in other castes. This situation leads to higher infant mortality rate of SC and ST children than in other caste children. The condition gets further worsened in case of the PTGs, which is the most deprived section of the society in all respects.

Here some relevant questions which naturally emerge, need to be explored and answered:

1. Is poverty a major reason for the high infant mortality rate in Jharkhand?
2. Whether there is inter-tribe disparity in infant mortality in Jharkhand within the tribes?
3. What sort of constraints produced by the infant mortality rate for containing the population of PTGs either as stagnant or diminishing state?
4. How inaccessibility to their abodes escalates the rate of child deaths?
5. What is the impact of poor infrastructural facilities on child deaths?

6. What is the impact of reproductive and child health intervention programme, national rural health mission etc. on the decline of infant mortality?
7. How education plays an important intervening factor in curtailment of child death?
8. Whether low intake of nutrition among the mothers and children lead to high infant mortality?
9. How economic prosperity is responsible for reducing post-neonatal mortality?
10. What is the role of unhygienic habits in escalation of excessive child mortality?
11. What is the role of dilapidated houses for creation of insanitation, which ultimately influences high neonate deaths?
12. Is infant mortality rate very high among the primitive tribal groups?
13. Which are the most neglected sections of society of the state and they are not properly enumerated as well?

This study will try to find out the actual picture in this regard. The analysis of the micro data will surely be helpful to the planners and programme managers to have an effective plan, while planning, formulating, implementing and monitoring the programmes.

Infant Mortality in International Perspective

Table 1.1 provides infant mortality rates in developed and developing regions of the world by continents that highlight the range of levels in two periods of time, i.e. 2007 and 2015. World's infant mortality rate of 52 per thousand live births in 2007 indicates that it needs time to lower infant mortality, and fortunately it has come down to 33 per thousand live births in 2015. Differences in infant mortality level across the world are substantial. Africa's rate of 86 is fourteen times higher than the average rate of 6 per thousand live births in the developed countries in 2007 and that kind of about six times disparity in IMR between the above two regions is also observed in 2015. The highest rates of infant mortality in the world have been reported in Africa. Both Europe and North America have low rates of infant mortality, with average rates under 6 per thousand live births in both periods of time. In Latin

Table 1.1: Infant Mortality rate (per 1000 live births) by region/ continent

Continent/Region	IMR in 2015	IMR in 2007
World	33	52
Developed Regions	5	6
Less Developed Regions	36	57
Africa	53	86
Asia	28	48
East Asia	10	25
West Asia	21	41
South Central Asia	40	64
South Asia	22	53
Europe	5	6
Latin America	17	24
Caribbean	26	61
North America	6	6
Oceania	20	42

Source: Retrieved from https://www.un.org/en/development/desa/population/publications/pdf/mortality/World-Mortality-2017-Data-Booklet.pdf and world population data sheet, population reference bureau.

America, the infant mortality rate was four times higher than North America in 2007 but that kind of disparity has drastically reduced in 2015 and it has decreased only three times lower. On average the rate in Asia (48 per 1000 live births) is somewhat lower than in Africa in 2007 and the infant mortality rate has got further reduced to the level of 28 per thousand live births in 2015. The average infant mortality rate in East Asia, West Asia, South East Asia, South Central Asia and South Asia was 25, 41, 32, 64 and 53 respectively in 2007. However, the IMR in the above-mentioned regions of Asia were 10, 21, 22, 40 and 41 respectively in 2015. In South Central Asia, the IMR was the highest in Asia in 2007 but the highest IMR was observed in the countries of South Asia in 2015. The reason behind lower rate of IMR in the South-Central Asia is that these Muslim dominated countries spent a large amount of money on the development of health sectors after separation from USSR but the health sector remained the lowest priority in South Asia, where meagre below 2 per cent of GDP was spent upon the above sectors whereas the corresponding figure in India remains below 1.3 per cent of its GDP.

The above statement is further substantiated by Appendix 1.5 that the infant mortality rate was below 4 per cent in most of the countries of Europe and North-East Asia in 2015/2020, which is lowest in the world. On the other hand, several Central African countries and South Asian countries have the IMR of above 40 per thousand live births, which is the highest in the world.

Infant Mortality in National Perspective

Chandrasekhar (1972) analysed that the infant mortality rate in India was close to 202 per 1000 live births in 1901. The trend of infant mortality got declined to 205 per thousand live births in 1911 but this trend got reversed in 1921, when the IMR was observed at 198 per thousand live births. However, the total population of India has shown negative growth of population due to spread of pandemic disease of Spanish Flue, i.e. influenza in 2018, which took toll of around 7 crore population in India. The gradual decline of IMR was noticed in 1931 and 1941, which was 179 and 158 per thousand live births respectively. It is further observed from Table 1.2 that the infant mortality rate was at 187 in 1951, which came down to 159 per thousand live births in

Table 1.2: Temporal trends of infant mortality rate (per 1000 live births) in India

Year	IMR in India
1951	187
1961	159
1971	140
1981	112
1991	87
2001	64
2011	43
2017	33

Source: Office of the Registrar General of India, Various Statistical Reports, Sample Registration System, Delhi: Controller of Publications.

1961. Again, it came down to 140 in 1971, 112 in 1981 and further to 87 in 1991. In the year 2001 infant mortality rate in India was 64 and in 2011 it was at 43 and finally, infant mortality rate was reduced to 33 in 2017 per 1000 live births. In India great disparity also exists among different segments of population. From the very early stage of society some castes were having higher socio-economic status than others (scheduled caste and scheduled tribe), with the result that the latter are facing very high under five mortality rates compared to the former. The first round of National Family Health Survey (1992-93) shows that the infant mortality rate is the highest among children belonging to scheduled castes (107 per 1000 live births) followed by scheduled tribes (91) and others (82) respectively. The third round of National Family Health Survey (2005-06) shows infant mortality rates are 66 and 62 per 1000 live births for children belonging to scheduled castes and scheduled tribes respectively, whereas the rates are 56 and 49 among children belonging to other backward castes and other communities respectively. Even in the latest fourth round of National Family Health Survey (2015-16) children belonging to scheduled castes, scheduled tribes and other backward classes have death rate of 56, 57 and 51 per 1,000 live births respectively, which is higher than others death rate of 39.

Table 1.3 indicates that infant mortality rate varies from state to state to a great extent because disparities exist between states with respect to socio-economic, cultural, demographic and physical structure. Starting from infant mortality rate of 10 per 1000 live births in Kerala, which is the lowest among major states to the highest in Madhya Pradesh (47 per thousand live births) in 2017. Infant mortality rate is high in the states of Assam, Orissa Arunachal Pradesh and Uttar Pradesh and all these five major states have infant mortality rate above 40 per thousand live births. It is followed by another group of states ranging from 33 to 40 per thousand live births consist of Chhattisgarh, Assam, Rajasthan, Meghalaya and Bihar, in which there is higher IMR than national average. The next group of states belongs to those states which have infant mortality between 20 and 33 per thousand live births consists of Andhra Pradesh, Gujarat, Haryana, Jammu and Kashmir, Jharkhand, Karnataka, Punjab, Uttarakhand, West Bengal, Himachal Pradesh, Tripura and Lakshadweep. Lastly, the lowest infant mortality having below 20 per thousand live births comprises mainly small states, namely Manipur, Mizoram, Nagaland, Sikkim, Andaman and Nicobar Islands, Chandigarh, Dadar and Nagar Haveli, Daman and Diu and Puducherry. Besides this, the major states, namely Delhi, Kerala, Maharashtra and Tamil Nadu also come under this group of lowest infant mortality rate. It is important to mention that IMR has come down to single digit in the states of Nagaland (7) and Goa (9). It is important to give more focus on these states for achieving the national population policy goals of IMR below 25 by 2020. Sample Registration System (SRS) data show that Punjab, West Bengal, Delhi, Tamil Nadu, Maharashtra and Kerala have already achieved the target of reducing infant mortality rate in 2017 but the states of Madhya Pradesh, Assam, Uttar Pradesh and Orissa have to implement new IMR policy so that infant deaths can be stopped at desirable level. Now the time has come to give special attention to the poorer states for achieving the national targets. More or less the same patterns of infant deaths among various states of India were observed in the year of 2012 and 2005, which is clear from Table 1.3.

Table 1.3: Infant Mortality rate (per 1000 live births) in various states of India

State	2017	2012	2005
Andhra Pradesh	32	39	57
Assam	44	55	68
Bihar	35	43	61
Chhattisgarh	38	47	63
Delhi	16	25	35
Gujarat	30	38	54
Haryana	30	42	60
Jammu and Kashmir	23	39	50
Jharkhand	29	38	50
Karnataka	25	32	50
Kerala	10	12	14
Madhya Pradesh	47	56	76

(*Contd..*)

State	2017	2012	2005
Maharashtra	19	25	36
Orissa	41	53	75
Punjab	21	28	44
Rajasthan	38	49	68
Tamil Nadu	16	21	37
Uttar Pradesh	41	53	73
Uttarakhand	32	34	42
West Bengal	24	32	38
Arunachal Pradesh	42	33	27
Goa	9	10	16
Himachal Pradesh	22	36	49
Manipur	12	10	14
Meghalaya	39	49	49
Mizoram	15	35	43
Nagaland	7	18	18
Sikkim	12	24	30
Tripura	29	28	31
Andaman and Nicobar Islands	14	24	27
Chandigarh	14	20	19
Dadra and Nagar Haveli	13	33	43
Daman and Diu	17	22	28
Lakshadweep	20	24	22
Puducherry	11	17	28

Source: Office of the Registrar General of India, Various Statistical Reports, Sample Registration System, Delhi: Controller of Publications.

Literature Survey

Theoretical Framework

A conceptual framework is useful to outline the relationship between the concepts. In a conceptual framework a set of concepts is linked in a planned manner to establish function and relationship. Conceptual framework may be considered as a relational model. Some frameworks given by prominent researchers are useful for the study of child survival. Among them Mosley and Chen's 'Analytical Framework for the Study of Child Survival in Developing Countries' is one of important framework (Mosley and Chen, 1984). This framework depicts a set of socio-economic and medical factors affecting child survival. Social and economic determinants of child mortality operate through a common set of biological mechanisms or proximate determinants to bring an impact on mortality. On the one hand, the social scientists mainly focused research on socio-economic aspects of child survival, while medical scientists focused research on biological aspects of child survival. Moreover, the above analytical framework for child survival brings an integration between socio-economic and biological factors, which determined child survival. The framework is based on the premise that all social and economic determinants of child mortality necessarily operate through a common set of biological mechanisms or proximate determinants, to exert an impact on child mortality and they considered altogether 14 proximate determinants. All these proximate determinants are grouped into five categories, such as:

(i) Maternal factors (age, parity, birth interval),
(ii) Environmental contamination (air, water, food, inanimate objects, insect vectors),
(iii) Nutritional deficiency (calories, protein, micronutrients),
(iv) Injury (accidental and intentional), and
(v) Personal illness control (personal preventive measures and medical treatment).

These variables directly influence the risk of morbidity and mortality. All social, economic and biological determinants must necessarily operate through these variables to affect child survival.

All the maternal factors have an influence on pregnancy outcome and infant survival. Survival of children is influenced by nutrients available not only to the child but also to the mother. Maternal diet and nutrition during pregnancy affect birth weight and during lactation influence the quantity and nutrient quality of breast milk, which affect child survival. Injury of the child includes physical injury, burns and poisoning. Injury may also be intentionally inflicted, the most extreme example being infanticide. Environmental contamination transmits infectious agents to children. The contaminated water and stale are the major factors behind the spread for diarrhoea and other intestinal diseases. The personal illness control is important for child survival. First, it influences the practices and the qualities of care during pregnancy and child birth and, secondly, measures taken to cure after child becomes ill. Along with this, physical infrastructure also influences child survival. The roads, electricity, water, sewage and telephone systems can influence health, particularly through their impact on the relative price of staples as well as of health-related goods, services, and information. For example, the poor pay more money, time and effort for poor quality water than the rich, who have access to an equivalent supply of pure piped water.

This framework depicts the linkages between various socio-economic, demographic, and environmental factors and infant survival. The socio-economic factors are affecting child survival mainly through intermediate factors. The economic status determines the type of food and cleanliness at the time of feeding the child which ultimately determines the nutritional status of a child. The demographic and biological factors determine the body mass index, nutritional status and immune system of a child, which influence child survival. People belonging to different castes are having different cultural values. The housing condition and sanitation factors also affect child survival. In *Kutcha* houses the bacteria and germs are more prevalent than *Pucca* houses which affect childhood diseases. In the same manner where sanitation condition is not good, the children are more likely to be affected by parasites, fungi etc. which leads to child morbidity and finally determines child survival.

Zakir and Wunnava (1999) examined the variables influencing the infant mortality rates using cross-sectional data for the year 1993. They use the number of births per women (fertility rates), female literacy rate, per capita GNP, percentage of women in labour forces and government spending on health-care as the dependent variables in explaining infant mortality rates. They conclude that infant mortality rate is influenced by fertility rates, female participation in the labour force, per capita GNP and female literacy rates.

Preston (1996) investigated the relationship between under

five mortality and socio-economic and demographic characteristics from world fertility survey data. He found that five socio-economic characteristics, such as mother's education, father's education, mother's labour force status, father's occupation and place of residence (rural/ urban) influence child survival. Mother's labour force status and place of residence were not as important as the other three socio-economic characteristics. The impact of mother's education on child mortality in Latin America and South East Asia was particularly important. The demographic factors such as sex of child, birth spacing and age of the mother have a substantial effect on child survival. Out of these factors birth spacing was most important for child survival. Potter (1988) while analysing World Fertility Survey (WFS) data found that birth spacing and child survival are positively and strongly correlated. Birth gaps affect child survival through two ways. On the one hand mother's good biological and health condition and on the other hand increasing the length of breast feeding by decreasing sibling competition increases the chances of infant and child survival.

Studies in Developing Countries

Stoeckel *et al.* (1972) studied 'neonatal and post-neonatal mortality in rural areas of Bangladesh' and found that the stage of development or modernization process influences the post-neonatal death rate substantially but not the neonatal mortality to that extent. The result also found that mothers in the oldest age group did not exhibit a neonatal mortality rate very different from that of mothers aged 25-39 and that post-neonatal mortality in the oldest age group decreased sharply after age 39. The births to women aged 40-49 years of high parity produced low levels of neonatal and post-neonatal mortality. Gubhaju *et al.* (1991) while analysing the Nepal fertility and family planning survey data found that demographic factors such as maternal age and birth orders are significant determinants of infant mortality, after controlling all other factors. Mothers less than 20 years of age were experiencing 51 per cent higher risk of infant mortality than mothers 20-29 years. First born children have the lowest risk of dying during infancy and risk increases with birth order. Drinking water and toilet facility are also significant factors affecting child survival.

Mostafa (1995) while applying odd ratios on demographic surveillance system data for Matlab Thana of Bangladesh found that biological factors have more influence on the perinatal mortality than socio-economic factors. Children born at an early age (less than 20) and old age (more than 34) of mother face higher risk of child death. Children of those women, who had foetal losses, are more at risk of child death. The results also show that birth interval between 2 to 5 years is very less risk for child death. The influences of socio-economic and demographic factors on infant mortality have been investigated in a number of populations. Some important studies from developing countries are reviewed first, followed by studies in India. Bairagi *et al.* (1999) using hazard model technique for Bangladesh Demographic and Health Survey 1993-94 data found that mother's education, age, birth order, sex of child and religion were important determinants of both infant and child mortality. Moreover, the different variables used to act differently in case of infant deaths and child deaths and their intensity and nature were also quite different. There was a U-shaped association between infant mortality and education level of mother and birth order whereas child mortality increased linearly with birth order. The infant mortality rate was higher for males and Hindus whereas child mortality rate was higher for females and Muslims in Bangladesh.

Chien *et al.* (2002) using Viet Nam Demographic and Health Survey (1997) data analysed disparities of perinatal mortality among different socio-economic and geographical groups of population. The study shows that perinatal mortality is high among mid-land/ mountainous population (30 per 1000 live births) and low among plain land population (19 per 1000 live births). The child of a low-income family has twice the risk of perinatal mortality than the child of a high-income family. The child of an illiterate mother faces three times higher risk of dying in prenatal period compared to the child of a higher secondary educated mother. Prenatal mortality rate was the highest among the Ba Na ethnic group (73 per 1000 live births) and lowest among the Kinh ethnic group (20 per 1000 live births). In Vietnam perinatal mortality was the highest in July, which is the hottest month, and also in February, the end of winter.

The acute poverty is generally observed in developing countries wherein malnutrition prevails in general and in females in particular and females during gestation period are not given sufficient food, which results in low-birth-weight babies. The intensity and frequency of deaths of low-birth-weight baby also influence the maternal and child care in developing countries. It is found that the entire world used to capitulate around 15.5 per cent of the occurrences of low-weight-babies, which was around 20.6 million babies in numerical figure being born every year whereas the developing countries only used to capture around 96.5 per cent of total occurrences of the said babies. Regional occurrences of ill-fated children manifest that 50 per cent are only born in South and Central Asia, 15 per cent in Sub-Saharan Africa, and 10 per cent in Central and South America. Whenever new-born baby has weight less than 2.5 kilogram, that baby is considered as under-weight baby. There is an inverse relationship between survival rate and low-birth-weight baby. That is why, the challenges of survival of under-weight baby increases so many times in compare to normal weight children. It is roughly estimated that the chances of early deaths among the low-weight-babies are as high as 20 times more than the normal weight children. Both life expectancy and survival rate of low-weight-babies become less due to faulty living style of mother. Thus, the weight of the new-born neonate depends on mother's lifestyle, nutrition, culture, and health thereby determine the outcome of pregnancy. The pregnancy outcome is also influenced by paternal education, income and social status of a family. It is further noticed that the use of alcohol, smoking, and drug by the respective mother have negative bearing upon the weight of baby. The mother living an impoverished lifestyle may have malnourishment, predisposing her to deliver a low-birth-weight infant (Gaiva, Fujimore, and Sato, 2014; WHO, 2004).

It is rightly addressed that the continuum of care framework aims to transcend the traditional emphasis on single, disease-specific interventions. It advocates a model of primary health care that embraces every stage of new born and child health. The success of this framework, however, depends on delivering essential services and implementing improved practices at key points in the life cycle, linking mothers, new-borns and their households and communities with quality basic health care and maternity services (Kerber, 2007). Veneman (2009) focused on maternal and neonatal health of African and Asian countries and came to conclusion that interventions and actions must be scaled up for saving lives of these countries. Most maternal and neonatal deaths can be averted through proven interventions such as adequate nutrition, improved hygiene practices, antenatal care, skilled health workers assisting at births, emergency obstetric and new born care and delivered through health system. It is found that two-thirds of all maternal deaths occur in just 10 countries and India and Nigeria together account for one-third of maternal deaths worldwide. Premature pregnancy and motherhood pose considerable risks to the health of girls. Finally, educating girls is one of the most powerful ways of breaking the poverty trap and creating a supportive environment for maternal and new born health.

It is usually observed that infant's survival depends on the socio-economic conditions of their environment. The Infant Mortality Rate (IMR) is defined as the risk for a live born child to die before its first birthday is known to be one of the most sensitive and commonly used indicators of the social and economic development. To reduce infant mortality significantly, it is required to focus on mother's level of education, which is inversely related to her child's risk of dying in Bangladesh. Significant differentials have been observed by different years in Gross Domestic Product (GDP), per capita health expenditure, mean age at marriage of female, literacy rate of female and source of pure drinking water attainment in mortality rate (Hossain and Kamal, 2010).

Since most of the South Asian women are suffering from anaemia, the utility of intaking of iron and folic acid tablets improve the health of mothers and newborns as well. A survey was conducted in Nepal to measure the effect of antenatal care through supply of Iron and folic acid to mother on infant mortality, the authors reported that the supplements of above dosage significantly reduced the risk of child mortality in Nepal. The beneficiaries were also the women who had taken the dosage of 120 Iron and Folic Acid tablets in early pregnancy (Nisar *et al.*, 2014). In another study of Bangladesh, it was observed that prematurity, respiratory illnesses and drowning were the most common cause of child death. Child death was inversely associated with socio-economic status. It highlighted the social distribution of different diseases in community (Adams *et al.*, 2013). The fundamental reasons behind excessive infant deaths in developing countries are due to scarce of income, lack of maternal care, insufficient resources, and less education. The lion's share of child deaths come under the component of neonatal mortality rate. It is rightly observed by the World Health Organization that around 45 per cent of deaths come under the components of perinatal, neonatal and post-natal mortality rate. It is further visualized that the variables, namely infection, asphyxia, and low birth weight only capture around 80 per cent of total infant deaths. It is found that there is an average acceleration of 4 per cent in infant deaths in the last six years but that kind of deviation in acceleration may be changed.

There is a vital role of nurses along with indigenous midwives in developing countries for providing antenatal care to the mothers and children. It is further observed that there is complete dearth of trained nurses and midwives in the developing countries whereby danger in childbearing and complications for mother and baby may increase so many times. The immediate need of health infrastructure is that the sub-centre of medical facility should be strengthened wherein nurse and medical personal with medicines of primary treatments may disrupt the cycle of infant and maternal morbidity and mortality. In fact, it is the nurse who can bring revolutionary amelioration in remote areas through the primary treatment and it will create conducive environment for promoting attitudinal change whereby a drastic change will occur at individual, family, and society level. Educating the indigenous nurses and health care workers in developing nations about appropriate hand hygiene, vaccinations, and sanitation practices is vital to decrease infant infection. Providing health care systems and communities with an educational awareness of proper treatment and the positive effect of Zn therapy and ORS in infants experiencing acute or chronic diarrhoea may be fundamental in eventual expansion or in availability to necessary resources. Basic nursing education, hospital orientation, and monthly in-services would be effective in promoting these interventions. These implications are feasible and necessary in providing the nurses at the frontlines of care with proper knowledge on how to provide quality service and decrease the risk of infant infection. Education for prevention of low-birth-weight infants during prenatal phase of pregnancy includes cessation of smoking, a nutritional diet, and treating mental issues. The nurse can visit these mothers in their villages, and counsel about these risk factors. The nurse can train the indigenous health care providers to give appropriate health advice. The local health personal may be educated by the nurse so that that indigenous health provider can give advice about diet of food and rest to the patient. The nurses play a great role regarding awareness of sanitation, hygiene, prevention of infections, intake of balanced nutritional food by the mother and need of parental health checks through their knowledge and skills so that maternal and infant mortality rate can be reduced at minimal level. They work in diversified field for improving the health of all indigenous people so that they can be stronger in all respects of physical, emotional and spiritual circumstances. They place better advice to a teenage mother about how to properly breastfeed a neonate. They also support to the grieving family members when premature infant and maternal death occur in the family, which is vital emotional support for the sustenance of other family members. The key to prevention of infant and maternal mortality rates is understanding the four main contributors which include preeclampsia, prolonged labour, low birth weight and natal infection (Newborns: Reducing Mortality, 2016).

Studies in India

It is to be mentioned here that medical infrastructure, financial position and mother's literacy account for lions share in case of tragic child deaths. Two individual level factors relating to medical care at birth and care during the post-neonatal period explain about 64 per cent of the regional variations in infant mortality as compared to 60 per cent explained by the two household level factors, i.e. poverty and adult women's literacy in India. The medical factors have shown a slightly high effect on infant mortality than the non-medical factors (Jain, 1985). It is found in case of rural Punjab that significant clustering of child deaths occurred only in the lower socio-economic and education groups of population. Education plays a great role in increasing awareness of healthcare. Mainly women's education results in more effective preventive and healthcare practices, which increases their productivity and affects infant mortality. Mother's education is a powerful factor that affects the clustering of child deaths. Significant heterogeneity in child mortality is found among uneducated women, but not among educated women. The study also showed that biological factors predominate in the causes of death of neonates, while post-neonatal mortality is more affected by child care practices than any other factors. There is significant clustering of deaths in both the neonatal and post-neonatal period but clustering is more prevalent during the post-neonatal period and it accounts for a large proportion of all child deaths. This shows that child care practices are more responsible for death clustering than biological factors (Das Gupta, 1997 and Monica, 1990).

Caldwell (1979) examined education as a determinant in mortality decline using the Nigerian data. He emphasized on the role of parental education, particularly, that of the mother, in reducing infant and child mortality. He argued that a well-educated mother can change the range of feeding and child care practices without imposing significant extra cost on the household. With increasing mother's education, the survival chances of children also increase. Mother's education has a greater effect on the survival of her daughters than it does on that of her sons. The effect of education was so much greater than that of place of residence (Bourne *et al.,*1991). Parental education particularly maternal education improves the survival chances of children in India. The improvement in the economic condition of the households measured through SLI and father's occupation is found to have enough potential to reduce child mortality (Singh *et al.*, 1998). Shetty and S. Shetty (2014) had interpreted census data from 1981 to 2011 that the states with higher female literacy have lower infant mortality rate and found that the states with higher female literacy are expected to progress better than the other variables in case of curtailment of infant deaths. Among the social variables, education of the mother is the most crucial determinant of infant mortality. All the existing literature demonstrates that there is a negative relationship between infant mortality and education of the mother. The level of infant mortality among babies born to illiterate mother is much higher than that among the offspring of mothers who had some years of schooling. The impact of education is found on both neonatal as well as post-neonatal mortality (Gandotra *et al.*, 1982; Ruzicka and Kantikar, 1972 and Khan,1988).

Rajna *et al.* (1998) using NFHS-2 data for Uttar Pradesh analysed the impact of maternal education and health services on child mortality. The study shows that maternal education plays a decisive role as a variable for neonatal and child mortality rate. The maternal education opens pandora box of health infrastructural accessibility for choosing the best health services on the basis of limited means and creates better environmental conditions for their children. The gross effect of maternal education on post-neonatal period shows that the chances of deaths in case of illiterate mothers' children are as high as 1.9 times than educated mother's children and that kind of relationship is also observed for semi-literate mother when they are having education level of middle school and above education. It is further observed that the illiterate women's offspring had 1.6 times of higher danger of probable deaths in compare to the children of semi-literate mother even after keeping other socio-economic variables as constant. Antenatal care of the mother during gestation period and maternal education are negatively related with infant mortality rate. The survival probability of those children, who are born from mothers with recipient of antenatal care during their gestation period had 30 per cent higher survival rate in compare to children of those mothers, who were deprived of antenatal care. It is also substantiated by the study that the children of Muslims/others had lower risk of infant deaths in compare to the children of SC and ST Hindus.

It is usually observed in India that there is differential treatment for the nourishment of boys and girls and girls are often ignored since their births. One study conducted by Arnold *et al.* (1998) on child mortality shows that, 45 per cent excess female child mortality over male child mortality was seen in Orissa, while 135 per cent excess female child mortality over male child occurs in Haryana. On the contrary, Kerala and Tamil Nadu show excess male child mortality over female. The scheduled caste and scheduled tribe children faced lower risk of dying in neonatal period but higher risk of dying in post-neonatal period compared to other caste children. In another study, the gender biased infant mortality inequalities have been examined in context of intra- and inter-states of India. It is observed that the inequality of infant mortality rate between boy and girl death rate are mainly determined by: (a) proportional share of female work force and; (b) policies, implementations and programmatic interventions to safeguard the interest of girl children (Narayan, 2008). The states of Tamil Nadu and Maharashtra had done praiseworthy work regarding discouraging sex selective abortion and depositing a handsome money on the name of girl children for their study and marriage. The girl children were further supported by implementing administrative and legal assistance through the Maharashtra Regulation of the Diagnostic Techniques Act of 1988, the Tamil Nadu Government's Baby Cradle Scheme, scaling up women's Self-Help Groups in order to carry out sensitization campaigns, surveillance of scan centres, and peer support of new mothers. In the northern and northcentral regions of India, excess female child mortality compared to the boys of respective rank is about onethird higher for the first girl child and even greater for girls of higher rank. Gender bias is more severe and selective in the north compared with the north-central regions of India. In the eastern, western and southern regions of India, excess female child mortality is marginal and does not rise systematically as the number of female children in the family increases. The improved education, economic status and exposure to mass media tend to reduce gender bias in these regions (Arokiasamy, 2004).

The micro level study at secondary sources of data is lacking due to unavailability of data in India. To meet the demand of data for infant and child mortality in India at district level, Rajan (2008) produced the report of district level estimates for IMR and CMR so that child level strategies can be chalked out smoothly. It is emphasized that India as a signatory to the Millennium Summit Declaration (2000) aims at achieving the Millennium Development Goals (MDGs) by the year 2015. Reducing child mortality is one of the 8 MDGs. The global recognition of infant mortality as an area of concern is well reflected in India's policy and programme documents. Reducing infant mortality rate has been given high priority in National Population Policy, 2000 as well as Rural Health Mission (2005-12). A new methodology has also been evolved for measuring the above parameter. Again, rural-urban differential and sex-differential at district level analysis of IMR and CMR are properly addressed.

A new method was evolved for measuring the causes of deaths in India by Bela Shah (2009), which is popularly known as verbal autopsy method and it improves in terms of coverage of death reporting, minimal use of residual categories, systematic screening of causes of death reports and timeliness of publication of reports. It is comparable as verbal autopsy based on similar interviews and the cause of death needs to be arrived at in the same way in all cases. The survey was conducted in some selected states, namely Assam, Bihar, Maharashtra, Rajasthan and Tamil Nadu. It basically addresses demographic and socio-economic profiles of death, causes of death and classification of deaths on the basis of communicable and non-communicable diseases.

Determinants of Infant Mortality Rate

Chandrasekhar (1972) rightly pointed out that high neonatal deaths are mainly due to ill-advised pregnancies, in view of the health of the potential mother, frequent and ill-spaced pregnancies, absence of antenatal care, malnutrition and low vitality of the expectant mother to begin with and malnutrition during her pregnancy, insanitary surroundings, absence of trained health visitors and midwives, *dais* and last maternal mortality itself as a cause of infant mortality. Manju Bhatt (2004) analysed the relationship between infant death and socio-economic factors on the basis of sample survey of India, where one-third of total deaths are engulfed by infant deaths only. It is seen that infant death is caused by diseases, lack of utilization of medical facilities and malnutrition of pregnant women and children. All these medical factors are influenced by socio-economic status of the person and their attitude towards health-care practices. Mortality is very responsive to social, economic and psychological factors. Historically, mortality has often used as a barometer of welfare. Statistical studies in the nineteenth and twentieth centuries showed concern for socio-economic differences in infant and crude mortality. Levels of death rate; more importantly, infant mortality reflects a society's status of well-being. Such aspects can be taken as indicators of quality of life (Hossain and Kamal, 2010).

In India considerable variations exist in terms of utilization of institutional health facilities by pregnant women. Scheduled caste and scheduled tribe women have higher probability of delivery at home.

So, the infant and child mortality among these groups is higher than in others. In rural India, the scheduled caste and scheduled tribe people are often forced to reside in isolated localities away from main village settlements reserved for the higher categories. Since health facilities are closer to the main settlement. They act as additional constraints for the women belonging to scheduled castes and scheduled tribes (Chakrabarti, 2005). Choe and Chen (2006) studied the effectiveness of reproductive and child health programme on child and maternal mortality in India and found that India could not achieve the goal 4 of United Nations of a reduction of under-five mortality by two-thirds (67 per cent). India may get reduction of 54 per cent by 2015 under the heading of under-five mortality on the basis of current trend of under-five mortality, which is also 13 per cent less than the target to be achieved. It is further examined that the said target can only be achieved through the effective implementation of family planning programmes. The programmes of early child bearing, short birth intervals, high order births, antenatal tetanus vaccination and child immunization should also come under the umbrella of family planning programme. However, sex discrimination against girl children may further increase the infant mortality in India, which is detrimental for civil society.

Primitive Tribal Groups

It has been rightly discussed earlier that no rigid fool-proof identification for the PTG has been evolved but for working purposes three criteria, i.e. pre-agricultural stage of economy, a low level of literacy and smallness of numbers have been adopted for identification and 52 primitive tribal groups including nine in Bihar have been identified. Distinct from the other tribes by virtue of their literacy, technology and population levels, the primitive tribes are still most distant from all kinds of development efforts and the so-called mainstream (Gupta, 1983 and Singh, 1995). The sudden decline of Sauria Paharias in 1991 Census was a matter of grave concern for demographers and the above situation was analysed by Sanyal that the recent and sudden spurt of concern for the Sauria Paharias is perhaps due to the dubious reputation that they are a dying tribe. If the census figures are to be believed the tribe should become extinct by the turn of the century. Fortunately, in this case, the figures are wrong. Whether they are actually dying out or not is a root point. It is further found by Bihar Tribal Welfare Research Institute that the enumerators during census operation could not differentiate among Parhaiyas, Mal Paharias and Sauria Paharias. Therefore, population of Sauria Paharias had been counted in population of Mal Paharias and Parhaiyas (Verma, 1991).

Health

A WHO Expert Committee (1965) pointed out that many parts of the world have illustrated a general association between low birth weights, high foetal and infant mortality rates and diets of poor nutritive value and it seems reasonable to conclude that under-nutrition and malnutrition among mothers especially in the developing countries contribute towards impaired maternal, foetal and infant health and vitality. It is also corroborated by Hari Mohan (1983) that most of the PTGs still believed that diseases are cursed by evil spirits and witches. When they suffer from any disease, the traditional diviner of the village is consulted, who tries to ascertain through divination, the names of the evil spirits and witches. The local traditional medicine-man is also consulted, who gives them herb. Further, it is observed that the primitive tribes are ready to accept the hospital facilities if the doctor visits their settlements and give them medicines. But the real problem is that the urban oriented doctors posted in rural primitive areas seldom visit the tribal settlements situated on the hills. However, the doctor always blames that the primitive tribes do not come to hospital for treatment as they are not ready to accept allopathic medicines prescribed by them.

Health is perhaps the most crucial aspect of human well-being. The 1948 UN Universal Declaration of Human Rights proclaims that "everyone has right to a standard of living, adequate for health and well-being of himself and of his family including food, housing and medical care". Health is very deeply related to natural and man-made factor, which have kept the Sauria Paharias as victims of marginalisation, neglect and exploitation. Moreover, India is a signatory to the Alma Ata Declaration of 1978. By it the country committed itself to the primary health care approach based on equity, access and social justice.

The national health policy subscribes to these principles. Yet the wide chasm that exists between these principles and their implementation, as far as the Saurias are concerned, is a sad commentary on the state of affairs (Chacko, 1991).

Maternal and child health care services form an integral component of the programme since long period. The regional poor food-in-take pattern of various tribal communities is largely responsible for their poor health in Jharkhand. The measurement of nutrition level for various tribal communities was carried out on a large scale. The importance of its role in lowering mortality and morbidity among women and children hardly needs any emphasis. If one has to single out one factor responsible for decline in child mortality, it should be adding to nutritional level of tribal women and children in the state (Kirk, 1996 and Mishra, 1997). Meharban Singh (2010) rightly pointed out that the health and well-being of the foetus is dependent upon the health and nutrition of the mother because she is both the seed as well as the soil wherein baby is nurtured for nine months.

Hygiene and Sanitation

It is rightly observed by UNICEF (1991) that 90 per cent of the deaths among the very young children in developing countries were caused by the combined factors of malnutrition, unsafe drinking water, inadequate sanitation and lack of immunization. There is acute shortage of good drinking water in the interior forest area of Singhbhum. The stream dries up after the rains and the poor villagers have to dig up sand in the stream bed to collect water (Upadhyay, 2005). The risk of infant infections gets multiplied when the birth attendants do not use proper washed hand, sterilized blade, sterilized cotton etc. during the delivery of child. It was observed that the birth attendants in Nepal usually practice unhealthy and unscientific practice during the process of bringing forth a new born-baby, which creates an environment wherein there is maximum risk of infections to the neonates. Institutional delivery is not common in Nepal. That is why around 63 per cent of childbirths happen in home setting without the help of Gynologist. That kind of home delivery is also accompanied by uncleanliness of equipments, dearth of birthplace in dark delivery room and mishandling of umbilical cord. The umbilical cord stump of new born baby is usually covered with traditional oils and spices in traditional society of Nepal, thereby the neonate become easy prey of tetanus and sepsis. It is notable that both within the home and healthcare setting, infection is a high risk (Joshi *et al.*, 2013). It is observed that people are used to open defection method for passing stools, which contributes the contamination of water supply, food, and environment. The bacteria, parasites, and viruses are usually grown on these filthy places and the children become easy victim of infections as they are more exposed to them. It is found that the poor countries of Asia and Africa capture around 72 per cent of child mortality having the age below two years. Complications from such infectious sources lead to infant morbidity and possible mortality (Bulled, Singer and Dillingham, 2014). A number of research papers reveal that the infant mortality can only checked, when there will be sufficient improvements in provision of safe drinking water and scientific sanitation programme. A research paper on Rwanda also manifests that when accessibility to safe drinking water in Rwanda is enhanced from 23 per cent to 41 per cent from 1992 to 2008 and availability of improved toilet facility from 9 per cent to 56 per cent from 2000 to 2008, there was tremendous decline in infant mortality rate. However, infant and child mortality in Rwanda declined steadily during this period regardless of whether households had access to safe drinking water, an improved source of water, or an improved toilet (Hong, 2009).

Social Milieu

It is found that the schools functioning on the hills of primitive tribes do not function regularly and the existing schools are in pitiable condition. The teachers remain absent for a long time without any leave but draw the salary regularly (Hari Mohan, 1983). Further, it is observed that the Sauria Paharia children do not attend schools because their traditional demands their presence in forest during school hour to learn folk songs, dances, hunting etc. They consider the Santhals and the non-tribals as their enemy hence they do not send their children to such schools where they are teachers. The irony of the fact is that the teachers are either the Santhals or the non-tribal. Further, the schools are located away from their areas in the plains (Narayan,

1991). Harding (1948) also found that a primitive tribal community in Sierra Leone registered a birth rate of 32.9 and a death rate of 32.9 with an infant mortality rate of 417, which is very high. When various components of infant mortality were not measured separately, Peller (1943) was of the view that the real neonatal mortality is in the first month of life. In view of its importance, he had proposed a separate term semantal mortality for mortality in the first week. His view is also substantiated by Padmanaban *et al.* (2009) that almost one-third of all deaths are accounted for by deaths among children before they reach their first birthday. Banerjee and Roy (2002) using National Family Health Survey data found that consanguineous marriage has a crucial genetic effect on offspring mortality. There is still some preference for marriage among biological relatives in India, particularly in the southern and western parts of the country. It is clear from the bivariate as well as multivariate analysis. The genetic effect of consanguinity on offspring mortality is detrimental only among close consanguineous couples and exclusively during the period of development of the foetus (stillbirths) and the early phase of infancy.

Malnutrition

Extensive studies of undernourished women have indicated that despite their poor dietary intake and low nutritional status, the lactational performance of these women is surprisingly satisfactory. It was found that the output of milk in these poor mothers was of the order of 400-600 ml. daily and the milk was of satisfactory quality at least with regard to proximate principles. The concentration of vitamins and minerals in the milk, however, was low. The growth rate and nutritional status of infant in poor communities were, therefore, relatively satisfactory during this period (Gopalan, 1962). The principal factors behind high maternal and child mortality are considered to high rate of malnutrition and undernutrition and almost all developing countries of the world are confronting with the above problems and both of them are main hurdles behind a large number of child deaths. The said finding is also applicable for India and the research paper on India corroborates that inequitable infant, child, and maternal mortality rates are due to insufficient intake of nutritional food by the mother. States and cities that have implemented micronutrient supplement, promoted breastfeeding, and reduced anaemia have fared better than other states (Claeson, 2000, Singh, 2011, Chatterjee, 2011 and Nguyen, 2013). Bhutta *et al.* (2013) analyzed that the lack of a coherent, integrated strategy on nutrition at both the federal and district levels, along with stagnating rates of stunting and undernutrition, as playing a role in Pakistan's struggle to improve maternal and child mortality rates.

Infant Deaths in Jharkhand

Even in Jharkhand the high infant mortality is observed among the general people and that rate becomes very high for scheduled tribes and scheduled castes and analysis through papers result in similar findings. The two states, namely Chhattisgarh and Jharkhand were created in 2000 by bifurcating the states of Madhya Pradesh and Bihar respectively on the idea of better performance of small states. It was thought that these states would perform better improvement in context of maternal and child mortality rate. It is further considered that independent status of administrative units would function for better prioritization of maternal and child health programmes. However, that notion of better performance by the smaller state completely failed. The similar kind of pseudo development occurs in case of Census Towns of India, when a large number of poverty-stricken rural people jump into these towns but facilities and infrastructural development do not expand accordingly in these towns. The poor people living in slums and unregularized colonies of towns did not have the accessibility of health sector due to their poverty and scarcity of resources whereas the native middle-class residents usually well-off attended the private health centres. The concept of Empowered Action Group of States was formulated after 2011 Census in place of BIMARU states of India. The relatively eight backward states in context of socio-economic parameter were included under it by the Federal Government of India for overall development of all sections of the societies and the states of Jharkhand and Chhattisgarh were also included under the above said scheme. The rural communities with special emphasis upon the scheduled caste and the scheduled tribe population were targeted especially by the National Rural Health Mission, which resulted in decline of infant and child mortality. But the lack of more significant progress is attributed to increase in mortality in higher wealth quintiles and urban areas (Minnery, 2013). Regarding the pathetic concern between high fertility and high infant mortality Hari Mohan (1960) rightly exemplified that most of the primitive women gave birth to six to nine children but mostly two to three survived. The infant mortality is, therefore, high. Child birth, therefore, affects the hearth of the primitive women. They are already suffering from malnutrition; hence giving birth to six to nine children is a matter of serious concern and considerations.

Introduction to Study Areas

Lying approximately between 21°59′ and 25°18′ N latitudes and 83°20′ and 87°57′ longitudes in the eastern part of India, the state of Jharkhand comprises a landlocked area of 79714 sq. km, which is 2.42 per cent of the total land area of the country and ranks 15th place in context of the area. Its length is extended to 380 km from north to south whereas its width is 463 km from east to west. It is encircled by Bihar through the contour line of 150 metre in the north, Orissa in the south, West Bengal in the east and Chhattisgarh and Uttar Pradesh in the west. The state had a total population of 3,29,88,134 in 2011 Census, which stands 13th position with the share of 2.72 per cent in term of country's total population. The general slope of the state is towards southeast but the north-western and north-eastern parts of the state slopes towards the north. According to 2011 Census there are five commissionaries, 24 districts, 37 tehsils, 260 blocks, 4562 panchayats, 228 towns and 32,394 villages. It happens to be one of the richest states from natural resources perspective, which owns about 40 per cent of the total mineral resources of the country. It accounts for nearly 48 per cent of copper, 80 per cent of uranium, 50 per cent of mica, kyanite, apatite, bauxite, 25 per cent of iron ore and bauxite and 36 per cent of coal reserves of the country. The state with its medium level of industrialization and urbanization is changing the contours of the rural landscape. Mining and industrial activities in many districts have brought prosperity to the areas.

The state of Jharkhand came into existence on 15th November, 2000 as the 28th state of India after the bifurcation of Bihar on the occasion of the birth anniversary of the legendry Bhagwan Birsa

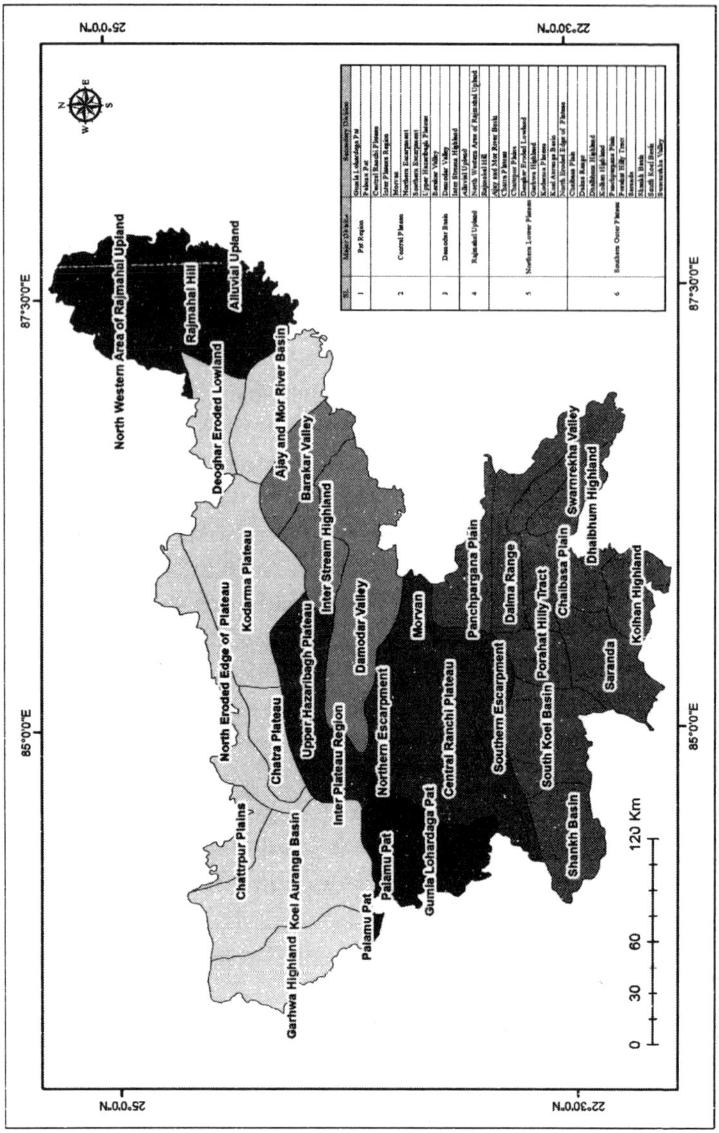

Fig. 1.1: Jharkhand: Physiography Divisions

Munda. The average density of population is 414 persons per sq. km against the national average of 382 persons per sq. km. Dhanbad with population density of 1284 persons per sq. km is the most densely populated district of the state whereas Simdega with population density of 160 persons per sq. km is the least densely populated district of the state. It has the literacy rate of 67.63 per cent against the national average of 74.04 per cent. The decadal growth rate of population in the last decade is 22.34 per cent against the national average of 17.64 per cent. Major part of population, i.e. 75.95 per cent lives in rural areas and the remaining 24.05 per cent of population reside in urban areas. It has sex ratio of 947 in comparison to national average of 941 whereas the tribal districts of Paschimi Singhbhum and Simdega account more females than males and all four dominating scheduled tribes, namely Santhal, Oraon, Munda and Ho have favourable sex ratio. It ranks 30th among 32 major states of India on per capita income. In fact, per capita income was only Rs. 76,019 and about 46 per cent of the total population still used to live below poverty line but it was as high as 60 per cent among the scheduled tribes in 2018-19. The forest occupies 29.6 per cent of the total land in the state. Around 7 per cent of land accounts for barren land, 9 per cent under non-agricultural use, 2 per cent under pasture, 3 per cent under culturable wasteland and 21 per cent under fallow land.

Jharkhand is a region of great physical diversities and presents a wide range of disparities in their various physical units. It has different areas of elevations ranging from 70 m to 1365 m at Parasnath hills. It is a region of great unevenness consisting of a succession of plateaus, hills and valleys drained by several large rivers such as Damodar, Suvarnarekha, North Koel, South Koel, Barakar and Sankh. The state has been divided into five major physiographic regions on the basis of elevation, morphologic feature and slopes. It is further subdivided into 11 first order regions and 21 second order regions (Prasad, 1973).

1. **The Pat Plateau:** The Pat plateau with an average elevation of 800 to 1100 metre is the highest region in the state. The most significant feature of the region is the mesa like flat-topped small plateaus, which are locally known as Pats. The Pats have a capping of Deccan Trap, which are the rich source of bauxite. It consists of flat-topped dissect hills like Netarhat, Ganeshpur

and Janira. The mesas and buttes are very common in this region. It is mainly made of basalt rocks and lavas erupted during Cretaceous Period. Now these rocks have been converted into laterite soil. The North Koel and the Sankh are important rivers of the region. It is primarily concentrated in the district of Gumla, Lohardaga and Latehar. The laterite soil is well spread over the region.

2. **The Central Plateau:** The Central plateau primarily consists of Ranchi Plateau and Hazaribagh Plateau. Ranchi Plateau is the largest plateau in the state with an average elevation of 650 metre. It covers the whole Ranchi and Khunti and north-western part of Paschimi Singhbhum district. It is a tableland intersected with numerous streams such as the Suvarnrekha, the South Koel etc., which are made of hard crystalline granite and gneiss rocks, where red soil is found in abundance. The uplands of the region are known as 'Tanrs' and the lowlands are locally known as 'Dons'. The pin pointed residual hills of the resistant rocks are known as 'Tongaris' where as the residual hills with dome shapes are called 'Dungaris'. Hazaribagh plateau is a continuation of the above plateau and has almost the same elevation but it is smaller in extent, which is separated from the above plateau by the Gondwana Trough of Damodar River. It is mainly drained by the Konar and the Bokaro River, which present glaring examples of eroded valleys and dissected uplands. Besides the above, Northern and Southern Fringe and Escarpment, Morvan and Inter-Plateau Ridges are also incorporated under it (Ahmad, 1965).
3. **Northern Lower and Southern Outer Plateau:** The Northern Lower and Southern Outer Plateau covers a very wide area of Palamu, Garhwa, Latehar, Chatra, Kodarma, Deoghar, Singhbhum and Simdega districts, which are basically concentrated in northern and southern portion of the Central Plateau. It has an average elevation of 150 to 600 m above sea level, which are further divided into two regions on the basis of location: Northern Lower Plateau and Southern Outer Plateau. The former region is further subdivided into Garhwa Highland, Koel and Auranga Basin, Chhatarpur Plain, Chatra

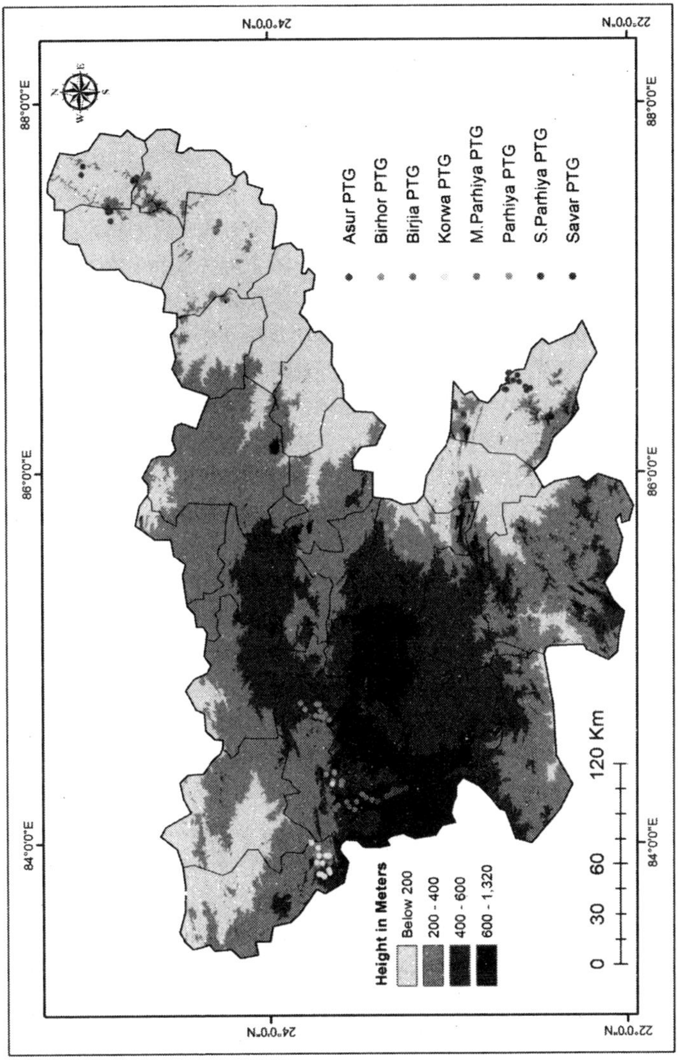

Fig. 1.2: Location of Villages under Altitude Zones in Jharkhand

Plateau, Kodarma Plateau and Giridih Plateau. The later region is also subdivided into Shankh Basin, South Koel Basin, Panchpargana Plain and Dharwarian Country. The last region is again subdivided into Porhat Hillu Tract, Saranda Hills, Kolhan Highland, Chaibasa Plain, Dalma Range, Suvarnarekha Valley and Dhalbhum Hills (Debi, 1979).

4. **Damodar Basin:** The morphology of the Damodar basin is the product of prolonged erosion over the Gondwana deposits. It is mainly concentrated in Dhanbad, Bokaro, Ramgarh and Hazaribagh district, where it has an average elevation of 150 to 600 m above sea level. Besides the above-mentioned river, it is drained by the Barakar and Jamunia River. The dome shape dungaris are common features, which are in fact isolated residual hill and Panchet Hill is an example of it. It is further subdivided into Damodar Basin, Barakar Basin and Inter-Stream Highlands.
5. **Santhal Pargana Highland:** Historically Santhal Pargana Highland was never a part of the Chotanagpur Plateau and people in this region speak 'Angika' as their mother tongue and the Santhals have arrived here in 19th century from West Bengal. The districts belonging to this region are Sahibganj, Jamtara, Pakur, Dumka, Deoghar and Godda. It has an average height of 70 to 300 m, which is upland tract with a hilly backbone. The Rajmahal hills is main hill range in the region. The hills comprise unregulated erosional depressions in the west side whereas the Ajay and the Mor rivers have scoured deep broad valleys in the southern part. In the east, the hill are broader by a narrow strip of alluvial deposits whereas the northern portion meets alluvial plain. The Ghatwals, the Khatoris, the Mal Paharias and the Sauria Paharias are the primitive inhabitants of the region. However, the primitive tribes are exclusively confined to Damin-i-Koh region, which are confined to certain blocks of Dumka Damin, Pakur Damin, Rajmahal Damin and Godda Damin. Figure 1.3 clearly conveys that the Asurs and the Birjias are concentrated in those regions of the state, which are situated above 600 metres of elevation whereas the Mal Paharias, the Sauria Paharias and the Savar

are agglomerated in those areas, which are located below 200 metres from mean sea level. However, the relative height of their settlements is quite high from their surroundings. The location of Korwa villages is generally found in between 200 and 400 metres height whereas the Parhaiyas and the Birhors are usually confined to those places, which have height between 400 and 600 metres.

Agriculture is the mainstay of people where the small landholders are found in preponderance and about 50 per cent of the farmers have a land holding of below 0.4 hectare. The total cultivable land of the state is 38 lakh hectares, which accounts for 48 per cent of the total geographical area of the state. The average rainfall is around 140 cm and about 20 per cent of the net sown area has assured irrigation facility. Consequently, the cropping intensity is only 126 per cent (Jharkhand Economic Survey, 2019). Poverty in Jharkhand is not due to lack of natural resources but due to poor governance, underutilization and non-utilization of resources, low opportunity for investment and unequal distribution of wealth.

Distribution of Scheduled Tribes

Almost all the Scheduled Tribes (STs) have the common religious and cultural characteristics of animism, totemism, shamanism, naturalism, polytheism, bongaism, witch-craft, customary laws, group dance and music, ancestor worship, endogamous society, geographical isolation and common territory in the state of Jharkhand. Further, the tribal economy is characterised by backward economy with much emphasis on forest products, use of simple technology in production process, absence of surplus economy with least desire of profit in economic dealings, community as a cooperative and collective functional interdependence, family as a unit of production, consumption and pattern of labour, much dependence on periodical markets for selling and purchasing of articles and joint ownership of property. They all belong to Proto-Australoid race and majority of them speak Austro-Asiatic languages barring few tribes, namely the Oraon, the Sauria Paharia, the Mal Paharia etc., who speak Dravidian languages. Again, some tribes have forgotten their original languages and they speak

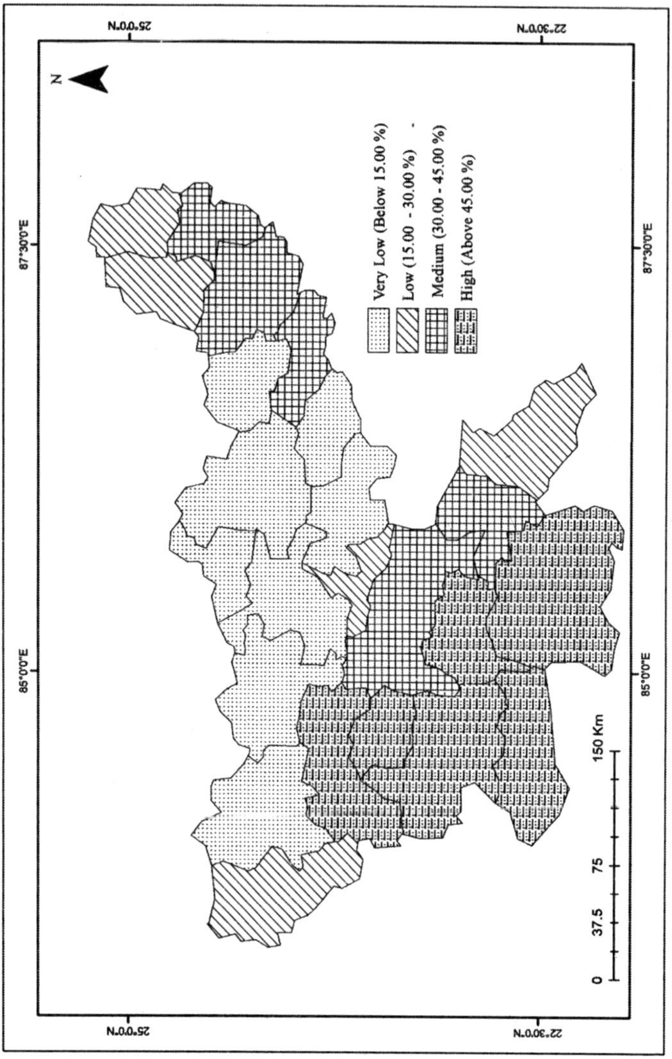

Fig. 1.3: Distribution of Scheduled tribes in Jharkhand, 2011

Sadri language along with other natives. Thus, they have developed a unique pattern of livelihood and culture (Vidyarthi and Rai, 1985 and Ahmad, 1999). They account for 26.2 per cent of the total population and their concentration level is very high in the difficult terrain of the Central Plateau, the Dharwarian Country and the Rajmahal Uplands in Jharkhand. However, the hilly, rugged and scarped area of the northern part of Chotanagpur Plateau is almost devoid of tribal population. In fact, the Damodar and the North Koel River act as demographic divide line between SC and ST population in the state wherein the northern region is the natural abode of the scheduled castes whereas the scheduled tribes dominate in the southern region. The total population of scheduled tribes in the state was 86,45,042 on the basis of 2011 Census, which is 8.3 per cent of the total tribal population of the country. Further, it is noticed that 78,68,150 persons reside in rural areas, which is 91.01 per cent of total tribal population. It is noticed that the sex ratio among the scheduled tribes in the state is 1003 against the state average of 947 and this is mainly due to least distinction made between the two sexes.

The decadal growth rate of tribal population is only 21 per cent in the last decade, which is below the state average. The tribal population constitute 32 tribal communities in the state and community-wise, the Santhal is the most populous tribe constituting about 31.9 per cent of the total scheduled tribe population in the state, which is clearly visible from Appendix-1.6. They are primarily concentrated in Dumka, Pakur, Jamtara, Sahibganj, Godda and Deoghar districts of Santhal Pargana division and they are also found in sizeable number in Purbi Singhbhum. In fact, they are historically inhabited along the catchment areas of the Damodar River, where *sal* trees are found in abundance. The Oraon, the Munda, the Ho, the Kharwar, the Lohra, the Bhumij and the Kharia stand at 2nd, 3rd, 4th, 5th, 6th and 7th position, which contain 19.9 per cent, 14.2 per cent, 10.7 per cent, 2.9 per cent, 2.5 per cent and 2.4 per cent respectively of the total scheduled tribe population of the state.

Historically, the Oraons are mainly concentrated in Pat region and they are densely concentrated in Lohardaga, Gumla and Latehar districts of Pat region whereas another numerically dominant group, i.e. the Mundas are traditionally concentrated in the region of Ranchi

Plateau. In term of population, the Hos are the fourth largest tribe in the state, who are basically confined to Singhbhum. These four mentioned tribes constitute around 85 per cent of the total tribal population of the state. The remaining four tribes, namely Kharwar, Lohra, Bhumij and Kharia, have heavy concentration in Palamu, Ranchi, Purbi Singhbhum and Simdega districts respectively and these communities have population around and above 2 lakh. On the other hand, there are eight such other tribes in the state, which have population less than ten thousand and their proportionate representations vary between 0.01 and 0.11 per cent. The lowest number and percentage are recorded for the Khond tribe, which comprises only 221 persons and its proportional share is below 0.01 per cent. It is followed by the Banjara, the Bathudi, the Baiga, the Gorait, the Birjia, the Kawar and the Savar. The other tribes on the basis of their numerical presence between 0.11 and 2 per cent belong to Mahli, Mal Paharia, Bedia, Chero, Karmali, Chick-Baraik, Gond, Kol, Sauria Paharia, Kisan, Korwa, Kora, *Parhaiya*, Asur, Binjhia and Birhor. Out of 32 tribes in Jharkhand, the eight tribes, namely Mal Paharia, Sauria Paharia, Korwa, Parhaiya, Asur, Birhor, Savar and Birjia are known as Primitive Tribal Groups (PTGs) on the basis of stagnation of population, low level of technology and low level of education, which altogether constitute about 3.4 per cent of the total tribal population. The distribution of scheduled tribes has been categorised into four groups for understanding their inherent patterns on the basis of district level agglomeration.

High Concentration of ST Population (Above 45%): Figure 1.3 reveals that Kunti has the highest share of tribal population to the total population, i.e. 73.25 per cent in 2011 Census. It is followed by Simdega, Gumla, Pashchimi Singhbhum, Lohardaga and Latehar districts, which have above 45 per cent of tribal concentration and these districts are categorised into the region of high tribal concentration. All these six districts are exclusively located in the Southern Outer Plateau, Central Plateau and Pat region of the state. The region is natural abode of Munda, Ho, Oraon and Kharia tribes since time immemorial.

Medium Concentration of ST Population (30-45%): The next group of medium concentration of scheduled tribes comprises those districts, which are situated in the Central Plateau and Rajmahal

Upland region and the concentration of ST varies from 30 to 45 per cent. It is remarkable to notice that Ranchi and northern Seraikella Kharsawan are confined to the former region whereas the remaining districts, namely Dumka, Jamtara and Pakur are located in the latter region. The former region is the abode of Mundas whereas the latter region is exclusively monopolised by the Santhals and the Mal Paharias.

Low Concentration of ST Population (15-30%): The districts with the distribution of ST varying between 15 and 30 per cent have been clubbed as low concentration of ST. The districts with low concentration of ST are located in a scattered pattern. Ramgarh district is basically confined to the Central Plateau region, Purbi Singhbhum in the Dharwarian Country and Garhwa in north-western part of the state. The other districts, namely Sahibganj and Godda are situated in the Rajmahal Upland region. In fact, large scale in migration of non-tribals from surrounding regions into these districts has made curtailment in the share of tribes due to high level of urbanization and industrialization in the region.

Very Low Concentration of ST Population (Below 15%): The districts having low level of ST concentration are spread either in the northern peripheral areas or mining cum industrial region of the state and these districts have ST concentration level of below 15 per cent. Bokaro, Deoghar, Giridih, Palamu, Dhanbad, Hazaribagh, Chatra and Kodarma are agglomerated in this group of very low concentration whereby Kodarma with only 0.96 per cent concentration of ST has enrolled the lowest proportion of ST population. It has already been discussed earlier that the region is primarily inhabited by the scheduled caste population. That is why, in spite of having hilly, rugged and scarped areas in the above-mentioned former region, it is almost devoid of tribal population due to a greater degree of accessibility, proximity and contiguity with the Ganga Plain. It is also an established fact that the north region of Damodar and North Koel Rivers is not the natural abode of scheduled tribes in Jharkhand.

The district-wise share of scheduled tribes to total tribal population of the state is nicely portrayed in Fig. 1.4. The highest share of ST population is found in Ranchi wherein its share to total tribal population was above 12.5 per cent in 2011. It is followed by Paschimi Singhbhum, which also accounts for around 11.7 per cent of

ST population of total ST population of the state. The other districts, namely Gumla, Purbi Singhbhum and Dumka have proportional share of ST population to total tribal population of the state of 8.17 per cent, 7.56 per cent and 6.61 per cent respectively. Thus, these five districts alone account for more than 46 per cent of ST population. On the other hand, the lowest share of ST population to total tribal population is found in the district of Kodarma, where it is found only 0.08 per cent and it is succeeded by Chatra, which also account for below 1 per cent of total tribal population of the state and the above statement is also substantiated by Appendix-1.7. The remaining seventeen districts of the state have ST population share to total tribal population fall between 1 and 5 per cent.

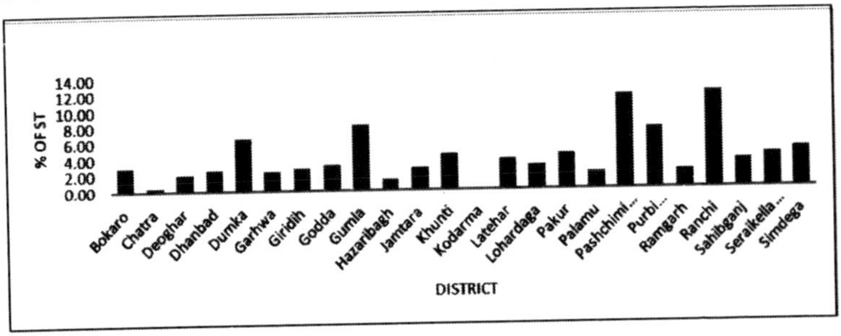

Fig. 1.4: Composition of Scheduled tribes in Jharkhand, 2011

Objectives

Several research scholars and authors have studied the socio-economic aspects of the primitive tribal groups residing in various regions of Jharkhand but the infant mortality rate among the above groups has not been analysed seriously and that is why, the present research work has been carried out to explore the hidden aspects of infant mortality among these groups. The specific objectives of this study are as follows:

1. To make a detailed study of the spatial patterns of infant mortality rate among the various primitive tribal groups in Jharkhand.
2. To assess the demographic and socio-economic factors of PTG accountable for high neonatal and post-neonatal mortality in Jharkhand.

3. To examine the role of environmental sanitation and hygienic practices used by the local people for the survival of children.
4. To investigate the role played by their low income level and dilapidated houses for high infant deaths.
5. To analyse the distributional aspects of health and infrastructural facilities availed by the various PTGs in their respective localities.
6. To examine the effect of various socio-economic, demographic and health care factors on neonatal, post-neonatal and infant mortality rate among the PTGs.
7. To develop a systematic analytical framework for reducing infant mortality through subsequent programmes and welfare measures.

Hypotheses

From the above discussion, it is found that the poor or vulnerable groups in the population are more susceptible to infant deaths. The following hypotheses have been made on this basis:

1. Infant mortality level is higher in the primitive tribal groups than the state average due to their relatively poor socio-economic conditions and social deprivation.
2. The neonatal mortality is influenced by biological variables whereas post-neonatal mortality is controlled by environmental variables.
3. The higher the share of low-income groups among the PTG, higher the share of infant mortality.
4. Mother's education plays an important role in the decline of infant deaths.
5. The infant mortality rate is higher for working mothers than for the non-working mothers among the PTGs in Jharkhand.
6. Immediate breast-feeding as pre-lacteal feed curtails reduction in neonatal mortality rate.
7. Antenatal care of mother creates a healthy environment whereby there will be reduction in neonate deaths.
8. The availability of safe drinking water leads to the lowering of the mortality of infants.

9. The longer the distance of medical centre from the village, the larger the share of infant mortality rate.
10. The risk of infant death is very high for fourth and higher order of child births.
11. Infant mortality in general and neonatal mortality in particular have lower infant mortality rate among the mothers having in the age group of 20 to 30 years at the time of child births.
12. Higher the share of immunization among the children of PTG, lower the proportion of infant deaths.
13. The inaccessibility of village from *pucca* road increases the infant mortality.
14. The dogmas and superstitions of the primitive tribal groups enhance the infant mortality rate.

Sample Design and Methodology

The purpose behind the selection of primitive tribal groups in Jharkhand as an area of study is that it is one of the backward states of India. Secondly, it includes 8 primitive tribal groups of the state, which stands at third position after Orissa and Andhra Pradesh in context of number. Thirdly, infant mortality rate of PTG is not properly enumerated. In addition to the above, the writer belongs to Jharkhand, where field survey has been easily done with the help of the local people and students of the state. The processes of data collection and solution of problems are sought here under this particular heading.

Database

The study is primarily based on primary data collected from sample households with the help of structured interview schedules. The information covers the availability of infrastructural facilities, the number of infant deaths, characteristics of infant deaths, patterns of infant deaths, impact of infant death on the place of households and villages as well. For primary sources of data, one of the important features of the present study is that most of the analysis is presented, taking into consideration the characteristics of the village, household, woman and individual infant deaths. In fact, the data utilized for geographical analysis of infant mortality in the state of Jharkhand are essentially based on field survey. Four types of schedules are used to obtain the data for the present study. These are: (i) village schedule, (ii) household schedule, (iii) woman schedule, and (iv) infant death schedule. The village infrastructural amenities such as facilities of education, medical services, transportation, distance from the nearest town etc. are incorporated in the village schedule. It is followed by the household schedule, which is used for socio-economic and demographic information regarding the concern families. The next woman schedule broadly covers the fertility, reproduction and natality characteristics of females and it also investigates the social value system for nurturing babies and adoption of family planning methods. Lastly, the infant death enquiry schedule inspects the components of infant deaths and determinants responsible for their deaths. However, for the secondary data, the main sources are:

1. Census of India,
2. Statistical Abstracts of Jharkhand,
3. Sample Registration System,
4. District Census Handbook of all districts of Jharkhand,
5. National Family Health Survey I, II, III and IV,
6. National Sample Survey,
7. Primitive Tribal Group of Jharkhand Survey Report, and
8. Jharkhand Economic Survey and Economic Survey of India.

Sample Design

Due to the empirical and spatial nature of the study and for providing proportional representation to each and every aspect of the local commons, certain sampling methods are used for selection of sample villages and sample households.

Selection of Villages: There are eight distinct primitive tribes in Jharkhand, namely Sauria Paharia, Mal Paharia, Korwa, Parhaiya, Savar, Asur, Birhor and Birjia. The total population of PTGs enumerated in 2011 Census were 2,92,359 and they were spread over in almost all districts of the state but their high level of concentration is restricted to few districts. That is why, only selected districts (11) were chosen for intensive field survey in which altogether 100 primitive tribal villages are surveyed for a detailed study of infant deaths among the PTGs in the state. Further, 14 villages, 11 villages,

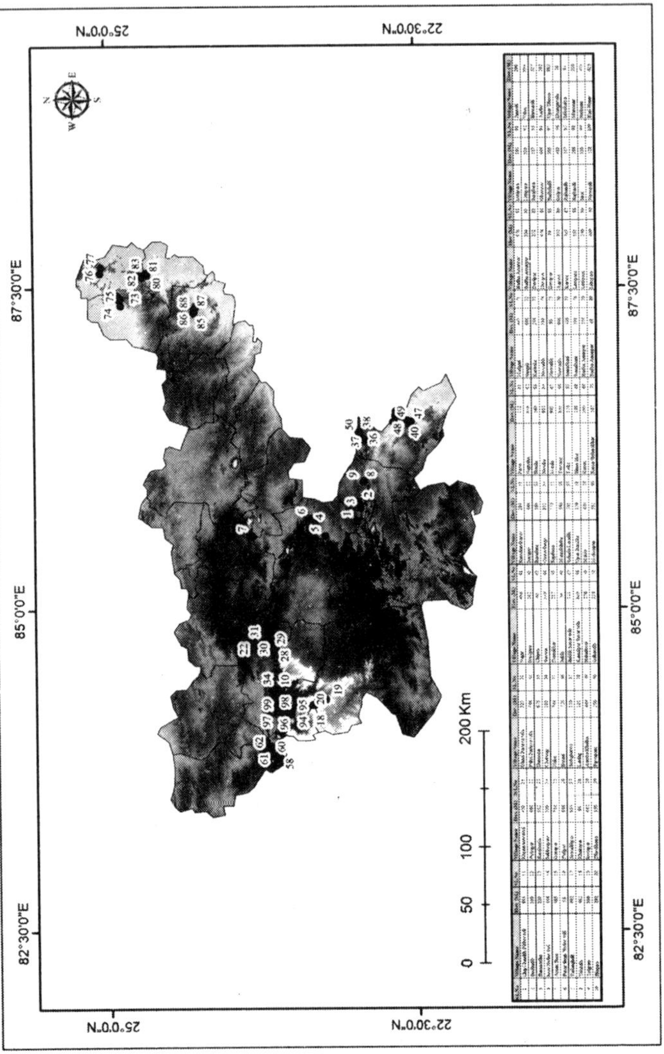

Fig. 1.5: Location of Surveyed Villages with Elevation in Jharkhand, 2017

13 villages, 15 villages, 15 villages, 10 villages, 10 villages and 12 villages have randomly been selected from the primitive tribal groups of Sauria Paharia, Mal Paharia, Korwa, Parhaiya, Savar, Asur, Birhor and Birjia respectively on the basis of convenience and security from Naxalites. Thus, areal random sampling method has been adopted for the selection of villages in the field survey. In addition to the above, selection of villages is also chosen on the basis of location of villages from the nearest urban centres, viz. within 10 km, 10-20 km and above 20 km. Lastly, average elevation has been taken into consideration for selection of villages for all PTGs through G.P.S. system.

Selection of Households: For selection of households, preliminary survey of households had been conducted on the basis of building material, economic activity and land holding status and on the basis of the above economic status of the households; they were classified into four categories. Households have randomly been selected from the above identified strata. Thus, stratified random methods of sampling have been used here for selection of households. Altogether 2209 households have been taken for the analysis of infant mortality in which 11051 persons live in for the PTGs of Jharkhand. However, it is likely to be mentioned here that the information regarding characteristics of households have been taken for both having infant mortality and not having infant mortality as well.

Measurement of Variables: The dependent variables are Neonatal Mortality Rate (NMR), Post-Neonatal Mortality Rate (PNMR) and Infant Mortality Rate (IMR) for correlation matrix and stepwise regression analysis whereas only infant mortality serves as dependent variable for binary logistic regression and each dependent variable is of dichotomous in nature. The independent variables are mother's literacy, share of infants with fourth and higher order of births, share of mother's age between 20 and 30 years, share of mothers with initial breastfeeding within one day, share of working mothers, proportion of mothers received antenatal care, proportion of addicted mothers, child-woman ratio, share of immunised infant deaths, percentage of households having handpump and tap facilities, percentage of households having houses with only one room provision, percentage of landless households, per capita income, distance of bus-stand facility and productivity per acre for the former two causal analysis methods. Similarly, the dependent variables, namely birth order of child, mother's age, care during delivery, breastfeeding, availability of food to mother during gestation period, size of household, source of drinking water, mother's education and per capita income have been chosen for the later mentioned causal analysis method.

Research Methods: Broadly the following research methods have been applied for analysing the topic entitled as 'Infant Mortality among the Primitive Tribal Groups in Jharkhand':

Location Quotient: The location quotient (LQ) is an index for comprising an area's share of a particular characteristic in relation to its position in the region. The concentration of primitive tribes at district level has been applied here with the context of its ratio on the state level. The location quotients of primitive tribes in Jharkhand are comparable to the location quotients of other states as they do not have any dimension. Thus, the regional character of distribution among the PTGs is investigated and determined through district-wise concentration index thereby to find out the pattern of their distribution in relation to their state-wise presence and it is measured through the following formula:

$$LQi = \frac{Pij / Pi}{Pj / P}$$

Where Pij= district-wise number of primitive tribal population
Pi = district-wise total population
Pj = state-wise number of PTGs
P = state-wise total population

Cross-Tabulation: Cross-tabulations analyse two variables, usually attribute and dependent or independent and dependent to determine if there is a relationship between them. The subcategories of infant deaths with demographic and socio-economic characteristics are cross-tabulated to ascertain if a relationship exists between the above in Chapter III. Usually, the absolute number of respondent and row and column percentages gives us a reasonably good idea as the possible association. Again, the relationship between dependent and independent variables have also been examined in Chapter VI with the help of cross-tabulation. It demonstrates comparison between groups.

In this study the neonatal mortality, post-neonatal mortality and infant mortality rate have been analysed by various social, economic, demographic infrastructural and sanitary factors through bivariate method.

Verbal Autopsy: The verbal autopsy method is applied here for filling up interview schedule wherein a systematic retrospective inquiry from the caregiver close to the deceased children about the signs and symptoms of illness prior to death of the deceased are used to help in determining the underlying medical cause of death. Usually such a caregiver is a close relative, who is knowledgeable about the events leading to the death of the deceased. It has been widely used to ascertain the causes of death among the children to have an effective mortality statistic.

Relative Risk: Exclusion can only be measured by comparing the circumstances of some individuals, groups and communities relative to others at a given place and time. Relative risk of mortality among children belonging to primitive tribal group compared with children belonging to other scheduled tribe community has been measured through this method.

Correlation and Regression: For verification of the hypotheses and for evaluation the role of various concepts, zero order correlation matrix and stepwise regression have been applied here to measure the relationship between the similar dependent and independent variables. The similar correlation analysis gives us an idea of the relationship existing among the variables. But the crux of the problem remains to be unsolved as to how much independent variables affect upon dependent variables; when they are working simultaneously. Stepwise regression procedure explains to obtain an optimum set of independent variables, which could explain maximum possible variation in the dependent variable. Together with regression coefficients, coefficient of determination and correlation coefficients are considered to understand the marginal usefulness of individual variables in increasing the predictive power of equation and to measure the influence of a particular variable when other variables are held constant. They are indeed naturally complimentary and perhaps inseparable. Firstly, it has been applied to test the hypothesis as an independent exercise. This has been done by using zero order correlation matrices with the help of correlation coefficient. The correlation coefficient has been calculated by using Karl Pearson's method.

$$R = \frac{\Sigma xy - \frac{\Sigma x.\Sigma y}{N}}{\sqrt{\Sigma x^2 - \frac{(\Sigma x)^2}{N}}\sqrt{\Sigma y^2 - \frac{(\Sigma y)^2}{N}}}$$

A 't' test has been applied to test the statistical significance of correlation coefficient.

$$t = r\sqrt{\frac{n-2}{1-r^2}}$$

Secondly, in order to ascertain the relative importance of the variable, the technique of stepwise regression has been applied. Stepwise regression is a procedure for selecting one regression equation from several possible combinations of independent variables. Even though a set of variables has been selected because they are theoretically relevant, a smaller subset of these variables may provide a satisfactory model of the process under examination.

$$Yi = \beta_0 + \beta_1 X_{i1} + \beta_2 X_{i2} + \ldots\ldots\ldots\ldots\ldots\ldots + \beta_k X_{ik} + E_i$$

Chi-Square: The chi-square test is applied here to measure the effect of infant mortality on deceased households. This test is one of the simplest and most widely used non-parametric tests in statistical work. This method is used to test the correspondence between certain observed and estimated frequencies. In the generalized notation, its formula is:

$$x^2 = \sum\frac{(O-E)^2}{E}$$

where O refers to the observed frequencies and E denotes to the expected frequencies.

Logistic Regression: The logistic regression is one that specifies a functional relationship between a basically dichotomous dependent variable and categorical or metric scaled independent variables. In fact, it is a method of multivariate analysis of the multiple regression model designed to deal with the situation when we have only the measurement of presence or absence, occurrence or non-occurrence of some factors. Logistic regression is concerned with modelling the odds of dependent variable and the parameters for logistic are most easily interpreted if they are expressed as odd ratios. In a logistic regression model, we assume that the P (probability of occurrence of events) is related to the independent variables in the form of logistic function instead of a linear function. Binary Logistic Regression is used to access the net effect of socio-economic, demographic and environmental factors on infant mortality rate. It is used to access the net effect of social, economic, demographic, sanitary and environmental factors on infant mortality. The basic form of logistic function is:

$$\mathrm{P} = \frac{1}{1+e^{-z}}$$

When numerator and denominator of the right side of the above equation are multiplied by e^z the logistic function can be expressed in the following manner:

$$\mathrm{P} = \frac{\exp\ (z)}{1+\exp\ (z)}$$

where z is the predictor variable and e are the base of natural logarithm, equal to 2.71828 and above equation is bivariate. If z is a linear function of a set of predictor variables than:

$$Z = b_0 + b_1X_1 + b_2X_2 + \ldots\ldots\ldots\ldots\ldots + b_2X_2$$

This expression is substituted in the formula for logistic function in the above equation.

$$\mathrm{P} = \frac{1}{1+\mathrm{e}^{-(b_0+b_1X_1+b_2X_2+\ \cdots\cdots\cdots\cdots\ -+b_kX_k)}}$$

In this analysis, both logistic regression coefficients and odd ratios are used. Odd ratio is the ratio of the probability of the event occurring to the probability of the event not occurring.

Odd Ratio = Probability of the event occurring/Probability of the event not occurring, defined as:

$$log\frac{P_1}{1-P_1} = \left(b_0 + b_1X_1 + b_2X_2 + \ldots\ldots\ldots\ldots\ldots\ldots\ldots + b_2X_2 + e\right)$$

where,

P_i = Probability of the event occurring.

B_o = Constant term representing the value of log ($P_i/1-P_i$) with the base line value of all values X_1 to X_n in the model.

X_1 to X_k = Independent variables associated with the process of infant deaths.

B_1 to B_k = Unknown regression coefficients associated with the independent X_1 to X_n.

E = Error term representing unobserved variables that influence dependent variable.

The quantity P/1 – P is called the odds, hence the quantity in P/1 – P is called the log odds or the logit of P. The coefficients are estimated using the method of maximum likelihood. The predictor variables should be numeric on a scale. If a predictor variable is in a categorized form, it needs to be converted into dummy variables. Computer packages of SPSS for logistic regression have a provision of doing so and it is adequate to specify categorised variables as such and note the reference category. In such cases, the ratio term exp (B_k) for a particular category k is the odd ratio, i.e. the ratio of odds for the category k to the odds for reference category (Retherford and Choe, 1993).

Scheme of Study

The present study entitled as 'Infant Mortality among Primitive Tribal Groups in Jharkhand' is a comprehensive attempt to analyse the conditions responsible for unprecedented high level of infant mortality, which ultimately creates that kind of environment whereby the primitive people have either slow or negative growth of their population. District-wise spatial distribution, growth and concentration of primitive people has been studied on secondary sources of data whereas the investigation of infant deaths is mainly carried out on the basis of primary data for other chapters. The entire work has been systematically organised into seven chapters in accordance with the aims and goals of the study.

Chapter 1 provides an introduction and background to the study. It deals with conceptual background, origin of the problem, general and specific objectives, hypotheses, database, sample design and methodology. Further, it presents a brief review of the work done so far on the area under study. Primarily, it highlights the studies conducted in the characteristics of PTGs, demographic and socio-economic characteristics, distribution of primitive tribes, infrastructural availability, spatial patterns and determinants of infant deaths. A brief introduction to study area is also presented here along with spatial distribution of scheduled tribes at district level on the basis of 2011 Census data. Again, it discusses the rationale behind the selection of area in general and the topic in particular.

Chapter 2 is a study of spatial distribution, growth and concentration of PTG at district level on the basis of census data in Jharkhand. It provides a brief description of physical traits found among all eight PTGs separately, viz. Asur, Birjia, Birhor, Korwa, Mal Paharia, Parhaiya, Sauria Paharia and Savar. It further presents the district level spatial pattern of all PTGs individually on the basis of the last two censuses of 2001 and 2011 and their distributional spatial variation at district level in both periods of time. Further, a micro-level distributional aspect of the above PTGs has also been analysed at block level on the basis of Primitive Tribal Group of Jharkhand Survey Report. Again, it discusses the population change of every PTGs separately in a historical perspective and it also examines the arithmetic growth rate from census data since 1872 simultaneously. It, further, looks into the concentration index of PTG through location quotient on the basis of 2011 Census.

Chapter 3 analyses the data on demographic, social and economic aspects of sample households based on data collected through extensive survey of 100 PTG villages found in different areas of the state. Demographic profile has been studied under the heading of mother's age at child birth, sex ratio of infant deaths, birth order of child and marriage age of females whereas social profile has been studied under the title of mother's education, size of household, type of family and religion. Again, economic profile has been examined under the topic of income, landholding possession, occupation of mother and father. Lastly, the availability of infrastructural facilities has been investigated under the caption of medical, communication, transportation, market, electricity, educational and drinking water facilities, which are somehow related with infant deaths and the above-mentioned parameter determine the quality of life. In fact, all these characteristics of households have been investigated with the tool of distribution and infant mortality rate. Moreover, some characteristics have exclusively been looked into with distribution only. Some of the characteristics of infant deaths have also further been examined here with cross-tabulation in order to provide complete characteristics of infant deaths. It also compares between the characteristics of households with infant deaths and the households without infant deaths in order to find out the differences between the two.

Chapter 4 attempts to examine the assessment and regional pattern of infant deaths on the basis of primary data. The former aspects of infant deaths do not only include the various components of infant deaths but they also consist of those unfortunate events, which happen in mother's womb after 20 weeks of conception and such foetal deaths are designated as still birth rate. Besides the above, the assessment of infant deaths also includes early neonatal mortality, late neonatal mortality, neonatal mortality, perinatal mortality, post-neonatal mortality and infant mortality rate. The regional pattern and magnitude of all seven components of infant deaths have been discussed at district level in detail. Basically, the whole exercise covers individual primitive tribe-wise and district-wise interpretation and causes behind differential rate of infant deaths.

Chapter 5 is devoted to examine health, hygiene, sanitation and morbidity condition among the PTGs in Jharkhand. The poor living condition in the former three parameters stimulate the children to fall ill by several diseases thereby the children become easy victims of diseases, which have been examined here under the topic of morbidity. It is thus devoted to mainly above four aspects of healthy lives, which are primarily associated with malnutrition and child deaths. In the first aspect reproductive health of tribal mothers and child care are studied under pre-lacteal food, addiction, and food eaten during pregnancy, family planning, supplementary food, low birth weight, immunization and medical check ups of children. It highlights community health needs, access and utilization of the services provided by the local health centres. In the second aspect, hygiene habit of PTG has been investigated under the topic of bathing, kitchen facility and toilet facility. Sanitation practises at community level has been introspected under sources and treatment of water, type of houses and sanitation of houses. It also discusses the role of local administration in the promotion of general health care. Lastly, it mainly focuses upon various diseases found among the children of PTG, which ultimately encourage to a very high level of infant deaths.

Chapter 6 under the head of Determinants of Infant Mortality determines the relations of various components of infant deaths, namely neonatal, post-neonatal and infant mortality rate with reference to various demographic, social, economic, sanitation and infrastructural variables through zero order correlation matrices and the quantity and magnitude of relationship among the above variables has further been examined in stepwise regression. Again, the role of various variables in explanation of infant mortality rate in Jharkhand has been established through applying binary logistic regression analysis. Thus, the impact of various variables on infant deaths has vividly been verified through the application of the above statistical techniques.

Finally, Chapter 7 includes summary, conclusion and policy implications. The findings, observations and problems discussed in each chapter are included in this chapter under the head Summary. The magnitude of either reproval or rejection of hypotheses has also been analysed under the head Conclusion. Several recommendations on the basis of previous findings have been summarised for the curtailment of child deaths among the PTGs in Jharkhand so that policy-makers and programme implementers can introduce the above suggestions while framing policies for the upliftment of primitive tribes in general and children and reproductive females in particular.

Significance of the Study

From the above observations, it is concluded that social, economic, demographic and environmental factors are important determinants of infant survival. The previous works are exclusively confined to the analysis of socio-economic characteristics of primitive tribes in the state. Again, some studies focused on level, trend and determinants infant mortality, while other focused on disparity of infant mortality among socio-economic groups and its causes for the whole population. Though some studies dealt with socio-economic disparity in infant mortality but whether this disparity has declined over time has not been properly addressed in any case of the studies. In this context, this study proposes to study the trends, patterns, causes and consequences of infant mortality among the primitive tribes in Jharkhand state in comparison to the state average and national average of India well, which is exclusively confined to the PTGs and thus presents a classical example of sectoral community-wise analysis of infant deaths in Jharkhand. The present study investigates a detail analysis of infant deaths among the PTGs and determines the role of child deaths in keeping the population of above communities as either stagnant or in declining mode, which is mainly produced through vicious circle of poverty.

REFERENCES

Adams, A.M., A. Rabbani, S. Ahmed, S.S. Mahmood, A. Al Sabir, S.F. Rashid and T.G. Evans (2013). "Explaining equity gains in child survival in Bangladesh: scale, speed, and selectivity in health and development", *Lancet*, 382:2027I 2037.

Ahmad, A. (1999). *Social Geography*, Jaipur: Rawat Publications, pp. 113-176.

Ahmad, E. (1965). *Bihar: A Physical, Economic and Regional Geography*, Ranchi: Ranchi University Press, pp. 22-26.

Arnold, Fred, Minja Kim Choe and T.K. Roy (1998). "Son preference, the family building process and child mortality in India", *Population Studies*, Vol. 52, pp. 301-315.

Arokiasamy, P. (2004). "Regional patterns of sex bias and excess female child mortality in India", *Population Studies*, Vol.59, pp. 833-863.

Bairagi, R., S.C. Sutradhar and N. Alam (1999). "Levels, Trends and Determinants of Child Mortality in Matlab, Bangladesh, 1966-1994 (Demographers' Notebook)", *Asia-Pacific Population Journal*, Vol. 14, No. 2, pp. 51-68.

Baneijee, K.S. and T.K. Roy (2002). "Parental Consanguinity and Offspring Mortality: The Search for Possible Linkage in the Indian Context", *AsiaPacific Population Journal*, Vol. 17, No. 1, pp. 17-38.

Bhatt, M. (2004). *Social Demography in India*, Delhi: Academic Excellence, pp. 1-17.

Bhutta, Z.A., Hafeez, A., Rizvi, A., Ali, N., Khan, A., Ahmad, F., Bhutta, S., Hazir, T., Zaidi, A., Jafarey, S.N. (2013). "Reproductive, maternal, newborn, and child health in Pakistan: challenges and opportunities", *Lancet*, 381: 2207I2218.

Bourne, K.L. and G.M. Walker (1991). "The Differential Effects of Mother's Education on Mortality of Boys and Girls in India", *Population Studies*, Vol. 45, No. 2, pp. 203-219.

Bulled, N., M. Singer and R. Dillingham (2014). "The syndics of childhood diarrhoea: a biosocial perspective on efforts to combat global inequities in diarrhoea-related morbidity and mortality", *Global Public Health, 9* (7), 841-853. doi :10.1080/17441 692. 2014.924022

Caldwell, J.C. (1979). "Education as a Factor in Mortality Decline: An Examination of Nigerian data", *Population Studies*, 33(3), pp. 395-413.

Chacko, P.A. (1991). "Healthy and Unhealthy Contradictions in the Lives of Sauria Paharias of Santal Parganas —Action Health Programmes of Rajmahal Hills", in S.P. Sinha (ed.), *Sauria Paharia of Rajmahal Hills: A Study in a Struggling Primitive Tribe for Existence,* Bihar Tribal Welfare Research Institute, Welfare Department, Government of Bihar, Ranchi, Vol. XXXI, Nos. 1 and 2, pp.159-66.

Chakrabarti, A. (2005). "Maternal Health Care Utilization: An empirical analysis based on Rural India", pp. 53-68, in B.B. Bhattacharya, *Studies in Macroeconomics and Welfare,* New Delhi: Academic Foundation.

Chandrasekhar, S. (1972). *Infant Mortality, Population Growth and Family Planning in India,* Chapel Hill: The University of North Carolina Press, pp. 100-213.

Chatterjee, A. and V.P. Paily (2011). "Achieving Millennium Development Goals 4 and 5 in India", *BJOG: an international journal of obstetrics and gynecology,* 118 Suppl 2: 47159.

Chien, Trung Thi Tran, Trinh Huu Vach, Robert Hanenberg, Luong Xuan Hien and BuiHuu Chuan (2002). "Perinatal Mortality in Viet Nam", *Asia-Pacific Population Journal,* Vol. 17, No. 1, pp. 116.

Choe, K.M. and J. Chen (2006). "Potential for Reducing Child and Maternal Mortality through Reproductive and Child Health Intervention Programmes: An Illustrative Case Study from India", *Asia-Pacific Population Journal,* Vol. 21, No. 1, pp. 14-44.

Claeson, M., E.R. Bos, T. Mawji, I. Pathmanathan (2000). "Reducing child mortality in India in the New Millennium", *Bulletin of the World Health Organization* 2000, 78: 1192-1199.

Monica, D. (1990). "Death clustering, mothers' education and the determinants of child mortality in rural Punjab, India," *Population Studies*, Vol. 44, No. 3, pp. 489-505.

Das Gupta, Monica (1997). "Socio-Economic Status and Clustering of Child Deaths in Rural Punjab", *Population Studies*, Vol. 51, No. 2, pp. 191-202.

Debi, P. (1979). *Scarps of Chotanagpur: A Study in Physiography and Human Geography,* Ranchi: Subodh Granthmala Karyalaya, pp. 1-8.

Gaiva, M.M., Fujimori, E., and Sato, A.S. (2014). "Neonatal mortality in infants with low birth weight", *Revista Da Escola De Enfermagem Da U S P*, 48(5), 778-786.

Gandotra, M.M., N. Das and D. Dey (1982). *Infant Mortality and its Causes in Gujarat*, Baroda: Population Research Centre.

Gopalan, C. (1962). *Bulletin of the World Health Organization*, 26, p. 205.

Gubhaju, B. (1991). "Socio-economic, Demographic and Environmental Determinants of Infant Mortality in Nepal", *Journal of Bio-Social Science*, Vol. 4, pp. 425-435.

Gupta, S.P. (1983). "Administering the Pre-farming and Marginal Tribes", *Bulletin of the Bihar Tribal Welfare Research Institute*, Vol. XXV, Nos. 1 and 2, pp. 109-124.

Mohan, H. (1960). "Economic Organization of the Mal Paharia and the Kumarbagh of Santal Pargana", *Bulletin of Bihar Tribal Research Institute*, Vol. 2, No. 2, pp. 33-66.

Harding, R.D. (1948). "A Note of Some Vital Statistics of a Primitive Peasant Community in Sierra Leone", *Population Studies*, Vol. 2, No. 3, pp. 373-77.

Hong, R.A. *et al.* (2009). "Childhood Mortality in Rwanda: Levels, Trends, and Differentials", Calverton, MD: ICF Macro.

Hossain, J. and Kamal, K.M. (2010). "An Econometric Investigation of Infant Mortality Scenarios in Bangladesh", *Journal of Business and Economics*, 5(1)2, 97-105.

Jain, A.K. (1985). "Determinants of Regional Variation in Infant Mortality in Rural India", *Population Studies*, Vol. 39, pp. 407-424.

Jharkhand Economic Survey, 2018-19, Planning-Cum-Finance Department, Centre for Fiscal Studies, Government of Jharkhand, pp. 1-15.

Joshi, R., Sharma, S., and van Teijlingen, E. (2013). Improving Neonatal Health in Nepal: Major Challenges to Achieving Millennium Development Goal 4, *Health Science Journal*, 7(4), 247-257.

Kerber, K.J. *et al.* (2007). "Continuum of Care for Maternal, New-born and Child Health: From Slogan to Service Delivery", *The Lancet*, Vol. 370, No. 9595, pp. 1358-1369.

Khan, M.E. (1988). "Infant Mortality in Uttar Pradesh: A Micro Level Study", in A.K. Jain and P. Visaria (eds.), *Infant Mortality in India: Differentials and Determinants*, New Delhi: Sage Publications, pp. 227-246.

Kirk, D. (1996). "Demographic Transition Theory", *Population Studies*, Vol. 50, No. 3, pp. 361-387.

Minnery M., E. Jimenez Soto, S. Firth, K.H. Nguyen, A. Hodge (2013). "Disparities in Child Mortality Trends in Two New States of India", *BMC Public Health*, 13: 779.

Mishra, J. (1997). "Nature of Food with Reference to Jharkhand Region", *Man and Life*, Vol. 23, Nos. 1-2, pp. 77-84.

Mohan, H. (1983). "Primitive Tribes: Problems and Prospects of Development", *Bulletin of the Bihar Tribal Welfare Research Institute*, Vol. XXV, Nos.1 and 2, pp. 125-134.

Mosley, Henry, W. and L.C. Chen (1984). "An Analytical Framework for the Study of Child Survival in Developing Countries", *Population and Development Review 10 (suppl.)*, pp. 24-45.

Mostafa, Golam (1995). "The Influence of Socio-biological Factors on Perinatal Mortality in a Rural Area of Bangladesh (Demographers' Notebook)", *Asia-Pacific Population Journal*, Vol. 10, No. 1, pp. 63-72.

Nisar, Y.B., M.J. Dibley, S. Mebrahtu, N. Paudyal and M. Devkola (2014). "Antenatal Iron-Folic Acid Supplement Reduces Neonatal and Under-5 Mortality in Nepal", Retrieved from https://pubmed.ncbi.nlm.nih.gov/26136588/

Narayana, D. (2008). "Intensifying Infant Mortality Inequality in India and a Reversal by Policy Intervention", *Journal of Human Development*, 9: 265I281.

Narayan, S. (1991). "Development and Tradition in Sauria Paharia", in S.P. Sinha (ed.), *Sauria Paharia of Rajmahal Hills: A Study in a Struggling Primitive Tribe for Existence*, Bihar Tribal Welfare Research Institute, Welfare Department, Government of Bihar, Ranchi, Vol. XXXI, Nos. 1 and 2, pp. 183-190.

Newborns: Reducing mortality (2016, January). Retrieved February 01, 2017, from http://www.who.int/mediacentre/factsheets/fs333/en/

Nguyen, K.H., E. JimenezISoto, P. Dayal and A. Hodge (2013). "Disparities in child mortality trends: what is the evidence from disadvantaged states in India?, The Case of Orissa and Madhya Pradesh", *International Journal for Equity in Health*, 12: 45.

Padmanaban P., P.S. Raman, D.V. Mavalankar (2009). "Innovations and Challenges in Reducing Maternal Mortality in Tamil Nadu, India", *Journal of Health, Population, and Nutrition*, 27: 202I219.

Peller, S. (1943). "Mortality, Past and Future", *Population Studies*, Vol. 1, pp. 405-456.

Potter, E. Joseph (1988), "Birth Spacing and Child Survival: A Cautionary Note Regarding the Evidence from the WFS", *Population Studies*, Vol. 42, No. 3, pp. 443-450.

Prasad, A. (1973). *Chotanagpur: Geography of Rural Settlements*, Ranchi: Ranchi University Press, pp. 8-30.

Preston, Samuel H. (1996). "Population Studies of Mortality", *Population Studies*, Vol. 50, No. 3, pp. 525-536.

Raj, Hans (2003). *Fundamentals of Demography, Population Studies with Special Reference to India*, Delhi: Surjeet Publications, pp. 1-43.

Rajan, S.I. *et al.* (2008). *Infant and Child Mortality in India: District Level Estimates*, New Delhi: Population Foundation of India, pp. 1-16.

Rajna, P.N., A.K. Mishra and S. Krishnamoorthy (1998). "Impact of Maternal Education and Health Services on Child Mortality in Uttar Pradesh, India", *Asia-Pacific Population Journal,* Vol. 13, No. 2, pp. 27-38.

Retherford, R.D. and M.K. Choe (1993). *Statistical Models for Causal Analysis,* New York: John Wiley and Sons, Inc, pp. 119-166.

Ruzicka, L.T. and T. Kanitkar (1972). 'Infant Mortality in an Urban Setting: The Case of Greater Bombay', in K.E. Vaidyanathan (ed.), *Studies on Mortality in India,* Madras: The Gandhigram Institute of Rural Health and Family Planning, pp. 186-204.

Sanyal, S. (1991). "Health Development of Sauriya Paharia", in S.P. Sinha (ed.), *Sauria Paharia of Rajmahal Hills: A Study in a Struggling Primitive Tribe for Existence,* Bihar Tribal Welfare Research Institute, Welfare Department, Government of Bihar, Ranchi, Vol. XXXI, Nos. 1 and 2, pp. 177-79.

Shah, B. (2009). *Study on Causes of Death by Verbal Autopsy in India,* New Delhi: Indian Council of Medical Research, pp. 3-25.

Shetty, A., and Shetty, S. (2014). "The Impact of Female Literacy on Infant Mortality Rate in Indian States", *Current Paediatric Research,* 18(1), 49-56.

Singh, A., P.K. Pathak, R.K. Chauhan and W. Pan (2011). "Infant and Child Mortality in India in the last two decades: a geospatial analysis", *PloS one,* 6: e 26856.

Singh, J. (1964). *Transport Geography of South Bihar,* Varanasi: B.H.U. Press, pp. 14-31.

Singh, M. (2010). *Care of the New-born,* (7th ed.), New Delhi: Sagar Printers and Publishers, pp. 1-12.

Singh, S.K. *et al.* (1998). "Socio-economic differentials in child mortality in three selected states of India", *Indian Association of Social Science Institutions (IASSI) Quarterly,* Vol. 16, pp. 53-73.

Singh, V.K. (1995). "Bihar Primitive Upliftment Project", *Bulletin of Bihar Tribal Welfare Research Institute,* Vol. XXXV, pp. 25-28.

Stoeckel, John and A.K.M.A. Chowdhury (1972). "Neo-Natal and Post-Neo-Natal Mortality in a Rural Area of Bangladesh", *Population Studies,* Vol. 26, No.1, pp. 113-120.

UNO (1948). *UN Universal Declaration of Human Rights,* Article No. 25, pp. 20-22.

UNICEF (1991). *Children and Women in India—A Situation Analysis,* UNICEF: India, New Delhi, p. 74.

UNITED Nations Children Fund (2006). *The State of World's Children 2007: Women and Children,* New York: UNICEF, pp. 1-34.

Upadhyay, V.S. (2005). *Hill Kharia/Sabar,* Ranchi: Jharkhand Tribal Welfare Research Institute, pp. 189-210.

Verma, U.K. (1991). "Sauria Paharia and Development", in S.P. Sinha (ed.), *Sauria Paharia of Rajmahal Hills: A Study in a Struggling Primitive Tribe for Existence*, Bihar Tribal Welfare Research Institute, Welfare Department, Government of Bihar, Ranchi, Vol. XXXI, Nos. 1 and 2, p. 197.

Veneman, A.M. (2009). *The State of the World's Children*, Colo Craft of Virginia, Inc., UNICEF, pp. 24-48.

Vidyarthi, L.P. and B.K. Rai (1985). *The Tribal Culture of India*, New Delhi: Concept Publishing Company, pp. 236-271.

World Health Organization (2004). *Low Birth Weight Country, Regional and Global Estimates*. Retrieved from https://www.unicef.org/publications/files/low_ birth_weight_ from_EY.pdf

World Health Organization-UNICEF (1978). Alma-Ata 1978, Primary Health Care, Report of the International Conference on Primary Health Care, Alma-Ata, USSR, 6-12 September, 1978.

Zakir, M. and P. Wunnava (1999). "Factors Affecting Infant Mortality Rates: Evidence from Cross-Sectional Data", *Applied Economics Letters, 6:* 271-273.

2
Distribution, Growth and Concentration of Primitive Tribes in Jharkhand

The distribution of population refers to the actual pattern of spacing of units of individuals. The state of Jharkhand is endowed with a wide variety of tribal people varying in concentration on environmental affinity, physiological construction, economic pursuits and cultural traits. The Dhebar Commission (1961) and the Shilu Ao. Committee constituted by the Planning Commission in 1969 for reviewing the tribal situation observed that a large number of tribal communities to be extremely backward and some of them were still in the primitive food gathering stage. It has emphasized that these communities needed special attention. Further, it was implemented in Fifth Plan, which is generally considered as the watershed in the task of tribal development because some major policies like tribal sub-plan, integrated tribal development project, identification of primitive tribes etc. were introduced in the plan. Now, there would be a separate budgetary head for the purpose and the central plan would supplement the state plan instead of replacing it. However, separate scheme for the PTGs in Jharkhand was launched in 1998-99. As a part of tribal sub-plan strategy, more than seventy-five tribal groups with a total population of about 13 lakh have been identified as the primitive groups in the country. Out of 32 tribal communities in Jharkhand eight tribes, namely Asur, Birhor, Birjia, Korwa, Parhaiya, Mal Paharia, Saruia

Paharia and Savar have been identified as primitives on the basis of pre-agriculture level of technology, low level of literacy and stagnant or diminishing population. They are simple artisan tribes, who still practise shifting cultivation and hunting as a way of living.

Composition, Physical Traits and Distribution of Separate Primitive Tribe

The structure of population plays a dominant role in shaping the socio-economic prosperity of the region. Its composition also performs a major game changer in a democratic country whereby elected government is constituted through majority-election. Since they are marginal in numbers, their voices are generally supressed through majority-form government. Again, the physical characteristics of any individual determine the involvement of any person in carrying out of a particular type of economic activity and selection criteria for the appointment of particular job like police etc. should be ascertained on the basis of their physical traits. Further, its isolated and juxtaposed distribution indicates what sort of welfare schemes are needed for their holistic development of the society. That is why, separate and detailed exercises of all eight primitive tribes have been analysed here.

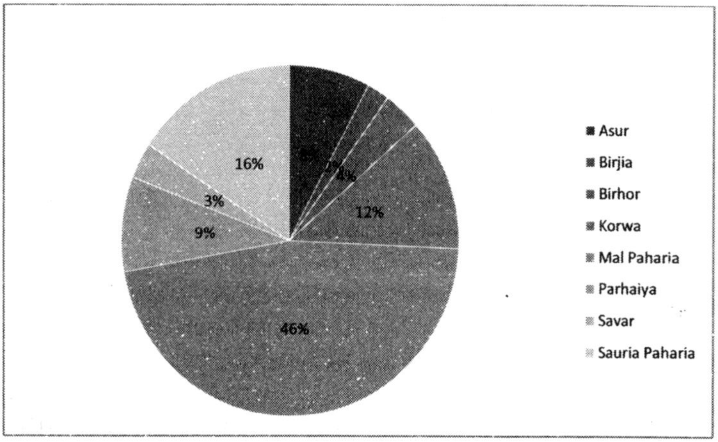

Fig. 2.1: Composition of Primitive Tribes in Jharkhand, 2011

Asur

The Asurs are Proto-Australoid race and their language belongs to Austro-Asiatic family. They are divided into three sections, viz. the Bir, the Birjia and the Agaria Asur. In our state, the Birjia has been treated as a separate tribe and the Agarias are mainly confined in Chhatisgarh. That is why, the Bir Asurs are represented as the Asurs in the state of Jharkhand. The Asurs are short statured, dolichocephalic, mesorrhine, deep chocolate brown skin colour, cymotrichy people on the basis of respective physical traits of statured, cephalic index, nasal index, skin colour and hair structure. They generally possess deep chocolate brown skin colour whereas the colour of eyes is deep brown black. Centuries of isolation coupled with exploitation and subjugation by one or the other alien elements have driven the Asurs into comparatively inaccessible tract of land amidst hills and mountains, forests and undulating slopes. They have traditionally been the iron-smelters and slash and burn cultivators but the unavailability of charcoal of green Sal and restriction imposed by the government on the slash and burn cultivation popularly known as Beora Panther have made them as the settled farmers (Gupta,1976).

Physical Traits of Asurs

The total population of Asurs was 22459 in 2011 Census, which is around 7.68 per cent of primitive tribal population. Again, Figure 2.2 elaborates the district level distributions of the Asurs in Jharkhand on the basis of 2011 Census and it is apparent that more than fifty per cent of them are concentrated in Gumla district itself. The other districts having population concentration between 9.33 and 50.74 per cent include Latehar and Lohardaga. Another medium level of concentration ranging from1.99 to 9.33 per cent consists of Hazaribagh, Garhwa, Ramgarh and Bokaro districts. There is only Palamu district, which falls in the category of low level of concentration ranging from 0.65 to 1.99 per cent. The remaining districts have very low level of agglomeration as the tribal concentration is found below 0.65 per cent in the state. Exploring the agglomeration of the Asurs at block level on the basis of Survey Report of Primitive Tribal Groups in Jharkhand,2002-03, the maximum concentrations are found in Bishunpur, Chainpur, Ghaghra and Dumri blocks of Gumla district. It is followed by Mahuadanr and Barwadih blocks of Latehar district and Senha and Kisko blocks of Lohardaga district. Although these blocks are concentrated in three districts but spatially, they are juxtaposed to each other through forming a compact belt in the Pat region of Jharkhand. Thus, that particular primitive tribe has made its presence throughout all the districts of the state by varying degree of intensity in 2011 Census but they were exclusively confined to the above mentioned three districts in 2001 Census. It is quite interesting to note that there is a basic difference between the Asurs and the Sauria Paharias that the former has no hesitation and fear psychosis in settling down in any place of the state whereas the later are reluctant to emigrate any other areas of the state than their place of origin. However, both of them are the consumers of beef and pork simultaneously, which are prohibited among the Hindus and the Muslims respectively. That is why, their population has increased more than doubled in the last decade and they possess 7.68 per cent of primitive tribal population, which is fifth ranking in term of their numbers. At state level, the Asurs take account of .07 per cent to the total population whereas its share to the tribal population was .26 per cent in 2011 Census.

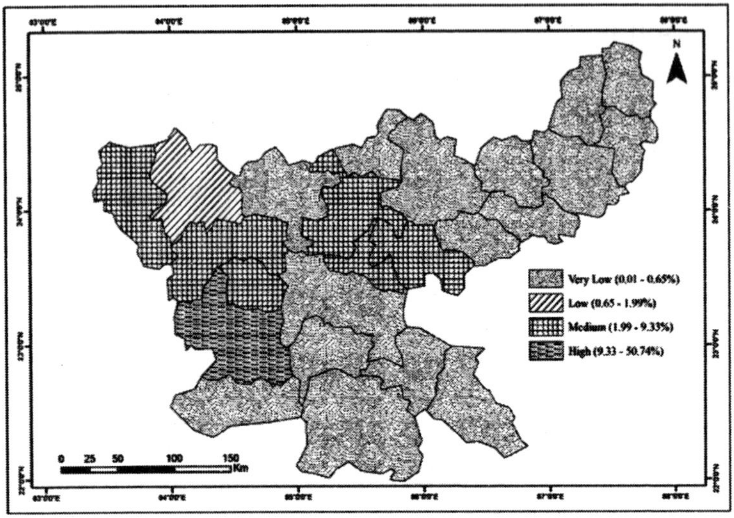

Fig. 2.2: Distribution of Asurs in Jharkhand, 2011

Birjia

The word Birjia is composed of two words Bir and Jia, which together mean the man of forest. It is already discussed earlier that the Birjia is a subgroup of the Asurs. They are Proto-Austroloid race and they speak the Birjia dialect, which is one of the Austro-Asiatic families and is a mixture of Mundari and Asuri dialects. They hold similar physical traits like the Asurs. They practise slash and burn cultivation earlier popularly known as Beora Panther but the prohibitions by the Forest Department have transformed them as the settled cultivators. They are divided into two groups on the basis of social organization: Sinduria Birjia and Teliya Birjia. The Teliya Birjias are further sub-divided into two groups: Dudh Birjia and Ras Birjia. The former only drinks milk from the cow whereas the later eats beef.

The Birjias had the total population of 6276 persons in 2011 Census, which is around only 2 per cent of total primitive people and it ranks the smallest PTG in numerical aspect in the state. The Birjias are exclusively confined to Latehar district where their population accounts far above 65 per cent, which falls into the category of very

Facial Features of Brijias

high concentration ranging from 20.19 to 65.7 per cent and they are again exclusively concentrated only in three blocks of the district, viz. Mahuadanr, Barwadih and Garu block (Appendix-2.4). It is followed by Gumla, which contains above 20 per cent of their population and it is placed in the category of medium level of concentration varying from 9.31 to 20.19 per cent. Bishunpur block of the district has almost all the population of the tribe. The low level of agglomeration comprises Lohardaga district only and 9.31 per cent of the Birjias population were found in 2011 but they were concentrated in Kisko and Senha blocks. Around 2 per cent of their population are found chiefly in the jungle tracks of the southern part of Garhwa, where the cultivation is done on Jhuming system, which is locally known as Beora Panther. They have no trace of their presence in the various districts of the Rajmahal Upland but they are found below 1 per cent in other districts of the state. However, while we visualize their concentration in Fig. 2.3, we find that they are exclusively agglomerated in particular area of Pat Region, which is juxtaposed in the above area but they are spread in different districts and blocks. They were the smallest marginal tribe in

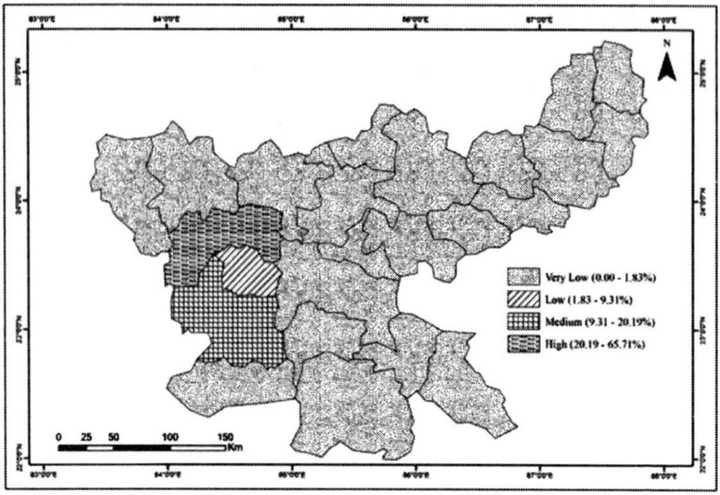

Fig. 2.3: Distribution of Birjias in Jharkhand, 2011

Jharkhand, which have its share to total population was only .02 per cent, whereas its ratio to tribal population was .13 per cent in 2011 Census at state level. However, its share to the PTGs was 2.15 per cent in 2011. They were limited to Latehar, Gumla and Lohardaga districts in 2001 Census but they were also found in the adjoining districts of the state in 2011 Census, which areclearly manifested in Fig. 2.3. Most probably they have out-migrated to other districts from their heartland as a part of their survival strategy.

Korwa

The Korwas are one of the Kolerian tribes, who are found in Jharkhand and Chhatisgarh as well. They are short statured people, whose skin colour varies from chocolate brown to black. They usually possess broad nose, long head and wavy hairs, which is also manifested from the following photo. The land they live in a combination of hills, valleys, well cultivated plains and forest covered hills. Living in and around the hills of north-west part of the state from time immemorial, they have been carrying on a strenuous struggle for bare existence and are constantly engrossed with the problems of food, shelter and immediate satisfaction of other material needs needed for bare existence. This led them to develop a primitive material culture of their own to secure a working control of their natural environment. Ancestors of the tribe used to practise shifting cultivation known as Beora cultivation but they are settled farmers due to constant discouragement by the government. They were once living in isolation in the hills but they are now living in such settlements, which are occupied by other castes and tribes. At present, there is not a single village, which is inhabited by this tribe only. Moreover, they are losing their identity and they are not able to speak their own dialect instead of they speak Sadri language. They are generally casual labourers and contract labourers in the forest (Prasad, 1961).

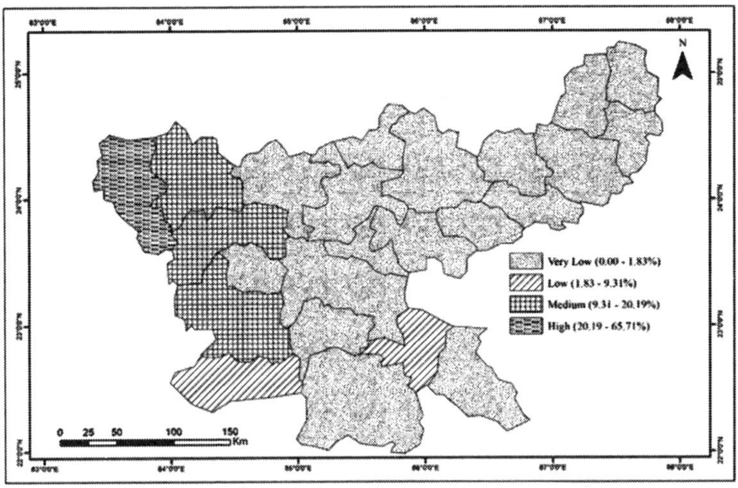

Fig. 2.4: Distribution of Korwas in Jharkhand, 2011

Physical Appearances of Korwas

The numerical strength of the Korwas in Jharkhand according to 2011 Census was 35,606 and it used to occupy the third largest group of primitive tribes which contains around 12.18 per cent of total primitive tribal population. Around 71 per cent of their population were found in the district of Garhwa itself, which is situated in the group of very high concentration ranging from 20.19 to 65.71 per cent. They are also found in the district of Palamu, Gumla, and Latehar, which inherit 9.54 per cent, 8.23 per cent and 7.68 per cent of their population respectively in which the former district is encircled under the category of medium level of concentration whereas the latter two districts fall in the group of low level of concentration. Their major concentration, therefore, is in those districts where they have been living in and around the hills for generations. So far block-wise concentration is concerned, they are observed in all blocks of the district but they are highly agglomerated in Chinia, Bhandaria, Ranka, Dhurki and Ramkanda blocks. It is to be mentioned that Palamu has the majority of the Korwas in Chainpur block. Thus, it clearly reflects that they are especially found in the hilly tracts of Kanhar and North Koel Interfluve, Pat Region and Sankh Basin. It is remarkable to investigate that the proportion of the Korwas to total population of the state was 0.11 per cent whereas the share of its population to total tribal population was 0.41 per cent in 2011Census.The analysis of the Korwas location in 2001 further manifests that they were thoroughly clustered in the districts of Garhwa, Palamu, Gumla, Latehar and Simdega, which are situated in the western part of the state. There is marginal dispersal of their population in the adjoining districts which had the similar physical environment and their out-migration owe to mainly extreme poverty and survival strategy. The positive increase in numbers was found high in those districts which had substantial population in 2001 Census.

Parhaiya

The Parhaiyas are one of the eight primitive tribes in Jharkhand, who are primarily extended over Kanhar-North Koel Interfluve and adjacent Pat region. They live on the forested tracts and hills since time immemorial. As they live in natural surroundings, their habitats, means of livelihood, thoughts and ideas have been shaped in the natural way. They are characterised by short stature, dolichocephaly, flat wide nose, short face, wavy or curly black hair and dark brown skin colour (Dash Sharma, 1928). Their chief means of livelihood is gathering and hunting, though some of them also practise the slash and burn type of cultivation popularly known as Beora and they are in a state of abject poverty. Now they have become labourers and work in the forest and field to earn wages and some of them are also marginal farmers. The forest economy of the Parhaiyas has received a setback due to strict forest laws. They are basically a Hinduized tribe, viz. their religious beliefs and practices reveal an intermingling Hinduism due to their long contact with the neighbouring Hindus. They speak a language, which is mixture of Sadri and Magahi dialects.

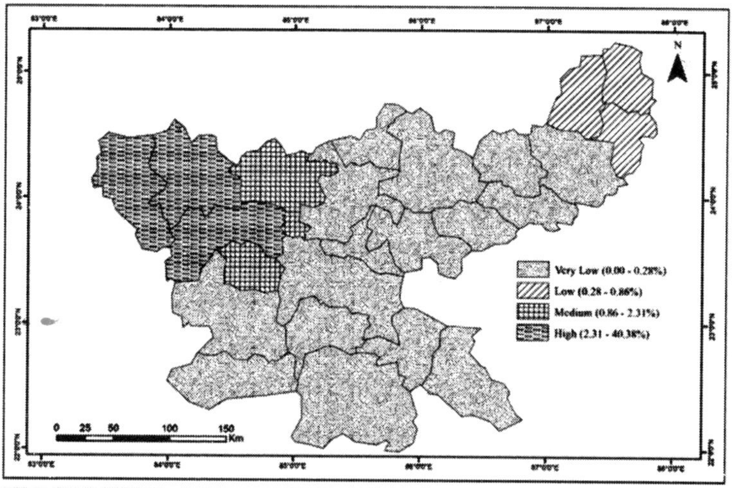

Fig. 2.5: Distribution of Parhaiyas in Jharkhand, 2011

Fundamentally, the Parhaiyas inhabit the districts of Palamu, Latehar and Garhwa, which are situated in north-western portion of the state and these districts contain high level of concentration ranging between 2.31 and 40.38 per cent of total PTG population at district level. Their total population was 25,585, which was just 0.3 per cent of the total tribal population whereas its share to total population was only 0.08 per cent in 2011 Census. It stands the fourth largest group through capturing the share of above 9 per cent of total primitive tribes and they are agglomerated in the western corridor of the state. Palamu alone contains more than 40 per cent of their population, which is the homeland of the Parhaiyas. It is followed by Latehar and Garhwa district where their share to their population is 27.18 per cent and 25.36 per cent respectively. It is also to be noticed that these two districts are neighbouring districts of Palamu. They are primarily found in Hussainabad, Chhatarpur, Manatu and Bishrampur blocks of Palamu, Latehar, Barwadih, Balumath and Chandwa blocks of Latehar district and Dandai, Ramna and Dhurki blocks of Garhwa district at block level. The other districts having the share of PTGs between 0.86 and 2.31 per cent are clubbed under the group of medium level of distribution and the districts are enumerated as Chatra and Lohardaga. The remaining districts of the state have population of PTGs below 1 per cent constitute low and very low level of concentration and their presence is completely negligible in the districts of Simdega and Khunti. It can be easily inferred from the above discussions that they are agglomerated in particular area of the state, i.e. Kanhar and North Koel Interfluve and adjoining areas of Pat Region, which are original habitats of the tribe. Even in 2001 Census they were exclusively confined to Palamu, Latehar, Garhwa and Chatra districts of the north-western portion of the state. There was gradual dispersal of their population in 2011 towards the adjoining districts of the state

Physical Traits of Parhaiyas

which had the similar physical and social environment. Broadly, their populations have expanded in almost all the districts of the state except Chatra, which experienced negative growth of population in 2011 Census.

Table 2.1: Composition of primitive tribal groups in Jharkhand

Primitive Tribal Groups	Population	% of PTG	% of PTG to Total Population	% of PTG to S.T. Population
Asur	22459	7.68	0.07	0.26
Birhor	10726	3.67	0.03	0.12
Birjia	6276	2.15	0.02	0.07
Korwa	35606	12.18	0.11	0.41
Mal Paharia	135797	46.45	0.41	1.57
Parhaiya	25585	8.75	0.08	0.30
Sauria Paharia	46222	15.81	0.14	0.53
Savar	9688	3.31	0.03	0.11
Total	**292359**	**100**	**0.89**	**3.38**

Source: Census of India 2011, Series I, Jharkhand, Social and Cultural Tables, Table A-II, District-wise Scheduled tribe Population for Each Tribe Separately, Delhi: Controller of Publications.

Mal Paharia

The Mal Paharia community living in the hilly and forest areas of the Southern Rajmahal Range, which is just south of the Bansloi river is one of the most backward primitive tribes. They are the Dravidian tribes, who belong to Proto-Australoid group. They are believed to have migrated here from Karnataka in ancient times. They speak Malto language, which is considered the language of the Dravidian people. Since the Mal and Sauria Pahrias belong to the same racial group, the Mal Paharias inherit the morphological characteristics of the Sauria Paharias. They do not have clan system but they are divided on the basis of hereditary background. Again, they avoid marriage among themselves. Culturally, the Paharia communities are broadly divided into three sections: Mal Paharia, Kumarbhag Paharia and Sauria

Paharia. However, the Kumarbhag community consider themselves as one community as the Mal Paharia for getting the benefit of reservation since they are not considered as separate group of scheduled tribes. The major source of their livelihood and pride of their tradition is Kurwa cultivation and their economic sub status is still based on it. Basically, they are Hinduized branch of Maler, who do not eat beef at all (Prasad, 1961).

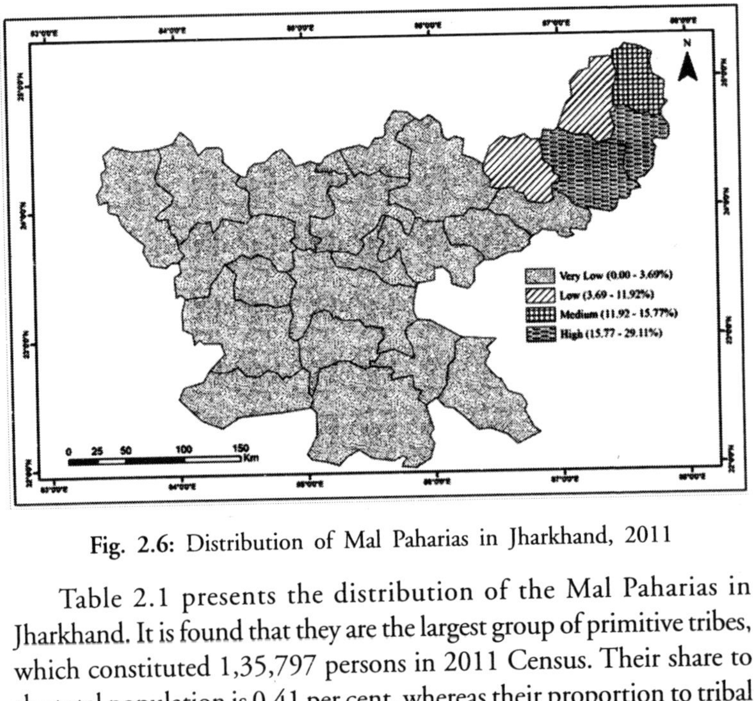

Fig. 2.6: Distribution of Mal Paharias in Jharkhand, 2011

Table 2.1 presents the distribution of the Mal Paharias in Jharkhand. It is found that they are the largest group of primitive tribes, which constituted 1,35,797 persons in 2011 Census. Their share to the total population is 0.41 per cent, whereas their proportion to tribal population is 1.57 per cent. Moreover, it is considered as the largest group of PTGs, which engulfs more than 46 per cent of primitive people. As it has been discussed earlier that they are found mainly in the Damin-i-Koh areas and the whole region consists of mainly into four parts on the administrative convenience, namely Dumka Damin, Pakur Damin, Rajmahal Damin and Godda Damin. Even today, the share of Dumka, Pakur, Sahibganj Godda and Deoghar district is 29.11 per cent, 28.07 per cent, 15.77 per cent, 11.92 per cent and 9.03 per cent respectively (Appendix-2.5). The Figure 2.6 vividly portrays that the former two districts, namely Dumka and Pakur belong to the group of high level of their agglomeration. Sahibganj district is recognised under medium whereas Godda and Deoghar districts are grouped under the heading of low level of concentration.At block level, they are primarily concentrated in Kathikund, Gopikandar, Shikaripara, Jama, Dumka, Ramgarh and Jarmundi blocks of Dumka, Hiranpur and Litipara blocks of Pakur, Taljhari and Barhait blocks of Sahibganj and Boarijor and Sundarpahari blocks of Godda district. The adjoining districts of the Damin-i-Koh are Deoghar and Jamtara which have their population—9.03 and 3.69 per cent respectively. It is almost absent in other districts of Chotanagpur Plateau, where their share is below 1 per cent. The same pattern of concentration was also observed in 2001 Census, when the four districts, namely Dumka, Pakur, Sahibganj and Godda used to capture the maximum concentration of their population. The analysis of growth of population also manifests that there was highest number of increases in population among the Mal Paharias between 2001 and 2011 Census. It also explains that they have also out-migrated to other districts of the state from the principal agglomeration of Damin-i-Koh area for their survival strategy.

Physical Looks of Young Mal Paharias

Sauria Paharia

The Sauria Paharias are one of the eight notified primitive tribes in the state of Jharkhand. They are primarily the inhabitants of the portion of the Damin-i-Koh, where they reside in the slope of the hills and the top of the hills. Their habitation is the wide sweep in the northern Rajmahal Hill Range. The river Bansloi, near Amarpara clearly demarcates the Sauria Paharias from the Mal Paharias. The former is concentrated on the northern side of it and the later on the southern side. They are Dravidian group of people, who usually speak Malto. Another group of the Paharias, namely the Mal Paharias consider the Sauria Paharias as untouchable because they eat beef. The main occupation is shifting cultivation, food gathering, and fishing, hunting and collecting of minor forest produce. The shifting cultivation is locally known as 'Kurwa' and has great love for it. They totally depend on it for their livelihood. They are generally short statured people having long limbs in proportion to their low stature. Their complex is light brown or black. Their noses are flat and broad at

Physical Portraits of Sauria Paharias

the base (Dalton,1872). They are also called the Malers and they have been driven from the plain by the most enterprising and industrious Santhals (Sinha, 1991).

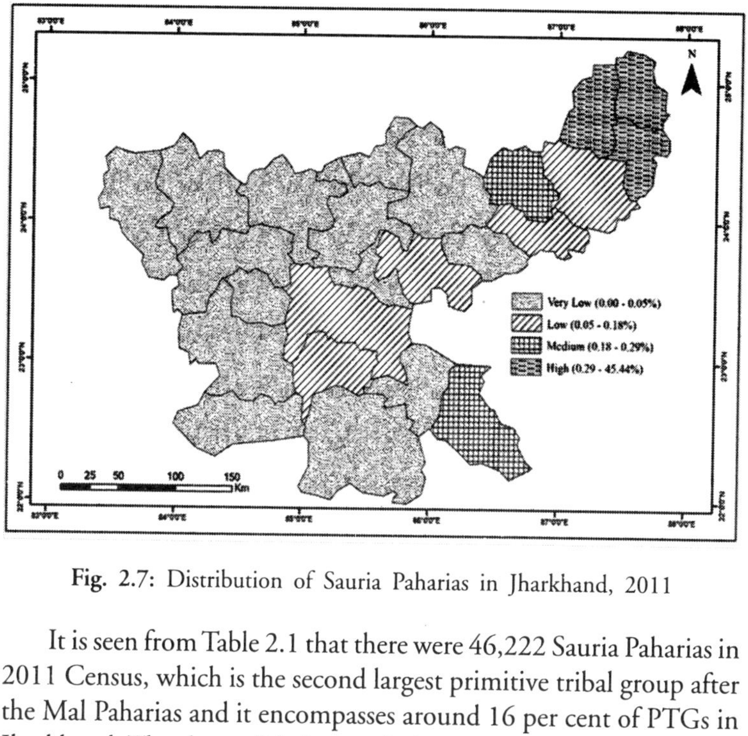

Fig. 2.7: Distribution of Sauria Paharias in Jharkhand, 2011

It is seen from Table 2.1 that there were 46,222 Sauria Paharias in 2011 Census, which is the second largest primitive tribal group after the Mal Paharias and it encompasses around 16 per cent of PTGs in Jharkhand. The share of their population to total population is 0.14 per cent whereas their share to tribal population is 0.53 per cent. Figure 2.7 clearly reveals that they are primarily confined to three districts only and they are Sahibganj, Godda and Pakur, which have their contribution of population 45.44 per cent, 29.61 per cent and 23.53 per cent respectively. In fact, these three districts contain the areas of Rajmahal Damin, Godda Damin and Pakur Damin, which were their original places of habitation since ancient times. It is further observed that their out-migration from their place of origin to other districts of the state are almost not found as they are very shy and uneducated people. They have fear psychosis of inferiority complex as they are the consumers of both beef and pork. That is why, they feel themselves secure in the midst of forested hills. The distribution pattern of the tribe in 2001 Census manifests the same kind of their agglomeration which was confined into the above-mentioned districts. Other districts of the state have almost no imprint of their population. It is a matter of anxiety that their population has reduced considerably in 2001 Census in comparison with1991 Census and the planners and policy makers should take cognizance of the decline of their population. However, their population has increased in 2011 Census, which may be due to overall development of scheduled tribes in the state after formation of state. The block level analysis reveals that they are basically located in Barhait, Taljhari, Mandro, Pathna and Borio blocks of Sahibganj, Boarijor and Sundarpahari blocks of Godda and Amrapara, Maheshpur, Hiranpur and Littipara blocks of Pakur district in the state.

Savar

The Savars and the Hill Kharias are two names of the same tribe. The Savars are also known as the Hill Kharias because they are mostly found in mountainous areas. They are living in the midst of forest and depend upon forest produces in the Dhalbhum Region of Jharkhand. Generally, their villages are situated at the foot of hills as well as on the bank of the stream surrounded by hill ranges covered with thick forest away from the mainland. They follow the Hindu rituals just like any other Bengali. The language spoken by them is known as Kharia, which is a branch of the Mundari family of languages. Their language has been deeply affected by the language spoken by their neighbours. That is why, they speak corrupt form of Bengali language, which is the mixture of the above two languages. The main source of livelihood is either wage earning as contract or casual labourer or marginal farming near the homesteads. In addition to the above, they are also involved in food gathering and hunting. Overall, they are submissive, shy, innocent and conservative. They do not like to mix with any outsiders and rather keep themselves aloof and isolated (Upadhyay, 2005). They are of Proto-Australoid race, which is characterised by dark brown to nearly black skin, long head, broad and flat nose with a slight depression at the root, wavy hair and short stature, which is reflected from the given snap.

Physical Traits of Savars

Table 2.1 presents that the Savars constitute 3.31 per cent of the total population of PTGs in the state of Jharkhand. The total population enumerated in 2011 Census was 9688 persons, which was 0.03 per cent and 0.11 per cent of the total population and the total tribal population of the state respectively. It clearly portrays that more than 83 per cent of their population is concentrated only in Purbi Singhbhum, which comes under the category of very high agglomeration of their population through Fig. 2.8. They are mainly distributed in Patamda, Ghatshila, Dhalbhumgarh, Baharagora, Potka and Chakulia blocks of the district. It is followed by Seraikella Kharsawan, where more than 5 per cent of their population is concentrated in Nimdih and Chandil block and that district has medium level of concentration of the above community. The population of the Savars ranging from 0.65 to 2.17 per cent belongs to Dumka, Paschim Singhbhum, Dhanbad, Pakur and Gumla where they are found in a scattered manner. The other districts of the state have negligible presence, which clearly conveys that they are the migrants from Purbi Singhbhum. The above concept can be verified by the minute investigation of 2001 Census, when they were primarily restricted to Purbi Singhbhum. But there was a widespread dispersal of their population in every district of the state due to their extreme poverty in 2011. They have become second smallest primitive tribe in the state. Again, it is a matter of great concern for the planners and the policy makers that their total population had decreased substantially in 2001 Census in comparison with 1991 Census but there is somehow an increase in their population in the current census. The above situation clearly reflects that their participation in mineral exploration and industrial activity is negligible but the above district is one of the richest districts in India in consideration of mineral resources and industrial development.

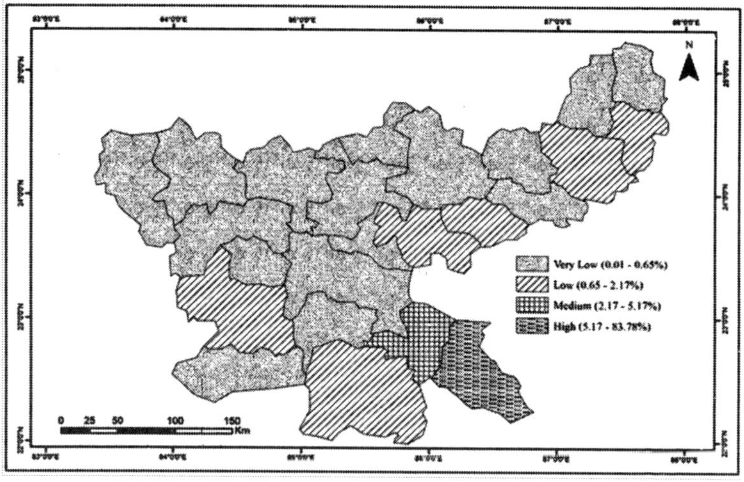

Fig. 2.8: Distribution of Savars in Jharkhand, 2011

Birhor

The Birhors are one of the nomadic primitive tribal groups in Jharkhand, which struggle hard for their existence even today. The word Birhor is made from two Mundari words wherein 'Bir' means jungle and 'Hor' means men. So, the word Birhor stands for the meaning of the jungle men. They are divided into two groups, i.e. Uthlu and Jaghis. The former has a wandering style of life and they move from one forest to another in search of food and rope materials, whereas the later has settled down on either some hill tops or the outskirt of a jungle. They belong to the Proto Australoid human group and are generally characterised by dark skin, short stature, long head, wavy hair and broad nose. Linguistically, they speak 'Birhori', which is one of the dialects of Mundari group but in the general conversation they use the local contact language (Kumar, 2004). The settlements are known as 'Tandas', which consist of about half dozen or more conical huts. They are further divided into exogamous clans named after animals and plants. They follow the Hindu rituals and also worship female deities and devils. Besides hunting and gathering, they trap the monkeys, hares, rabbits, peacocks etc. and sell them in the market. The also collect honey, wax etc. for selling them in markets.

Physical Traits of Birhors

It is the only primitive tribe in the state, who is found in almost all the districts of the Chotanagpur Plateau due to their nomadic habit and abject poverty and their share to total population of PTGs was 3.67 per cent in 2011 Census. The total population enumerated in

2011 Census was 10726 persons, which was 0.03 per cent and 0.12 per cent of the total population and the total tribal population of the state respectively. Fig. 2.9 manifests that the districts with the ratio of population above 12.32 per cent are comprised of Chatra, Hazaribagh and Kodarama in the Outer Plateau Edge. The region is endowed with rich forest resources, which are the principal livelihood for them. It is followed by another group of districts where their population is found between 3.20 and 2.32 per cent, which is inherited from Ranchi, Gumla, Ramgarh, Giridih and Pashchimi Singhbhum. The districts with the population from 1.22 to 3.20 per cent includes Purbi Singhbhum, Simdega, Dhanbad, Bokaro, Latehar, Seraikella Kharsawan and Lohardaga, where their habitats are semi-sprinkled settlements. The remaining districts of the state have population below 1 per cent, which clearly leads one to think that they have migrated to these districts for selling the forest produces. Further, it is observed that they are found in almost all blocks of Chatra district but they are densely agglomerated in the block of Chatra, Simaria, Lawalaung, Itkhori and Hunterganj. The situation is the same for Hazaribagh, where there is a high concentration in Katkamsandi and Chauparan block but they are observed in all blocks of the district. In addition to the above, they are also observed more in number in all blocks of Bundu of Ranchi, Noamundi of Pashchimi Singhbhum, Kodarma of Kodarma and Bagodar of Giridih and Gumia of Bokaro district. Even in 2001 Census, the patterns of distribution of the Birhors were more or less in the same manner. They were heavily concentrated in Hazaribagh and Chatra, whereas the districts, namely Deoghar, Godda, Sahibganj, Pakur, Dumka and Jamtara of the Rajmahal Upland Region were completely devoid of their population. Beside this, there was substantial concentration in Kodarama,Ranchi and Pashchimi Singhbhum and their presence was also observed in other districts of the Chotanagpur Plateau. It is interesting to note that there was positive growth of population in almost all the districts of the state barring Garhwa and Pashchimi Singhbhum, where there was minor decline from 2001 to 2011 Census.

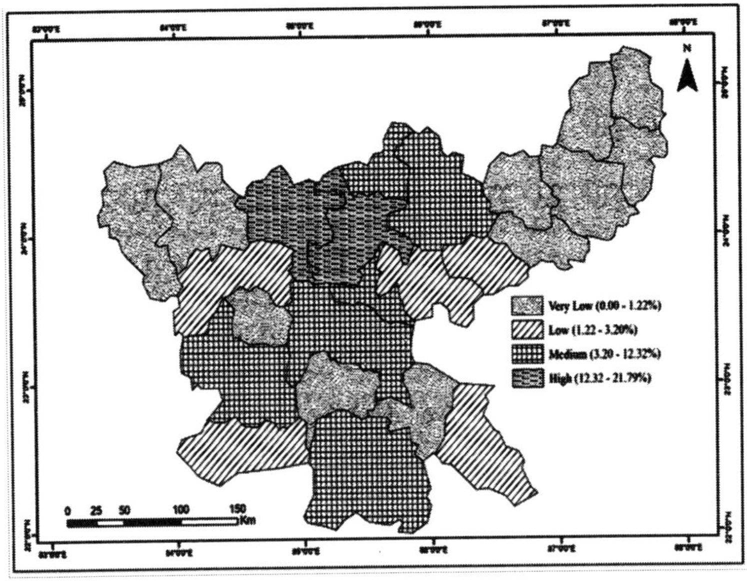

Fig. 2.9: Distribution of Birhors in Jharkhand, 2011

Distribution of Composite Primitive Tribal Groups

It is essential to know the overall numerical strength of primitive tribal groups in comparison to the total strength of scheduled tribes. That is why, the percentage share of PTGs to scheduled tribes has been calculated at district level of Jharkhand and their proportional representation has been portrayed in Fig. 2.10. The districts which can be grouped under the heading of high share of PTGs in comparison to scheduled tribes belong to Pakur, Sahibganj, Dumka, Garhwa, Godda, Gumla and Latehar and all these districts have the percentage of PTGs more than 5 per cent of ST population. In fact, Pakur has the lowest level of economic development but it has the highest share of PTGs, i.e. 16.84 per cent and all these districts with high concentration of PTGs are situated either in Pat or Damin-i-Koh region and they form compact belts through juxtaposition of the blocks. The next group of districts with medium level of PTGs (3-5 per cent) are located in scattered pattern. Palamu is situated in the region of the Outer Edge of Plateau whereas Deoghar and Purbi Singhbhum are located in

Santhal Pargana and Dhalbhum region respectively. The low level of concentration of PTGs varies between 1 and 3 per cent and the districts are located in a haphazard manner. On the one hand Jamtara is located in Santhal Pargana region whereas Lohardaga is situated in Pat region and the remaining two districts, namely Chatra and Hazaribagh are confined to north-central part of the state. The districts with very low level of PTGs are concentrated thickly in central part of the state through juxtaposition of districts extending from north to south and the rest ten districts, namely Ramgarh, Seraikella Kharsawan, Bokaro, Kodarma, Ranchi, Simdega, Pashchimi Singhbhum, Giridih, Dhanbad and Khunti have concentration of PTGs below 1 per cent. Thus, the higher concentration of PTGs is found in peripheral areas of either eastern or western side of the state whereas the lower agglomeration is noticed in the middle part of the state.

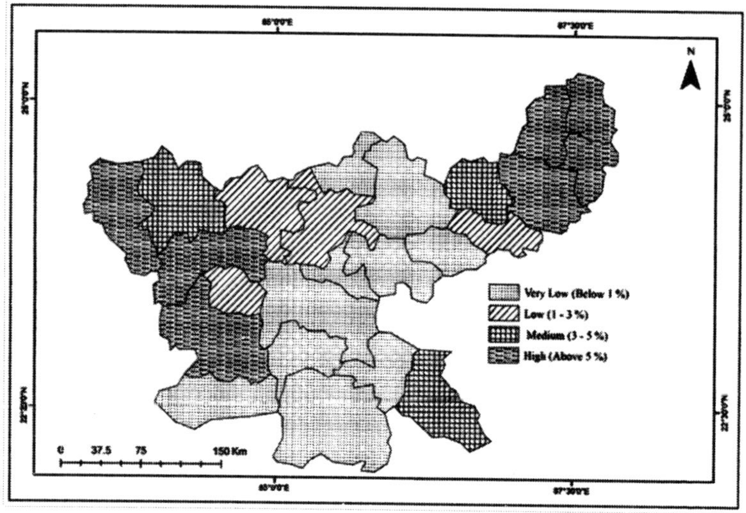

Fig. 2.10: Distribution of Primitive Tribal Groups in Jharkhand, 2011

Population Growth of Primitive Tribes

The growth of population for any society or region is determined by migration, births and deaths. Under the existing study of the PTG in Jharkhand, the migration component does not make significant differences to the growth of population and hence this aspect of population change has been ignored here. In contrast, natural increase, i.e. cumulative effect of births and deaths play an important role in deciding the population growth of primitive tribes. The very high birth and death rates of primitive tribes have resulted in young population in which the proportions of the population in younger ages are much larger than the older ages, which is basically non-existence. The decennial growth of population has been applied here to measure the size of population since 1872 to till the current Census of 2011.

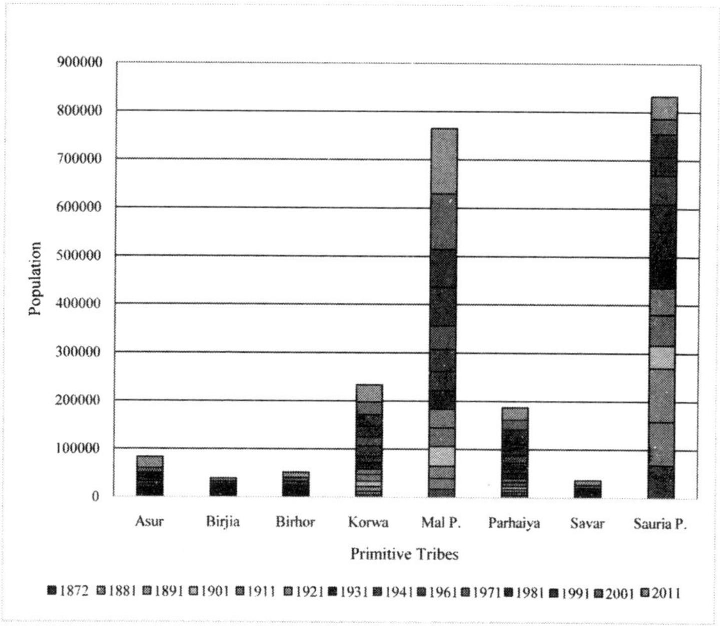

Fig. 2.11: Growth of Primitive Tribes in Jharkhand (1872-2011)

At the beginning of 1872 Census, the total population of primitive tribes exceeded in lakh in which the Sauria Paharias itself attributed to more than two-thirds of total population and it was followed by the Mal Paharias, which accounted for more than one-sixth of total population. In 1881 Census the overall decennial growth rate of primitive tribes was 27.1 per cent in which the Korwas has the highest positive growth rate, i.e. 45.01 per cent whereas the Asurs experienced negative growth rate, i.e. -23.7 per cent. It is further observed the population of Sauria Paharias had substantial positive growth rate, which was around 25 per cent and other PTGs experienced slow growth of population among the PTGs, the situation got reversed in 1901 Census, when there was deceleration of population, i.e. -29.60 per cent. It was mainly due to widespread prevalence of malaria and plague in their localities, which had taken a heavy toll on the lives of primitive tribes. The situation was further aggravated by the famine of 1896-97, which was basically more acute in their inaccessible areas. The above environmental hazards were more pathetic for the Sauria Paharias and the Birhors, who witnessed more than 50 per cent decline in growth rate of their population. However, the other primitive tribes had undergone marginal increase in their population during the next decade, 1901-11.The primitive tribal localities of the state were comparatively normal when the growth of population increased steadily at the rate of 17.58 per cent as the region recovered from onslaught of plague, malaria and famine. On the one hand, the highest growth rate was noticed for the Birhors due to their migratory attitude. On the other hand, negative growth rate was observed for the Mal Paharias due to spill over the effects of the above determinants and the other tribes recorded medium growth rate of population ranging from 6 to 34 per cent in 1911. The census of 1921 recorded a serious drop of population, i.e. -6.90 per cent owing mainly due to influenza and cholera epidemics and frequent famines in their localities. The highest drop of population, i.e. -39.59 per cent was noticed in the Asurs whereas the marginal positive variations were watched in the Savars, the Parhriyas, the Birjias and the Mal Paharias and the other tribes experienced negative growth of population. The population of primitive tribes rose steadily even in 1931 and 1941 Census which was 3.54 per cent and 5.16 per cent respectively. The population growth rate was noted negatively in the Savars, the Asurs, the Mal Paharias and the Sauria Paharias whereas the remaining tribes recorded marginal positive variation of population growth in both periods of time.

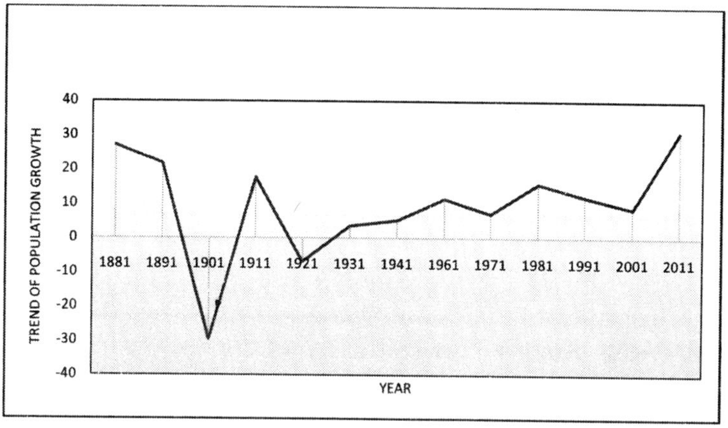

Fig. 2.12: Trend of Population Growth among Primitive Tribes in Jharkhand, 1881-2011

The population growth of primitive tribes remained almost stagnant in 1961 and 1971 Censuses, when population grew at the rate of 5.74 per cent and 7.02 per cent in the above-mentioned periods of time. There were fluctuating growth rates of population among the various primitive tribes. The PTGs, namely the Sauria Paharias, the Savars and the Birhors registered negative variation in population change whereas the remaining tribes reported low to moderate growth of population in 1961. More or less the same trend is noticed for 1971 Census when the Korwas and the Birjias enrolled negative growth in place of the above-mentioned tribes. A substantial growth of population among the PTGs (15.79%) was noticed in 1981 Census owing to special provision assigned to the PTG during the Fifth Five Year Plan. In spite of the special provisions, negative growth rate was reported for the Sauria Paharias but the other tribes recorded considerable growth in their size. Further, abnormal fluctuations in the population figures depicted in the census records in respect of some of the primitive tribes could be attributed as due to faulty enumeration. A large increase of the Parhaiya population in Santhal Pargana and decrease of the Sauria population in the above region in 1981 Census indicate towards the shortcoming of enumeration.

The tempo of growth rate again reduced to 11.97 per cent in 1991 but the remarkable characteristic of the above census may be considered for positive trend for the majority of PTGs except for the Savars and the Mal Paharias, who suffered below 1 per cent of their growth rate. The declining trend of growth rate reached to 8.53 per cent in 2001 Census when the Sauria Paharias, the Savars and the Birhors suffered a heavy causality of lives, which is manifested by their negative growth rates. Otherwise, the medium positive variations among the remaining primitive tribes were noticed in the above year. Lastly, the current 2011 Census illustrates the different picture for the PTGs in Jharkhand, which had recorded a very high decennial growth rate of 30.91 per cent against the state average of 22.34 per cent. Almost all the PTGs have scored a substantial increase in their population, which was quite high from the other tribal groups of the state. That is why, the eight primitive tribes constitute about 3.4 per cent of the total tribal population, which was around 3 lakh in 2011 due to assured supply of food grains and improved sanitary and health conditions after becoming a separate state on 15th November, 2000. Further, this increase in population seems to be due to the increase in their birth rate and also a large section of the PTGs started becoming sedentary cultivators. Thus, the growth rate of PTGs remained either quite slow or stagnant up to 2001 but afterwards there was a phenomenal increase in their population in 2011.

Concentration of Primitive Tribes

The Location Quotient (LQ) is an index for comprising an area's share of a particular characteristics in relation to its proportion in the region. The concentration of primitive tribes at district level has been applied here with the context of its ratio on the state level. The main advantage of the above method lies in the fact that it will enable the planners to understand the areas of specialization of primitive tribes in the state in 2011 Census, which is the recent enumeration carried out by the Government of India. Again, the location quotients of primitive tribes in Jharkhand are comparable with the location quotients of other states as they do not have any dimension. The primitive tribes were known as the marginal tribes earlier but they were defined as primitive tribes on the basis of low level of education, primitive method of agriculture and decline or stagnant population in the Fifth Five Year Plan in India. Now they are also known as Particularly Vulnerable Tribal Groups (PVTG) since 2006 by the Supreme Court of India. The districts with various kinds of location quotients for primitive tribes have been arranged into four categories for their studies in detail:

High Concentration of PTG (2.00-6.50): The districts which can be grouped under the heading of high concentration of primitive tribal groups are Pakur, Sahibganj, Godda and Latehar where location quotients vary between 2.00 and 6.50 in 2011, which is revealed from Fig. 2.13. The first three districts are located in Rajmahal Hilly Region whereas the last district is located in Pat Region. The above enlisted districts are very poor in term of infrastructural, social and economic development. The above kind of development is more miserable in those areas where the primitive tribes live in abundance. The former first three districts are the abode of the Mal and the Sauria Paharias whereas the Asurs, the Korwas, the Parhaiyas and the Birjias are agglomerated in the latter district. These districts have very large share of forested areas and the terrains are rugged where the Naxalites find themselves the as save heaven due to inaccessibility through transportation routes.

Moderate Concentration of PTG (1.00-2.00): There is only one district, i.e. Gumla, which falls in the category of moderate concentration of primitive tribal groups, which is located in Pat Region. While analysing the concentration of various primitive tribal groups, it is found that it is only the district where all seven primitive tribes barring the Sauria Paharias are found in various numbers. It is one of the most backward districts in context of industrial, infrastructural and economic development, which is densely forested and forms a part and parcel of the Barve Plain where the Upper Sankh and the South Koel drain the areas.

Low Concentration of PTG (0.10-1.00): The maximum number of districts in the state comes under the category of low concentration of primitive tribal groups, which have the value of location quotient ranging between 0.10 and 1.00. They are scattered in a dispersed manner since the districts, namely Chatra, Kodarama, Giridih, Deoghar, part of Hazaribagh, Palamu are situated in the Lower Plateau Region. The above kind of concentration is also observed in

Lohardaga and Ramgarh, which are located in the Central Plateau Region. Simdega also comes under this kind of concentration, which is located in the South Koel-Sankh Basin. The Dharwarian Country comprising Purbi Singhbhum and Seraikella Kharsawan also contain the above pattern of concentration. Further, Jamtara is another district, which falls under this group and it is located in the Rajmahal Upland.

Very Low Concentration of PTG (Below 0.10): The districts, namely Giridih, Dhanbad, Bokaro, Ranchi, Khunti and Pashchimi Singhbhum also come under this group of very low concentration of primitive tribes. It is remarkable to note that these districts have high level of urbanization and economic developments. These districts are mainly concentrated in the Damodar Basin and the Central Plateau Region, where mining, industrial and service sectors play an important role for the livelihood of people. The literacy level is also high in these districts and the inhabitants are economically well off.

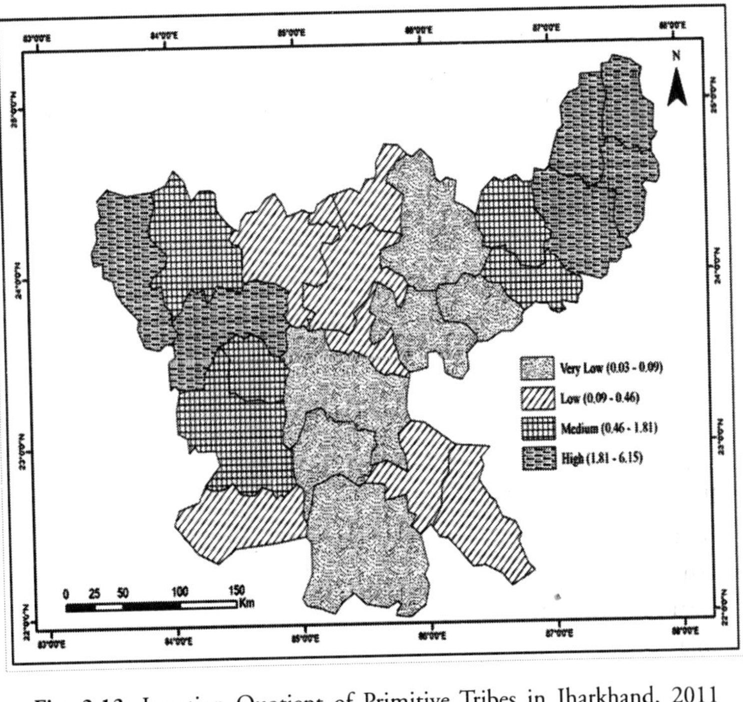

Fig. 2.13: Location Quotient of Primitive Tribes in Jharkhand, 2011

Summary

On the basis of the above discussion, it can be easily inferenced that each of eight primitive tribes in Jharkhand is agglomerated in particular area of the state. The Asurs and the Birjias are primarily found in Gumla and Latehar districts of the Pat region whereas the Korwas and the Parhaiyas are basically concentrated in Garhwa, Palamu and Latehar districts in the north-western part of the state. So far, the concentration of the Sauria Paharias and the Mal Paharias is concerned; they are exclusively confined to Rajmahal Upland. Under the similar pattern of isolation, the Savars have their habitation in the Dhalbhum region of Purbi Singhbhum. However, the Birhors are noticed throughout the areas of Chotanagpur Plateau due to their nomadic habit but more than 53 per cent of population are agglomerated in Chatra, Hazaribagh and Kodarma of the Lower Plateau. In a nut shell, the higher concentration of PTGs is found in peripheral areas of either eastern or western side whereas the lower agglomeration is noticed in the middle part of the state.Barring the negative growth in 1901 and 1921 Censuses, the growth rate of PTGs remained either quite slow or stagnant up to 2001 but a phenomenal increase in their population was manifested in 2011 Census, which is the result of carving out of Jharkhand as a separate state from Bihar in 2000. Further, it can be also established from the location quotient that high concentration of primitive tribes is found in Pakur, Sahibganj, Godda, Garhwa and Latehar districts. The first three districts are located in the Rajmahal Upland, where the Mal Paharias and the Sauria Paharias live in abundance. The last two districts of the Pat region have the abode of the Asurs, the Birjias, the Korwas and the Parhaiyas. On the other hand, there is negligible presence of primitive tribes in the Damodar Basin. Thus, high concentration of the PTGs is confined to Damin-i-Koh and Pat region whereas the lowest level of concentration is mainly centred in and around the Damodar Basin and the Central Plateau Region, where mining, industrial and service sector play an important role for the livelihood of people.

REFERENCES

Dalton, E.T. (1872). *Descriptive Ethnology of Bengal*, Calcutta, pp. 264-73.

Dash Sharma, P. (1996). *The Parhaiyas of Palamu: An Ethnographic Study*, Ranchi: The Bihar Tribal Welfare Research Institute, p. 9.

Gupta, S.P. (1976). *The Asurs: Ethno-Biological Profile*, Ranchi: Varma's Union Press, pp. 49-63.

Kumar, S. (2004). *The Birhors of Chotanagpur Region*, New Delhi: Rajesh Publication, pp. 48-61.

Oraon, P.C. (2003). *Land and People of Jharkhand*, Ranchi: Jharkhand Tribal Welfare Research Institute, Government of Jharkhand, p. 350.

Prasad, N. (1961). *Land and People of Tribal Bihar*, Ranchi: Bihar Tribal Research Institute, Government of Bihar, pp. 155-167.

Prasad, N. (1961). *op. cit.*, pp. 193-196.

Risley, H.H. (1891). *The Tribes and Castes of Bengal*, Vol. II, Calcutta, pp. 66-73.

Sinha, S.P. (1991). *Sauria Paharia of Rajmahal Hills: A Study in a Struggling Primitive Tribe for Existence*, Ranchi: Bihar Tribal Research Institute, Government of Bihar, pp. 1-8.

Upadhyay, V.S. (2005). op. cit., pp. 1-4.

Vidyarthi, L.P. and B.K. Rai (1985). *The Tribal Culture of India*, New Delhi: Concept Publishing Company, pp. 1-488.

Jharkhand Tribal Welfare Research Institute (2002-03). *Primitive Tribal Groups of Jharkhand Survey Report*, Ministry of Welfare, Government of Jharkhand, Ranchi.

3
Demographic and Socio-Economic Profile and Infrastructural Facilities

An analysis of the basic demographical and socio-economic features of selected primitive tribal villages where the infant mortality occurs, helps to explain the structural factors behind their early demise of the children. As the rate and incidence of mortality are not independent, the nature of a given demographic and socio-economic characteristics determines as to which particular section of children are more prone to demise. In this context, it is necessary to find out how and what way the propensity of child death differs significantly among various socio-economic groups of the society. The socio-cultural milieu in which the villages exist, their compositions and distributions in the villages and the resulting social differentiations and stratifications affect the rate of infant mortality. Furthermore, to understand the nature of occurrences, causes and consequences of infant death, it is necessary to examine some of the demographic and socio-economic characteristics of the deceased (Kumar, 2005). The infant mortality and its effect on social, economic and demographic aspects have recently occupied a considerable place in social science research. It has a significant implication on regional as well as national planning. A variety of approaches depending upon the conceptualization of various stages of infant deaths and the scale of investigation have been used in the past to analyse data on the aggregate levels.

The study also analyses the manpower resources and their allocation in the economic system of these villages. Most of the child deaths occur in the primitive tribal villages of Jharkhand due to poor living condition, less exposure to mass media and non-availability of modern medical system at their villages, which are generally isolated and inaccessible through modern transport system. The Shilu Ao Committee, constituted by the Planning Commission in 1969 for reviewing the tribal situation, had observed that a large number of tribal communities are extremely backward and some of them are still in the primitive food gathering stage. It has emphasized that these communities needed special attention. As a part of tribal subplan strategy, 75 tribal groups have been identified as the primitive groups in 14 states and one Union territory. Earlier they were known as the marginal tribes by the Anthropologists due to their relative isolation, educationally and socio-economically backwardness. In 2006, the Government of India renamed the Primitive Tribal Groups (PTG) as the Particularly Vulnerable Tribal Groups (PVTG). They were reframed with the purpose of enabling improvement in the condition of certain tribal communities with particularly low development indices. However, 8 tribal communities in Jharkhand, namely Asur, Birhor, Birjia, Korwa, Parhaiya, Mal Paharia, and Sauria Paharia have been identified as primitive tribes.

Demographic Characteristics

Mother's Age at Child Birth

Mother's age at child birth has a significant impact upon infant's survival and it is significantly associated with the risk of infant death. The infants of mothers aged less than 20 years are expected to a higher-than-average risk of dying during the neonatal period of their life whereas the infants of older mother are also exposed to a higher-than-average risk of dying during the post-neonatal period. It is an established fact that there is a U-shaped relationship between Infant Mortality Rate (IMR) and the age of mothers. Moreover, there is a less disparity of infant mortality among the various primitive tribal communities. It is evident from Table 3.1 that the neonatal mortality was 150 per thousand births in survey year of 2017 whereas the post-neonatal was 115 per thousand births and overall, the infant mortality was 265 per thousand live births at the time of survey in the age group of below 20 years.

The above finding is also corroborated through the percentage distribution of neonatal, post-neonatal and infant mortality rate whereby they stand at 16.54, 12.64 and 29.8 per cent respectively. The probability of pregnancy-related complication is high among the adolescent mothers as the young mother is not biologically mature to bring forth a new born baby. It is further observed that the adolescent mothers are unable to take care of their child since they have less exposure and experience about the rearing of small baby. Moreover, the joint family system is still prevailing in India wherein the small children get considerable support from the old members of family. That kind of support may be curse or boon for the new born baby. Since the old family members take care of children in traditional outlook wherein superstitions also prevail in certain circumstances. That is why, the life and health of small children sometimes become risky through traditional rearing by the old members of the family. It is further observed that the neonatal, post-neonatal and infant mortality have decreased under the age group of 20 to 30-year females, which are 68, 48 and 116 per thousand live births respectively and this age group of females is considered the best age group in term of their reproductivity among the primitive tribes whereby the infant mortality rate is the lowest. The above result is also substantiated through the percentage distribution of infant deaths (19.26%), which is the lowest among all age groups of the PTGs.This trend of least infant deaths gets slightly accelerated in all three components of neonatal, post-neonatal and infant mortality in the age group of from 30 to 40-year females, which are 164, 139 and 303 per thousand live births. Again, the percentage distribution of infant deaths is 45.33 in the above age group. Moreover, the above trend of acceleration gets further increased in the age group of above 40-year females and the neonatal, post-neonatal and infant mortality raises to 396, 208 and 640 per thousand live births. Beyond the age of 40, the risk of pregnancy complications apparently increases because of the increasing inflexibility of the female reproductive organ.

Thus, the above analysis corroborates the earlier findings that the infant mortality in general and the neonatal mortality in particular is of the lowest level in the age group of 20 to30-year females.

Overall, the neonatal, post-neonatal and infant mortality rate are 130, 100 and 230 per thousand live births and the above finding is also illustrated through the percentage distribution of infant deaths, which accounts for 56.4 per cent among the PTGs in Jharkhand. The similar result was also found by Ezra and Gurum (2002) in case of Ethiopia that births to mothers in the age group of 15-19 face higher mortality risk than births to mothers in the age group of 25-29 or 30-34. The risk of IMR has decreased as mother's age at first birth increased; that is, the risk of IMR has been high for new-borns who was the first child at younger age. As mother's age at first birth increased, the risk of IMR was reduced and mothers who gave birth to their first child at younger age also faced high mortality risk due to social and reproduction immaturity. If we further analyse primitive tribe -wise, it is observed that the highest infant mortality is noticed among the Parhaiyas, which is followed by the Birhors, the Korwas, the Sauria Paharias, the Mal Paharias, the Asurs, the Birjias and the Savars.

Table 3.1: Mother's Age at Child Birth among the PTGs in Jharkhand at the Time of Survey

Age Group	Component	Live Births	Infant Deaths	IMR	% of Infant Distribution
Below 20 Years	Neonatal Deaths	567	85	150	16.54
	Post-Neonatal Deaths	567	65	115	12.64
	Infant Deaths	567	150	265	29.18
20-30 Years	Neonatal Deaths	851	58	68	11.28
	Post-Neonatal Deaths	851	41	48	7.98

(*Contd.*)

Age Group	Component	Live Births	Infant Deaths	IMR	% of Infant Distribution
	Infant Deaths	851	99	116	19.26
30-40 Years	Neonatal Deaths	768	126	164	24.51
	Post-Neonatal Deaths	768	107	139	20.82
	Infant Deaths	768	233	303	45.33
Above 40 Years	Neonatal Deaths	53	21	396	4.09
	Post-Neonatal Deaths	53	11	208	2.14
	Infant Deaths	53	32	604	6.23
All	Neonatal Deaths	2239	290	130	56.42
	Post-Neonatal Deaths	2239	224	100	43.58
	Infant Deaths	2239	514	230	100

Birth Order

Infant mortality is generally high in the first order birth but it declines gradually up to third birth order and it takes again an upward turn in fourth and higher order of births. In normal circumstances, infant mortality rates construct either a U-shaped or reverse J-shaped curve with birth order. An analysis of neonatal and post-neonatal at various birth orders reveals that it is again the neonatal mortality level which decrease with increase in birth order and brings about a decline in overall infant mortality. The changes in the post-neonatal mortality level, however, are not of the same order of magnitude. As a matter of fact, that repetitive child bearing affects the biological capacity of women, which ultimately affects succeeding births. It is assumed that women, who give a smaller number of births, their children will be healthier than the mother, who gives more births and this means that children at higher order are disadvantaged. It is apparent from Table 3.2 that the neonatal mortality was of 184 per thousand live births, the post-neonatal mortality was 73 per thousand births and the infant mortality rate was 257 per thousand live births in 2017 in case of the first order of child among the primitive tribes in the state. The first order of child takes into account of around one-third share of child deaths among the PTGs in Jharkhand. The second order of birth was 92, 58 and 150 per thousand births for neonatal, post-neonatal and infant deaths respectively. Further, its share to total infant deaths are 14.2 per cent. The trend of neonatal, post-neonatal and infant deaths goes up even at third order of child birth, which are 104, 86 and 190 per thousand live births respectively, which engulfs around 15 per cent of infant deaths. Lastly, the trend of increment of neonatal, post-neonatal and infant deaths reaches to the crest, which are manifested by the share of 133, 150 and 283 per thousand live births respectively, which captures around 40 per cent of infant deaths. Thus, it can be easily summed up that the higher order of child birth leads to the higher infant mortality rate and caring of children at high order lessens due to scarcity of resources among the primitive tribes in Jharkhand. The females become old at very early age due to less in taking of nutritional food. It is also substantiated by R.N. Pandey (1997) that short birth intervals, high birth orders and mother's young at the time of giving birth have all increased mortality and morbidity risks.

Table 3.2: Birth Order of Children among the PTGs in Jharkhand at the Time of Survey

Birth Order	Component	Live Births	Infant Deaths	IMR	% of Infant Distribution
1.	Neonatal Deaths	631	116	184	22.57
	Post-Neonatal Deaths	631	46	73	8.95
	Infant Deaths	631	162	257	31.52

(*Contd.*)

Birth Order	Component	Live Births	Infant Deaths	IMR	% of Infant Distribution
2.	Neonatal Deaths	487	45	92	8.75
	Post-Neonatal Deaths	487	28	58	5.45
	Infant Deaths	487	73	150	14.2
3.	Neonatal Deaths	406	42	104	8.17
	Post-Neonatal Deaths	406	35	86	6.81
	Infant Deaths	406	77	190	14.98
Above 4.	Neonatal Deaths	715	95	133	18.48
	Post-Neonatal Deaths	715	107	150	20.82
	Infant Deaths	715	202	283	39.3

Marriage Age of Females

Normally girls are married at socially determined ages just after puberty among the primitive tribes in Jharkhand and those married at higher ages usually face adverse criticism. Marriages are usually arranged by parents on the basis of clan. The brides have little scope to express their views regarding the matter. Most of the marriages in tribal villages are usually arranged in the neighbouring villages depending on the availability of suitable partners. No marriages are permissible between males and females belonging to the same clan among the Birhors, the Asurs, the Birjias, the Parhaiyas, the Korwas and the Mal Paharias whereas there is no clan system among the Sauria Paharias and the Savars. Hence marriage with relatives up to third generation is avoided in the latter two tribes. Moreover, the child marriage is prevalent among the primitive tribes, which ultimately leads to higher infant mortality. It is apparent from Table 3.3 that the average age of females for marriage was 16.7 years at the time of investigation for the primitive tribes in the state. As a matter of fact, that the females who get married at adolescent age generally produce a weak child in general. Simultaneously, they are not capable of taking care of their children in early age. Again, it is noticed that nuclear family is more prevalent among them and there is no other elderly female, who can co-operate in rearing of the children just like other traditional Indian families.

The above statement is corroborated by the neonatal, post-neonatal and infant mortality rate, which are 174, 112 and 286 per thousand live births respectively for the females under 18 years and more than fifty per cent of infant deaths occur in this group of mothers. The high rate of neonatal and post-neonatal mortality clearly reveals that they are forced to marry at the age of school going days. Again, they have to work as labourers in the field besides rearing of children and domestic works. The situation remains more or less the same for the women, who are married at the age of 18-20 years and all three components of infant demises, viz. neonatal, post-neonatal and infant mortality rate comprise 112, 94 and 206 per thousand respectively and the females in this group engulfs around 33 per cent of infant deaths. Suddenly, there is an abrupt change of neonatal, post-neonatal and infant mortality for the females married at the age between 20 and 22 years, which are 82, 86 and 168 per thousand live births respectively and the occurrence of infant deaths is only 13.62 per cent. In this group of females, that kind of amelioration in mortality rate is also observed among those females married at the age of above 22 years and the corresponding figure for neonatal, post-neonatal and infant mortality are 65, 87, and 152 per thousand live births respectively and it accounts only below 2 per cent of infant deaths. The above finding is also endorsed by Pandey (1997) that young age at birth for the mother is the main factor leading to heightened risk of infant and child mortality. Young mothers (less than 20 years of age) are not fully biologically capable for child birth. If they conceive the child faces many biological problems, which decrease the survival chances of child. Thus, demographic dividends have become demographic liabilities for the primitive tribes in Jharkhand.

Table 3.3: Mother's Marriage Age among the PTGs in Jharkhand at the Time of Survey

Marriage Age	Component	Live Births	Infant Deaths	IMR	per cent of Infant Distribution
Below 18	Neonatal Deaths	916	159	174	30.93
	Post-Neonatal Deaths	916	103	112	20.04
	Infant Deaths	916	262	286	50.97
18-20	Neonatal Deaths	814	91	112	17.71
	Post-Neonatal Deaths	814	77	94	14.98
	Infant Deaths	814	168	206	32.69
20-22	Neonatal Deaths	417	34	82	6.62
	Post-Neonatal Deaths	417	36	86	7
	Infant Deaths	417	70	168	13.62
Above 22	Neonatal Deaths	92	6	65	1.17
	Post-Neonatal Deaths	92	8	87	1.55
	Infant Deaths	92	14	152	2.72

Social Characteristics

Mother's Education

Among the social variables, education of the mother is the most crucial variable of infant mortality. It is a tool which helps the people in breaking some of the traditional taboos and makes them more independent in taking decisions within the family setup. It is a crucial input for development as it enables a person to understand his surroundings and environment and acts as a very strong catalyst in the process of keeping good health, which ultimately reduces infant mortality. It is generally believed that those mothers who have no education face relatively higher mortality risk of children than those with some level of education. It influences the proper nourishment of children which finally influences in reduction of infant deaths. It not only improves her own level of awareness and knowledge but also changes her attitudes and values towards family. Education is the most important variable in this study because the effect of mother's education for child survival is high. It is associated with the release of the individuals from the bonds of tradition, with the progressive differentiation of society, with emergence of civil society, with social equality, and with innovation and change. It helps people to escape from superstition and religious dogmas. Mother's education is more important than father's education for child survival as proved from previous studies (Caldwell, 1979). More educated women inclined to seek antenatal care and will be more willing to choose the trained medical personal to assist them during delivery and post-natal care. Educated women are more conscious of the proper feeding practices for their children and also might be better informed about the symptoms of child illness and therefore more likely to give proper treatment to babies.

Table 3.4 shows that the primitive tribal females is one of the least educated females in India and not even a single female had education above middle class. On the whole, 77.8 per cent of tribal mothers were illiterate and the infant mortality was of the highest level, i.e. 242 per thousand live births at the time of survey. Again, the neonatal mortality was 136 per thousand lived births whereas the post-neonatal mortality was 106 per thousand live births, which clearly implies that mother's education is highly related to the infant mortality. Next to this is the group of primary-passed mothers, whose offspring had infant mortality of 204 per thousand live births, whereas the neonatal and post-neonatal mortality were 119 and 85 per thousand live births accordingly. This group of mothers incorporates 23.15 per cent of infant deaths. Further, the lowest level of infant mortality, i.e. 190 per thousand live births found among those females, who were middle passed. Naturally, the neonatal and post-neonatal mortality are 95 and 95 per thousand live births accordingly. It only takes into account of below 2 per cent of infant deaths. Thus, female education plays a crucial role in reducing the infant deaths among the primitive tribes in Jharkhand in spite of having very low level of education among the primitive tribe mothers.

Table 3.4: Mother's Education among the PTGs in Jharkhand at the Time of Survey

Mother's Education	Component	Live Births	Infant Deaths	IMR	% of Infant Distribution
Illiterate	Neonatal Deaths	1597	217	136	42.22
	Post-Neonatal Deaths	1597	170	106	33.07
	Infant Deaths	1597	387	242	75.29
Primary	Neonatal Deaths	582	69	119	13.42
	Post-Neonatal Deaths	582	50	85	9.73
	Infant Deaths	582	119	204	23.15
Middle	Neonatal Deaths	42	4	95	0.78
	Post-Neonatal Deaths	42	4	95	0.78
	Infant Deaths	42	8	190	1.56

Size of Family

The size of a family has a significant effect on the interrelationship among its members and can play a major role in the nurturing of a child's survival. The children of large families have a greater opportunity to learn cooperation at an early age than children of smaller families as they must learn to get along with siblings. They take more responsibility for younger brothers and sisters and by doing so they reduce infant mortality. Table 3.5 manifests that the small size of households consisting of less than 4 members had moderate kind of infant mortality, i.e. 245 per thousand live births among the primitive tribes in Jharkhand at the time of survey. Even the neonatal and post-neonatal present the different figures, viz. 139 and 106 per thousand live births accordingly for small family but its share to total infant deaths embodies 45.14 per cent, which manifests that the total infant deaths are very high in this group of households. Next to this is the medium size of households having family members ranging from 5 to 7 incorporate the infant mortality of 195 per thousand live births, which is further classified as neonatal and post-neonatal mortality account for 110 and 85 per thousand live births respectively. The next group designated as large size of households having 8 to 10 members present a sharp rise in neonatal, post-neonatal and infant mortality rate, which are substantiated by the rate of 195, 150 and 345 per thousand live births respectively. So far, the per centile share of the group is concerned; it includes only 13.42 per cent of infant deaths. Another group of family belongs to extended family having more than 11 family members where the NMR, PNMR and IMR consist of 89, 101 and 190 per thousand live births respectively. Moreover, total number of live births and infant deaths are very less in the group. That is why; it encompasses less than 3 per cent of infant deaths. Thus, it can be easily summarized that the highest share of infant deaths comprises small size of family whereas the highest infant mortality rate is found in large size of family among the primitive tribal households in Jharkhand.

Table 3.5: Size of Family among the PTGs in Jharkhand at the Time of Survey

Size of Family	Component	Live Births	Infant Deaths	IMR	% of Infant Distribution
Small (< 4)	Neonatal Deaths	946	132	139	25.68
	Post-Neonatal Deaths	946	100	106	19.46
	Infant Deaths	946	232	245	45.14
Medium (5-7)	Neonatal Deaths	1014	112	110	21.79
	Post-Neonatal Deaths	1014	86	85	16.73
	Infant Deaths	1014	198	195	38.52
Large (8-10)	Neonatal Deaths	200	39	195	7.59
	Post-Neonatal Deaths	200	30	150	5.83
	Infant Deaths	200	69	345	13.42
Extended (>11)	Neonatal Deaths	79	7	89	1.36
	Post-Neonatal Deaths	79	8	101	1.36
	Infant Deaths	79	15	190	2.92

Type of Family

The family among the primitive tribes of Jharkhand is a biological one with father and mother along with unmarried children forming the family bond and thus presents glaring examples of nuclear family. The greater predominance of the nuclear family may be another cause of higher mortality of children among the primitive tribes. The married sons and daughters form separate households after their marriage and are given a different and distinct social position among the primitive tribes. Family is the more important unit in the primitive tribes because their major economic, social, religious and reproductive activities are concentrated in family itself. Their emotional attachment with family members, villagers, tribes and the villages are further integrated due to these traditions. Moreover, joint families are also found in their locality. The pattern of relationship between husband and wife may also be considered in terms of their tradition. When the wife gives birth to a child, the husband also shares pollution and as the tradition goes, the counterpart also undergoes confinement till the purification.

There are mainly three types of families found in the state: joint, nuclear and single parent family. Almost all people subsist on nuclear family and around 72.22 per cent people live in the above kind of family. Again, the joint family is not prevalent among them in which children are taken care of within the joint family system. It is possible that the support provided by other members is found in joint family in the nourishment of children, which reduces the infant mortality. Moreover, the above kind of family comprises only 22.06 per cent among them. Another kind of family, i.e. single parent family is also popular among them, which incorporates slightly less than 6 per cent. That kind of family is found either by accidental death of counterpart or the plight of counterpart with another male, which is associated with negative effects on a child's health. It is apparent from Table 3.6 that the infant mortality is very high in case of nuclear family, which encompassed around 237 per thousand live births at the time of survey and neonatal and post-neonatal mortality separately stood at 142 and 95 per thousand live birth accordingly at the time of survey. Since most of the primitive tribal people reside in nuclear family system, most of the deaths (74.71%) are observed in that category itself. As a matter of fact, those children in neonatal and post-neonatal phase are not properly taken care of owing to parents' engagement outside the home. That is why, both components of infant deaths occupy mortality rate of 142 and 95 per thousand live births. It is followed by the joint family, which captures the infant mortality rate of 210 per thousand live births and neonatal and post-neonatal mortality rates capture around 121 and 89 per thousand live births. More than 20 per cent of infant deaths are engulfed by the joint family. Even in case of single parent family system, the infant mortality rate is found around 203 per thousand live births and all infant deaths were exclusively confined to post-neonatal stage but the total share of infant deaths is around 5 per cent. Thus, it can be easily visualized that the highest share of infant deaths and infant mortality rate are found in the category of nuclear family among the primitive tribes in Jharkhand.

Table 3.6: Type of Family among the PTGs in Jharkhand at the Time of Survey

Type of Family	Component	Live Births	Infant Deaths	IMR	% of Infant Distribution
Joint	Neonatal Deaths	494	60	121	11.67
	Post-Neonatal Deaths	494	44	89	8.56
	Infant Deaths	494	104	210	20.23
Nuclear	Neonatal Deaths	1617	230	142	44.75
	Post-Neonatal Deaths	1617	154	95	29.96
	Infant Deaths	1617	384	237	74.71
Single	Neonatal Deaths	128	0	0	0
	Post-Neonatal Deaths	128	26	203	5.06
	Infant Deaths	128	26	203	5.06

Religion

Religion plays a vital role in determining the complexes and attitudes of their life. Its basic notions are environmental ethics, cosmic integrity of man-nature, symbolism and perceptions, which are translated into belief systems under religious ecology. It produces a distinct attitude towards life, which affects the further development of the society and proper nourishment of children (Singh, 2009). The primitive tribes hold that they are surrounded by a number of gods and spirits and they strive to satisfy the whims and caprices of these supernatural powers. They believe that their all activities are guided and controlled by these supernatural powers and as such they very much dread their displeasure. They believe that if due propitiations are made to them at every ritual and ceremony the gods and spirit would help them by all occasions.

Table 3.7: Religion of the PTGs in Jharkhand at the Time of Survey

Religion	Component	Live Births	Infant Deaths	IMR	% of Infant Distribution
Hindu	Neonatal Deaths	716	82	115	15.96
	Post-Neonatal Deaths	716	71	99	13.81
	Infant Deaths	716	153	214	29.77
Christian	Neonatal Deaths	627	60	96	11.67
	Post-Neonatal Deaths	627	72	115	14.01
	Infant Deaths	627	132	211	25.68
Sarna	Neonatal Deaths	896	148	165	28.79
	Post-Neonatal Deaths	896	81	90	15.76
	Infant Deaths	896	229	255	44.55

Table 3.7 exhibits that the primitive tribal are primarily the followers of three religion, viz. Hindu, Christian and Sarna religion. The highest rate of infant mortality, i.e. 255 per thousand live births is perceived among the people of the Sarna religion. They have great love for their tradition and ecological environment. The people are usually worshippers of Nature and they consider the Singbonga (sun) and the Burubonga (mountain) as their supreme deity. They have neonatal and post-neonatal mortality at 165 and 90 per thousand live births. It is followed by the Hindu religion in which the IMR is observed 214 per thousand live births.The neonatal mortality is recorded at 115 per thousand live births whereas the post-neonatal mortality is reported at 99 per thousand live births independently. In fact, they are residing in the periphery areas of primitive localities,

where economic exploitation by the money lenders is of extreme level and the primitive people are in debt traps. The lowest level of infant mortality is noticed among the Christianity, which are only 132 per thousand live births. The neonatal mortality rate is also found only 96 whereas the post-neonatal rate accounts for 115 per thousand live births. If we dig up the reason behind it, we find that the spread effect of modernization and Westernization through the mission school and the church have diminished the infant deaths of all components. This is due to the fact that so many superstitions prevailing among the original PTGs regarding the nourishments of infants have been wiped out with the contact of them. The nurses and doctors are also arranged through the churches, which are usually present during the delivery of child for their followers.

Economic Characteristics

Per Capita Income

Income plays a crucial role in the determinator of child mortality because a number of factors like food, hygiene, sanitation, housing and affordability of medical aid influence infant mortality. Several economic indices are devised to measure individual's needs. In this regard, per capita income is considered more telling index in India than their absolutes. Generally, it is directly correlated with the standard of living and areas of high level of living tend to be areas of low infant mortality while areas of low level of living tend to areas of high infant mortality. The complexity of income among the primitive tribes gets further multiplied by several other factors like simultaneous pursuit of more than one occupation, changes in occupation in different seasons, lack of continuity of employment throughout the year and payment of wage in kind. Further, the primitive tribes do not generally know how to save or how to plan for their future. Whatever they earn they spend in merry making. They think of the present only, forget the past and do not care for the future and they are very easy going.

Table 3.8: Per Capita Income among the PTGs in Jharkhand at the Time of Survey

Income in Rs.	Component	Live Births	Infant Deaths	IMR	% of Infant Distribution
Below 2000	Neonatal Deaths	1367	190	139	36.96
	Post-Neonatal Deaths	1367	160	117	31.13
	Infant Deaths	1367	350	256	68.09
2000-5000	Neonatal Deaths	605	75	124	14.59
	Post-Neonatal Deaths	605	46	76	8.95
	Infant Deaths	605	121	200	23.54
5000-10000	Neonatal Deaths	180	20	111	3.89
	Post-Neonatal Deaths	180	14	78	2.72
	Infant Deaths	180	34	189	6.61
Above 10000	Neonatal Deaths	87	5	57	0.97
	Post-Neonatal Deaths	87	4	46	0.78
	Infant Deaths	87	9	103	1.75

Table 3.8 reveals that majority of people are living in abject poverty whereby they have annual income below two thousand rupees and this group of households comprise of 61.05 per cent in 2017. Obviously, this group of people contains the IMR of 256 per thousand of live births in which neonatal and post-neonatal mortality stand for 139 and 117 per thousand live births respectively. Again, the infant deaths constitute the share of 68.09 per cent of child deaths. It is followed by those households in which people have annual per capita income between Rs. 2,000 and Rs. 5,000 and this group of households takes into account of 27.02 per cent. The infant mortality is of moderate level (200 per thousand live births) wherein the NMR and the PNMR account for 124 and 76 per thousand live births respectively. The

proportion of child deaths under the umbrella of this particular group constitutes of 23.54 per cent, which is lower than their total share of households. The other income group of households having the range of annual income between Rs. 5,000 and Rs. 10,000, which contains 8.04 per cent of total households. The IMR, the NMR and the PNMR are at 189, 111 and 78 per thousand live births in which the share of infant deaths constitutes only 6.61 per cent. Lastly, the households having income above Rs. 10, 000 include only less than 4 per cent and it contains the IMR, the NMR and PNMR of 103, 57 and 46 per thousand live births but it encompasses below 2 per cent.

Land Ownership

Land ownership is one of the basic measures of economic status in a primitive tribal village. In an economy where most people earn their living from the land, land-ownership is relevant in determining the rate of infant deaths. Land is greatly valued in rural life not only as an important source of production but as a continuous source of income and security also. As in the majority of cases rural livelihood pattern is determined by agriculture-based employment, the landholding pattern among the primitive tribes may be influential variable in the study of infant mortality. The landholding of a household plays an important role in their household income in an agrarian economy where people are mostly dependent on land for their survival and thereby influence the child's survival strategy.Unfortunately, most of the PTG households are either landless or marginal farmers in the state, which is also substantiated from Table 3.9 that 81.71 per cent of households fall in the category of landless and small farmers among the PTGs in Jharkhand. The infant mortality rate is 184 per thousand live births in the group of landless whereas its share is around 35.8 per cent in the survey year of 2017. It captures 107 and 77 per thousand live births for NMR and PNMR respectively. Again, the IMR, NMR and PNMR stand at 240, 132 and 108 in the class of small farmers, who have possession of less than 2 acres of land and simultaneously their shares in the above groupings are 45.9 per cent, 25.29 per cent

Table 3.9: Landholding Pattern among the PTGs in Jharkhand at the Time of Survey

Land Status	Component	Live Births	Infant Deaths	IMR	% of Infant Distribution
Landless	Neonatal Deaths	785	107	136	20.82
	Post-Neonatal Deaths	785	77	98	14.98
	Infant Deaths	785	184	234	35.8
Small (<2 Acres)	Neonatal Deaths	984	130	132	25.29
	Post-Neonatal Deaths	984	106	108	20.62
	Infant Deaths	984	236	240	45.9
Medium (2-4 Acres)	Neonatal Deaths	283	31	109	6.03
	Post-Neonatal Deaths	283	28	99	5.45
	Infant Deaths	283	59	208	11.48
Large (>4 Acres)	Neonatal Deaths	187	22	118	4.28
	Post-Neonatal Deaths	187	13	70	2.53
	Infant Deaths	187	35	187	6.81

and 20.62 per cent for the small farmers. In fact, the medium and large size of households incorporate only around 18 per cent of households combinedly but meagre amount of land possession in the above groups also manifests that they actually fall in the category of marginal farmers in all India perspective.The IMR is found around 208 per thousand live births whereas the NMR and PNMR capitulate 109 and 99 separately in the group of middle farmers. Moreover, the share of infant deaths in the middle group of farmers is below 12 per cent and the proportion of neonate and post-neonate deaths also remains at negligible level. More or less, the same pattern of infant deaths is

noticed for large farmers, whereby the IMR, NMR and PNMR are recorded 187, 118 and 70 per thousand live births and the ratio of infant deaths is found below 7 per cent among the PTGs in the state. Thus, it can be easily concluded from the above discussion that the landholding possession also play an important role in all components of infant deaths whereby the inverse relationship is established between infant deaths and size of landholding among the PTGs in Jharkhand.

Mother's Occupation

Occupation refers to a set of activities which predominately engage one's time for primary motive of earning livelihood. The classification of rural primitive tribal female workers according to their specific occupation is beset with problems, as in the majority of cases female workers are engaged in several economic activities instead of a single pursuit. The workers are considered those persons who are participating in any economic productive activity. Apart from domestication of cattle, household work, lac collection, basketry work, mat making, selling forest produces in the local market etc., the main source of livelihood of the primitive tribal females belong to farming, food gathering and working as daily wage labourers. It is believed that the babies of working mothers as wage earners face a higher risk of infant mortality than babies born to non-working mothers. However, it is only possible when the support provided by other members of a joint family reduces the effect of the work status of the mother. They also prepare mats and collect forest produce like oilseeds, lac, gums, resins, kendu leaves, tasar cocoons, tamarinds etc. Since the division of work is very simple among the primitive tribes in Jharkhand, they classified into three categories for females: collection of forest produce and housewife, cultivator, labourer and artisan worker. As a matter of fact, that the females are engaged in all sort of arduous work beside domestic work. It is the female who bring drinking water daily through the rugged dissected terrain of the scarped forested zone. In fact, they always stand along with their counterparts in every walk of life.

Rope Making through Plastic for Selling in a Local Market by Birhor Women

Apart from household engagement, they bring a variety of produces from forest either for self-consumption purpose or selling them in the local hats. A small proportion of females is engaged in the work category of housewife and the infant mortality is observed as high as 242 per thousand live births in this group of females and the share of neo-natal and post-natal used to stand at 134 and 108 per thousand live births separately and the share of infant deaths, neonate deaths and post-neonate deaths comprises of 17.9 per cent, 9.92 per cent and 7.98 per cent respectively. The next group of work category belongs to the female cultivators, which has the infant mortality rate of 195 per thousand live births and the respective share of neonatal and post-neonatal mortality use to command 82 and 78 per thousand live births. Sunita and Parsuraman (1998) using data from the 1992-93, National Family Health Survey, found that mother's income translates into greater control over the expanding of resources, increased exposure and access to relevant information about childbearing and childrearing practices. Their study showed that mothers who are employed have 10 per cent higher infant mortality rate and a 36 per cent child mortality rate than mothers who are not

Table 3.10: Mother's Occupation among the PTGs in Jharkhand at the Time of Survey

Mother's Occupation	Component	Live Births	Infant Deaths	IMR	% of Infant Distribution
Housewife	Neonatal Deaths	380	51	134	9.92
	Post-Neonatal Deaths	380	41	108	7.98
	Infant Deaths	380	92	242	17.9
Cultivator	Neonatal Deaths	364	39	107	7.59
	Post-Neonatal Deaths	364	32	88	6.22
	Infant Deaths	364	71	195	13.81
Labourer	Neonatal Deaths	1258	175	139	34.05
	Post-Neonatal Deaths	1258	129	103	25
	Infant Deaths	1258	304	242	59.15
Artisan	Neonatal Deaths	237	25	105	4.86
	Post-Neonatal Deaths	237	22	93	4.28
	Infant Deaths	237	47	198	9.14

employed. Again, there is a constant rate of infant mortality, i.e. 242 per thousand live births in the work category of labourers and they mainly work as the labourers in the forest but the share of infant deaths is as high as of above 59 per cent. The above trend of stability is also observed for neo-natal and post-neonatal mortality in above occupation, which are 34 and 28 per thousand live births respectively. The last category of artisan workers includes the share of infant deaths is as low as below 10 per cent in which neonate and post-neonate deaths consist of 4.86 per cent and 4.28 per cent. Moreover, the IMR, NMR and PNMR remain at the constant rate of 198, 105 and 93 per thousand live births. Thus, heavy engagement and low caloric intake of mothers are mainly responsible for high infant mortality in all category of mother's occupation among the primitive tribes in the state.

Processing of Mahua Seeds for making Oil by Mal Paharia Females

Father's Occupation

The unemployment and underemployment affect all groups of primitive tribal people. There is not enough work available in the area due to low productivity of agriculture and mono cropped agricultural pattern. The poor tribal people seek whatever opportunities are available outside the tribal area and the state where wages are low and exploitation intense and manifold. A child's nourishment is affected by his parents' economic, educational and occupational status. Low education and low occupational status of the father may result into death of infants.The primitive tribes have different traditional occupations. The Asurs are iron smelters subsisting mainly on primitive agriculture. The Birhors make ropes, okhli, kathot, musical instruments like drums and enjoy hunting birds and other animals. The Birjias are slash and burn cultivators, prepare bamboo pans, small baskets, broom and are agricultural labourers. They subsist on primitive agriculture, collection of wild roots, tubers, leaves, flowers and fruits and hunting of wild animals. The Mal Paharias and the Sauria Paharias are traditional shifting cultivators. The Parhaiyas are mainly hunters and food gatherers, cutters of woods and bamboos.

The Savars are mainly food gatherers, hunters and collectors of honey. Almost all the PTG males are engaged in traditional artisan works.

Table 3.11: Father's Occupation among the PTGs in Jharkhand at the Time of Survey

Father's Occupation	Component	Live Births	Infant Deaths	IMR	% of Infant Distribution
Mining and Factory Worker	Neonatal Deaths	244	28	115	5.45
	Post-Neonatal Deaths	244	22	90	4.28
	Infant Deaths	244	50	205	9.73
Govt. Employee	Neonatal Deaths	324	34	105	6.61
	Post-Neonatal Deaths	324	28	86	5.45
	Infant Deaths	324	62	191	12.06
Cultivator	Neonatal Deaths	492	67	136	13.04
	Post-Neonatal Deaths	492	41	83	7.98
	Infant Deaths	492	108	219	21.01
Labourer	Neonatal Deaths	1047	143	136	27.82
	Post-Neonatal Deaths	1047	120	115	23.35
	Infant Deaths	1047	263	251	51.17
Artisan	Neonatal Deaths	132	18	136	3.5
	Post-Neonatal Deaths	132	13	99	2.53
	Infant Deaths	132	31	235	6.03

The maximum number of primitive tribal males are engaged as labourers and the share of infant deaths in this group encompasses of

51.17 per cent in the survey year of 2017 and this particular group also inherits the highest rate of infant mortality, which is as high as 251 per thousand live births among the PTGs in Jharkhand. Further, this group also contains both the highest rate and the share of neonate and post-neonate deaths, which is visible from Table-III.11. It is followed by the artisan workers in which the IMR, NMR and PNMR stand at 235, 136 and 99 per thousand live births whereas the share of above-mentioned groups contains 6.03 per cent, 3.5 per cent and 2.53 per cent of infant deaths respectively.The group of cultivators includes the share of around 21 per cent of total infant deaths but the IMR is 219 per thousand live births. The proportional share of neonate and post-neonate deaths are 13.04 and 7.98 per cent whereas the NMR and PNMR stand at 136 and 83 per thousand live births. Almost all the farmers practice broadcasting method of paddy cultivation. Besides this, they grow coarse crops in which productivity per person is very low. The next group belongs to mining and factory workers, which represents the lower IMR of 205 per thousand live births and the contribution of neo-natal and post-neonatal mortality, persist at 115 and 90 per thousand live births individually. The proportionate share of infant, neonate and post-neonate deaths remains at very low level of 9.73 per cent, 5.45 per cent and 4.28 per cent. The last group of workers is the government employee in fourth grade and the share of infant mortality is quite meagre quantity of 12.06 per cent in which the contribution of neonate and post-neonate deaths incorporate 5.45 per cent and 4.28 per cent of total infant deaths. Nevertheless, the ratio of IMR, NMR and PNMR persist as high as 191,105 and 86 per thousand live births respectively. Thus, the share of infant mortality in the latter two categories of workers is minimal as the father gets assured and handsome salary in the above occupation.

Infrastructural Facilities in Primitive Tribal Territories of Jharkhand

Even after the frequent use of term infrastructure, it is not well defined in precise and greatly acceptable manner. The terms, namely 'Social Overhead', 'Economic Overhead', 'Overhead Capital', 'Basic Economic Overhead' etc. are used as synonym of infrastructure, which usually denote services. Nurske (1955) delineated 'infrastructure as basic for any productive activity, cannot be imported, require large and costly installation, call for public assistance, have long maturity period, lumpiness and high operational capital intensity and generate external economies.' However, some basic characteristics that infrastructural services possess can be identified. They are: (a) essential but not directly productive, (b) pre-requisite of development, (c) non-importability, (d) lumpiness, (e) external economies, and (f) provision by state. In the field of infrastructure availability, regional imbalances both at inter-district and intra-district level have been characterized through rural development in Jharkhand, which are accompanied by equally sharper variations in infrastructural facilities. Infrastructural facilities available in a village may be taken as an index of the general advancement of economic conditions and improvement in the facilities provided to the people. The financial funding is basically focussed on infrastructure under article 275(1) in the remote primitive tribal areas to bring at par with other areas of Jharkhand. Most of the hill tops and the hill slope villages and majority of other villages in the plains are seriously lacking of government-driven infrastructural amenities in the remote and inaccessible villages of Jharkhand. Since banking, agricultural credit societies etc. are not available within the vicinity of 5kms from the surveyed villages, they are not taken consideration for the measurement of infrastructural amenities in the territories of primitive people in Jharkhand. That is why, only five amenities, viz. educational facility, transport facility, communication facility, medical facility and marketing facility have been examined here, which are somehow related to the infant mortality.

Medical Facility

The norms prescribed for medical facilities are not very appropriate in the primitive tribal region because of the hilly terrain, inaccessible areas and dispersal of population in small settlements over a large area. It is further observed in Fig. 3.1 that the average distance of primary health centre was 8.16 kms whereas the average distance of government hospital, private hospital and trust hospital were located at 17.38, 43.68 and 45.57 kms respectively in 2017. That kind of scenario is found in the region of Jharkhand where there is an extreme kind of deficiency of transportation facility, which is virtually inaccessible. Again, Appendix 3.1reveals that the situation is further aggravated in case of the localities of the Sauriya Paharias, the Asurs and the

Korwas. In the circumstances of far located medical institution, the poor primitive tribal still depend upon their primitive system of medicine which encourages quacks. It is generally not true to say that a primitive tribal does not accept modern system of medicine. Actually, his resources do not permit to avail of it. That is why, Lewis (1966) mentioned that good health increases the number of main hours of work that can be performed; secondly it improves the quality of work and thirdly by clearing uninhabitable areas, it makes possible the use of natural resources which would not be otherwise utilised. However, general health of primitive tribes in Jharkhand appears to be very poor and badly suffering from the effects of malnutrition and widespread incidence of chronic diseases.

The distance should be the main criteria in setting up primary health centres because firstly lack of transportation facilities in the areas isolate many remote villages in the rainy season. Even in fair weather journeys are long and hazardous in the forested and hilly terrain. Secondly, there is complete absence of private medical facility as the people are devoid of wealth resources through which they can hire the above. Lastly, Ayurveda and indigenous tribal medicines have not been evolved even after independence whereby they can easily get the above medicine within the territory of their localities at cheaper rate.

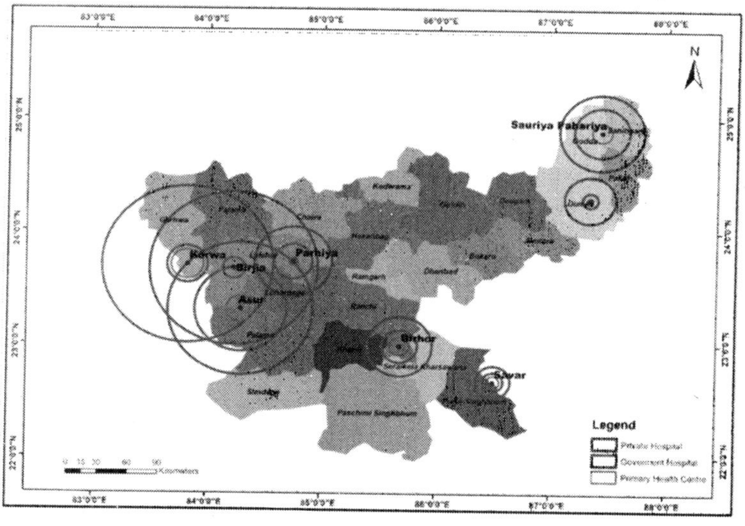

Fig. 3.1: Medical Facilities among Primitive Tribes in Jharkhand, 2017

Communication Facility

Infrastructural facilities available in the territory of the primitive tribes may be taken as an index of the general advancement of the economic condition and improvement in the facilities provided to the people. In this context the availability of communication facilities like post office, mobile and internet play an important role for infrastructural development. As Appendix 3.2 shows that there is only one means of communication facility, i.e. mobile, which is spread in almost all one hundred sampled villages. Again, the share of prevalence of mobile facility is 82 per cent, which are less prevalent in the villages of the Birjias and the Savars. However, the role of post office and internet as means of communication are negligible in the villages of primitive tribes. It is generally said that cheap and extensive network of communication is the greatest blessing for any region from the economic point of view. Unfortunately, the above territories are completely devoid of communication facilities.

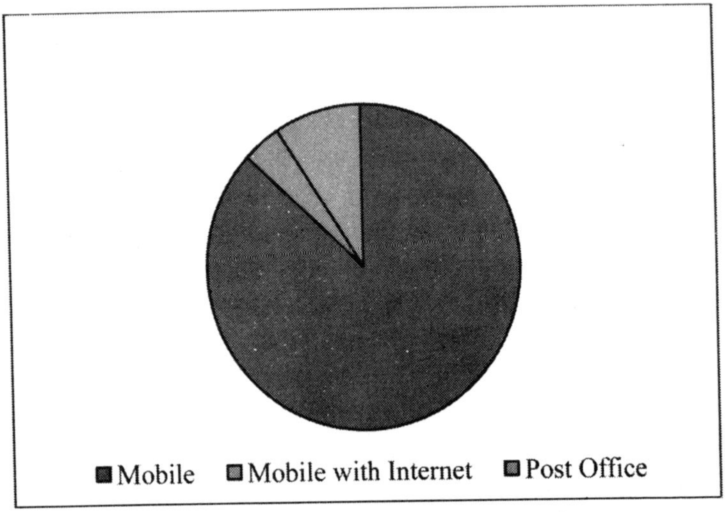

Fig. 3.2: Distribution of Communication Facilities in Primitive Tribal Villages of Jharkhand, 2017

Transportation Facility

Transportation is an essential a type of service involving spatial interaction. It has been an essential accompaniment of human socio-economy at some scale and intensity according to the stage of development. The modes of transport are most substantive parts of infrastructure. Today they create intimate bond among local, intra-national, regional and global spatial socio-economy people and products from surplus areas to deficit areas (Singh and Siddiqui, 2012). In absence of medical facilities surrounding the tribal village, the primitive people can not avail the medical facilities of urban areas since there is complete dearth of transport facilities in the territory of tribal areas.

This pathetic situation can be easily visualised from Appendix 3.3 that they have to travel around fifteen kms for riding on a bus. The situation can be further worsened when the availability of bus stand is taken into consideration of the surrounding areas of the Sauria Paharias, which is around 25 kms from their residential areas. Again, it is a matter of great concern regarding the availability of railway station. The people have to travel at least 50 kms to catch a train in the areas of primitive people in Jharkhand. The situation gets further deteriorated when the territories of the Asurs, the Sauria Paharias and the Korwas are taken into consideration, which are above 75 kms. It is observed that 62 per cent of villages do not have *pucca* road facilities and not even a single village of primitive tribes is connected through the railway line. It is a matter of shame on the civilized society of the state that even 13 per cent of villages are devoid of unmetalled road. Moreover, the absorbing capacity of a particular destination, especially in terms of medical opportunities also plays an important role in determining the characteristics of the deceased. It is rightly remarked by Youngson (1967) that the transport system helps to determine the scope and direction of economic development and to improve in creating new opportunities and new incentives. Furthermore, transport plays a very important part in opening up markets for local commodities without which their value of output could not be increased.

Market Facility

The periodic market or *haat* has an unavoidable part in the economy of primitive tribes. It is the only channel through which local agricultural commodities are sold and necessary implements as well cash are received. The markets are generally held in the open ground regularly in the very fixed day of the week in the market space. The *hat* keeps them busy throughout the week. They cut wood from the jungle, get them dried up and cut them into several pieces from an axe and lastly tie them into bundles of different sizes from fibres of any tree. Finally, they sell these fuel woods, bamboos, seasonal fruits, grains, cattle, birds, vegetables, *handias* etc. in the market. It is evident from Appendix 3.4 that the markets are generally held within the vicinity of about 9 kms from their residential villages. So far, the location of towns is concerned that they are far away, i.e. 58.4 kms from their native land. This way, there is no question of transferability of their products in the city. That is why, the middlemen play an important role in exchange of their products. Nevertheless, these poor and illiterate people have haphazard and whimsical life style without any planning in expenditure. Major part of their income from agriculture goes to the middlemen at the time of harvest and that from forest products to the traders during sale in village market. The moment money in cash comes to their hand, wine and alcoholic drinks become the first item of expenditure, exhausting a considerable part of their income.

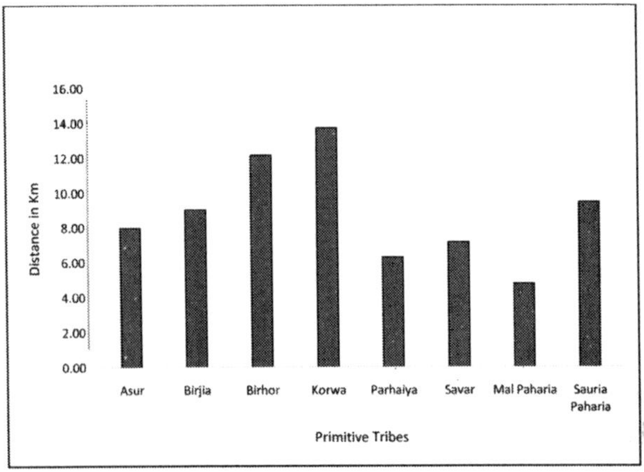

Fig. 3.3: Distance of Markets in Primitive Tribal Villages of Jharkhand, 2017

Educational Facility

Education besides bringing about number of changes in attitude to work, family size, tradition etc. also affects the process of capital formation through its effect on consumption preferences and expenditure on social ceremonies (Joshi, 1990). It is regarded as an important asset for an individual since it provides the key to the understanding of the wide world and equips him better to assert his rights and to claim his due share from others. It not only improves his own level of awareness and knowledge but also changes his attitudes and values since economic benefits and social prestige are generally derived from formal education.

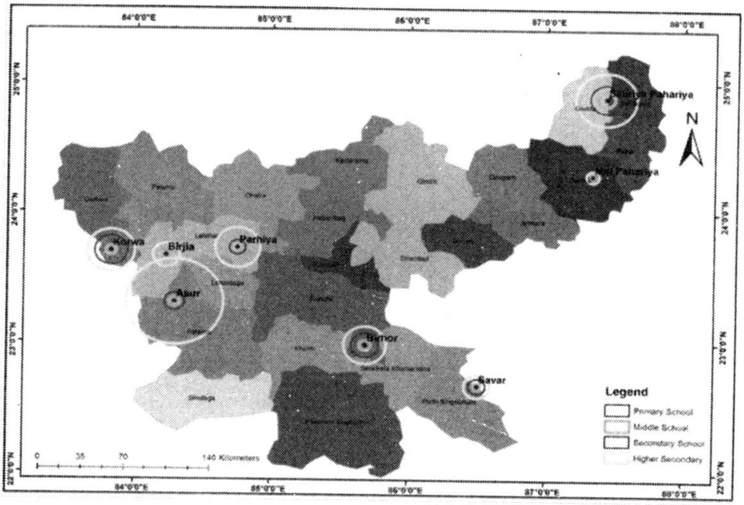

Fig. 3.4: Educational Facilities among Primitive Tribes in Jharkhand, 2017

The norms fixed by the government of setting up school on the basis of area and physical distance will not work here. Fig. 3.4 illustrates the observations of educational facilities available for the primitive tribes in Jharkhand. It is observed that there is complete destitute of schooling amenity in the areas where the primitive tribes reside. It is found that 23 per cent of primitive tribal villages have no access of any kind schooling facility. However, 40 per cent of villages have primary schooling facility whereas the share of middle school, secondary school and higher secondary school occupies 32 per cent, 3 per cent and 2 per cent respectively. The position is very bad among the Birjia and the Birhor villages where about half of the villages have no primary schools. It further reveals that the hidden constraint of drop-out rate at middle school level among the primitive children. The location of middle schools, secondary schools and higher secondary schools is so bad that many students of poorer families have to abandon their studies because the nearest school is at a distance which can't possibly be covered on and no hostel facilities are available. The average distance of secondary school and higher secondary school are 8.63 and 16.44 kms respectively.

The situation is more pathetic for the localities of the Asurs and the Sauria Paharias. The qualitative aspect of the existing educational facilities is also depressive. It is a common complaint in the interior rural areas that the teachers do not attend schools and many of them remain away from areas for months together. The teachers recruited from non-tribal areas do not like to work in the distant and inaccessible tribal areas with poor amenities. The physical distance and lack of transport, inefficiency and corrupt practises have made a mockery of supervision carried out in respect of these schools. The position of building for schools is also alarming. Even if some schools have their own buildings, the repairs have not been attended to for years and the building is in a dilapidated condition. Many schools do not have even such elementary facilities like blackboard, duster, chalk and drinking water. Even if there are schools in the villages and non-tribal are recruited as teachers. The primitive tribe children do not attend the school because their tradition demands their presence in the forest during school hour to learn folk songs, dances, hunting etc. They consider the non-tribal as their enemy hence they do not send their children to such schools where they are teachers. The irony of the fact is that the maximum teachers are the non-tribal. The schools are generally located in the plains but the children are not coming because they believe that if they attend to these schools, they will become alien to their culture.

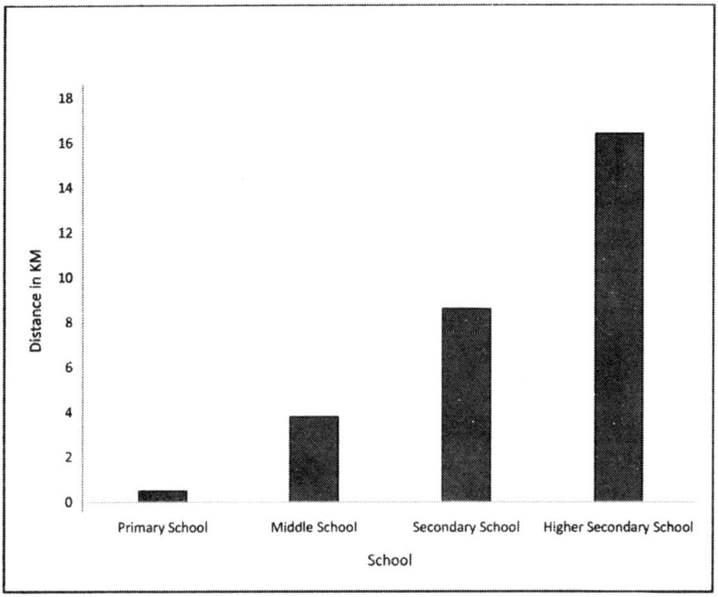

Fig. 3.5: Distance of Education Facilities in Primitive Tribal Villages of Jharkhand, 2017

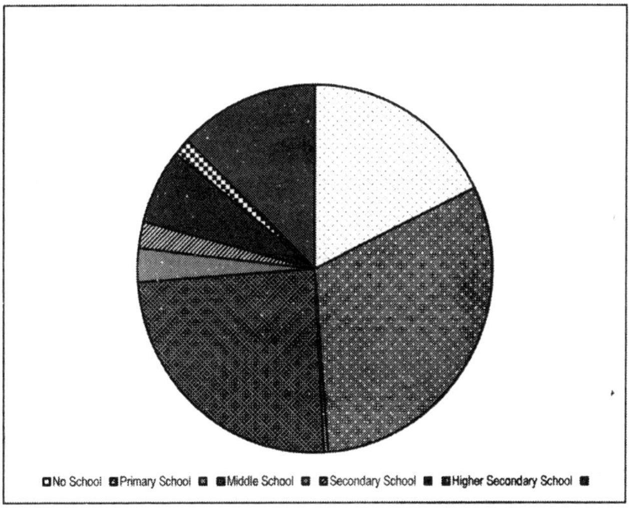

Fig. 3.6: Distribution of Education Facilities in Primitive Tribal Villages of Jharkhand, 2017

Summary

The present study focuses mainly on four parameters of infant deaths, viz. mother's age at child birth, child birth order and marriage age of female under demographic profile of infant deaths. The above study elucidates the hypothesis that the biological variables, namely share of either young or old age mothers, proportion of first and above fourth order of child births, ratio of lower marriage age enhances the neonatal mortality rate whereas post-neonatal mortality is controlled by environmental variables, namely percentage of illiterate mothers, share of large size family, quota of single parent family, portion of low per capita income and proportion of landless households. It is found that more than 51 per cent of infant deaths are exclusively confined to those unfortunate children whose mothers were more than 30 years old whereas the lowest infant mortality rate, i.e. 116 per thousand live births are found in the age group of such mothers, who are having the age between 20 and 30 years. So far birth order of infant death is concerned, it is perceived highest, while the children are born in the category of fourth and higher order of births. Again, the early age of mother, i.e. below 18 years is detrimental for the survival of children wherein the IMR is 286 per thousand live births and the NMR is also above 174 per thousand live births.

The variable, namely mother's education has negative impact upon child deaths. Further, it is noticed that the large size of household augments the IMR but its share to total death is small. Another conspicuous feature is noticed in case of the type of family, where the highest PNMR is found in single parent family, wherein mother usually flees away with their lovelorn and leave the children with their father. Moreover, religion does not play a decisive role in context of infant deaths but the largest IMR is perceived among the people of Sarna religion. Next to this is the income status of the people, which manifests that the enormous IMR is watched in lower income people whereas paltry amount of IMR is concentrated in high income group of people, which is universal truth.The next parameter namely landholding status reveals that high level of IMR is found in small landholding households in lieu of landless households. Lastly, occupation of mother and father elucidates that the highest mortality rate of infants, viz. NMR, PNMR and IMR are found among those primitive tribal children, when their parents are engaged in particular occupation of labourers.

It can be inferred from the above discussion that the availability of medical facility is very poor in the locality of primitive people. It is found that even ill-equipped primary health centre is around ten kms from their residence. The scenario of transportation and communication amenities are further aggravated as approachable *pucca* road is fifteen kms away from their dwellings and there is no trace of post office in their habitations. It is a matter of dismay that even VI class towns are located around sixty kms from their surroundings. In case of electricity amenity, their villages are completely devoid of it. Of all the infrastructural amenities, the drinking water appears to be the most important means for their livelihood and sustenance. Unfortunately, one-third villages did not have even that basic provision. That is why, they mainly rely on polluted spring and stream water. However, the education facility of primary school was observed in almost all the villages but the enmity towards non-tribal teachers and location of schools in the plains lead to rethink about their development by the policy maker so that the local tribal teachers may be recruited and the schools would be established in their territory.

REFERENCES

Cladwell, C. J. (1979). *op. cit.*, pp. 395-413.

Ezra, M. and E. Gurum (2002). "Breastfeeding, birth intervals and child survival: Analysis of the 1997 community and family survey data in southern Ethiopia", *Ethiopian Journal of Health Development*, Vol. 16, No. 1, pp. 41-51.

Joshi, B.M. (1990). *Infrastructure and Economic Development*, New Delhi: Ashish Publishing House, p. 27.

Kumar, S (2005). *Rural Male Out-Migration*, Delhi: Vista International Publishing House, p. 111.

Lewis, W.A. (1966). *Development Planning: The Essentials of Economic Policy*, London: George Allen and Unwin, pp. 97-102.

Mukherji, A.B. (1980). *The Chamars of Uttar Pradesh: A Study in Social Geography*, Delhi: Inter-India Publications, p. 14.

Nurkse, R. (1955). *Problems of Capital Formation in Under-Developed Countries*, Oxford: Basil Blackwell, pp. 46-47.

Pandey, R.N. (1997). "Levels and Patterns of Infant and Child Mortality in Mongolia", *Asia-Pacific Population Journal*, Vol. 12, No. 3, pp. 49-64.

Singh, K.N. and A.R, Siddiqui (2012). *Economic Geography*, Allahabad: Prayag Pustak Bhawan, p. 570.

Sunita, K. and S. Parsuraman, (1998). *Mother's employment and infant and child mortality rate in India*, National Family Health Survey, No 8, IIPS, India.

United Nation Development Programme (2005): *Human Development Report 2003*, International Cooperation at a Crossroad: Aid, Trade and Security in an Unequal World, New Delhi: Oxford University Press.

Youngson, A.J. (1967). *Overhead Capital: A Study in Development Economics*, Edinburough: Adams and Charles Black, pp. 72 -93.

4
Assessment and Regional Patterns of Infant Deaths

Infant mortality plays an important role in determining the prevailing mortality conditions in primitive tribal groups of Jharkhand. The greatest incidence of all deaths in the PTG is infant death. More than one-third of all deaths in a year of 2017are of infant deaths. Although, the assessment of infant deaths takes into account of the various components, namely Early Neonatal Mortality Rate (ENMR), Late Neonatal Mortality Rate (LNMR),Neonatal Mortality Rate (NMR),Post-Neonatal Mortality Rate (PNMR) and Infant Mortality Rate (IMR) under the heading of its components directly but Still Birth Rate (SBR) and Peri Natal Mortality Rate (PMR) also affect child deaths indirectly. That is why, all seven components of infant deaths have been analysed here for the primitive tribes of Jharkhand. Again, the pattern of infant deaths for various components has been analysed on the basis of various orders of geographical regions, districts, blocks and villages level through proper spatial investigations. Malnutrition, insanitation, unavailability of medical and transport facilities, poverty and unhygienic condition are mainly responsible for ill health and death of children among the primitive tribes. Further, as a consequence of high infant mortality, the risk of experiencing child deaths for a household increases. The incidence of child loss not only disturbs the family emotionally, it also leads to excess childbearing, which ultimately is responsible for ill health of mothers. It was rightly, said by Weinstein and Pillai (2017) that because the very young are the most vulnerable to infectious disease, malnutrition, and other illness that can prove fatal, the rate at which deaths occur among them is an especially sensitive indicator of socio-economic conditions.

Still Birth Rate

Although the Still Birth Rate (SBR) does not come directly under the gamut of Infant Mortality Rate (IMR) but the factors of SBR such as pregnancy and labour complication, problem with placenta, umbilical cord, birth defect, infection, high blood pressure and so on and so forth are associated with infant deaths. Therefore, a glimpse of SBR has been presented here in context of the primitive tribes in Jharkhand. The SBR refers to foetal death in the womb of mother after 20 weeks of pregnancy per thousand births. It encompasses any death of a foetus after 20 weeks of gestation till the delivery of baby with no signs of life. It is mainly caused by placenta cord disorder, high blood pressure, infections, birth defects and poor life styles. Foetal deaths can also be divided into death prior to labour known as antepartum death and death during labour known as intrapartum death.

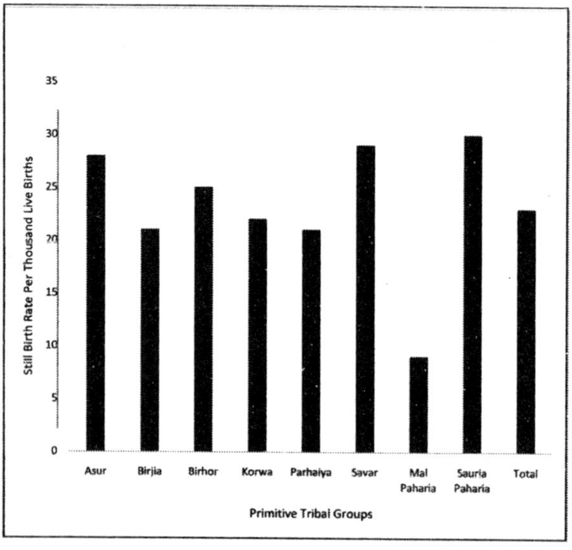

Fig. 4.1: Still Birth Rate among Primitive Tribes in Jharkhand, 2017

Table 4.1: Assessment of Infant Deaths among Primitive Tribal Groups in Jharkhand

Component of Infant Deaths	Primitive Tribe								
	Asur	Birjia	Birhor	Korwa	Parhaiya	Savar	Mal Paharia	Sauria Paharia	Total
Live Births and Still Births	216	340	202	279	287	239	329	399	2291
Still Births	6	7	5	6	6	7	3	12	52
SBR	28	21	25	22	21	29	9	30	23
Live Births	210	333	197	273	281	232	326	387	2239
Early Neonatal Deaths	25	26	21	33	27	22	24	58	241
ENMR	119	78	107	121	96	95	74	150	108
Still Births and Early Neonatal Deaths	31	33	26	39	33	29	27	70	293
PNMR	144	97	129	140	115	121	82	175	128
Late Neonatal Deaths	6	4	5	7	5	6	6	10	49
LNMR	29	12	25	26	18	26	18	26	22
Post-Neonatal Deaths	19	29	34	28	31	13	26	49	224
PNMR	90	87	173	103	110	56	80	127	100
Neonatal Deaths	31	30	26	40	32	28	30	68	290
NMR	148	90	132	147	114	121	92	176	130
Infant Deaths	50	59	60	68	63	41	56	117	514
IMR	238	177	305	249	224	177	172	302	230

It is disclosed from Table 4.1 that the SBR was found as high as 23 per thousand births among the primitive tribes in Jharkhand at the time of survey against the national average of 22 per thousand births. It is further noticed that only 52 babies were stillbirths against 2291 live births in the survey of 2017 among the primitive tribes. The highest still birth deaths, i.e. 30 per thousand births are observed among the Sauria Paharias living exclusively in the Hill Tops of Damin-i-Koh region in Santhal Pargana. On the contrary, the lowest foetal deaths, i.e. 9 per thousand births are found among the Mal Paharias, who are also concentrated in the Plains and Scarps of Damin-i-Koh region, where they have mingled with the Hindus and naturally, they receive maximum government support. Again, their preconceived notion regarding child rearing has been changed into scientific temperament of child's nourishment. The other primitive tribes of the Savars, the Asurs, the Birhors, the Korwas, the Birjias, and the Parhaiyas, have their proportionate share of the SBR as 29, 28, 25, 22, 21, and 21 per thousand births respectively. Thus, the high level of still birth rate among the Sauria Paharias, the Savars and the Asurs is apparently exhibited from Fig. 4.1 and these three tribes are completely backward in all aspects. Arokiasamy and Gautam (2008) had also shown that full antenatal care is an important factor that helps reduce neonatal mortality for eight empowered action group states of India in which Jharkhand is also one of the states of empowered action state.

The district level analysis from Table 4.2 reveals that the highest concentration of SBR is found in the district of Khunti whereas the lowest agglomeration of SBR is confined to the district of Dumka. However, it is to be bring to mind that total number of stillbirths was only one but total number of live births was also very low, i.e. 15. That is why, Khunti encompasses the highest SBR. The district of Sahibganj comes as the next district in term of high SBR which is followed by Seraikella-Kharsawan, Purbi Singhbhum, Godda, Gumla, Ranchi, Latehar, Garhwa, and Pakur. That is why, district level analysis of SBR does match with tribe-wise explanation of SBR in the present study. Thus, the districts with the primitive tribes in context of SBR do not form any pattern; rather they are located in a scattered manner. This is mainly due to non-proportional representation of household surveys on the basis of district as criteria rather the present survey completely relies on proportional representation of community-wise distribution. In fact, they are located in all major physiographic regions of the state. Again, it can be concluded that the SBR of the PTGs corresponds to national average of SBR, which manifests that the biological factors responsible for child deaths remain the same among all ethnic communities of India.

Early Neonatal Mortality Rate

The Early Neonatal Mortality (ENMR) is defined as the death of a new born baby between zero and seven days after birth against per thousand live births. It is Herculean task to know the ENMR and their inherent causes of deaths among the primitive tribes in Jharkhand, where people have tremendous faith in Bongaism and Shamanism whereby it means that the disease is caused either by the branch of taboo or the hostile spirit, which can be cured by the village shaman, i.e. priest. On an average, the early neonatal mortality rate was found 108 per thousand live births, which explicitly manifests towards very high early neonatal deaths among the primitive tribes in Jharkhand. Almost all people dwell in a fragmented settlement on the rugged scarps, forested areas and hill tops, which are mostly concentrated in remote areas. Again, the area is covered with dense forest, where there is complete absence of means of transportation and communication. The people are thoroughly dependent upon agriculture. Unfortunately, that agriculture is also uncertain and the coarse crops are generally grown. As a result, per person productivity is of meagre amount. Subsequently, they have pitiable low socio-economic status wherein the women are basically illiterate and mingled with superstition tradition.

The chief causes of ENMR are asphyxia, prematurity, bacterial infection and congenital malformation. In fact, almost all tribal mothers give prelacteal food to their new-borns for few days. Moreover, no prelacteal food is probably required during the first few days and the breasts secrete yellowish fluid milk called colostrum. Colostrum is good for the baby and will take care of its first hunger. Though the amount of colostrum available at each feed is small, the act of sucking during these days promotes the flow of milk and soon the breasts start secreting milk. The primitive tribal mothers think that colostrum has remained in the breast during the nine months of pregnancy and is, therefore, harmful. These mothers have to be educated that colostrum is not only harmless but it is richer in body-building nutrients than natural milk and it is possible that it may provide valuable materials needed for the protection of the baby against infection. Therefore, WHO recommends initiation of breastfeeding as soon as possible after childbirth, within the first hour after delivery. The primitive tribe-wise analysis of ENMR divulges that the highest ENMR, i.e. 150 per thousand live births are found among the Sauria Paharias. It is followed by the Korwas, the Asurs, the Birhors, the Parhaiyas, the Savars, the Birjias and the Mal Paharias, which have substantiative figure of ENMR as 121, 119, 107, 96, 95, 78 and 74 per thousand live births. Above all, what is noticeable in case of ENMR that there is universal very high ENMR among all the tribes varying from 74 to 150 per thousand live births but the difference is not that much noticeable.

The above pattern of ENMR among the various ethnic groups of PTGs is also reflected in Fig. 4.2. It clearly substantiates that there is complete dearth of medical facilities and the females are not given proper and nutritious food during their gestation period across all primitive tribes. Regular antenatal check-ups, health education to pregnant and lactating mothers, healthy and nutritious diet to mother during gestation period, free delivery of iron and folic acid tablets, free delivery kit to all pregnant mother, compulsory vaccination of tetanus, institutional child delivery and timely referral of pregnancy complication to well-equipped hospital may cut down on early neonatal mortality rate but the above processes of child rearing are not completely taken into account among the PTGs in the state. There is complete dearth of medical, transportation and communication infrastructural facilities in their localities.Therefore, institutional delivery is not popular among the PTGs in the state. People can reach their localities only after walking of at least five kms distance from the metalled road. The situation is further aggravated in the localities of Damin-i-Koh and Pat region. Not to speak of availability of doctors, even the nurses are not deployed in these inaccessible areas of PTG.

The district level analysis of ENMR manifests that Sahibganj ranks the first position, which is followed by Seraikella Kharsawan, Godda, Purbi Singhbhum, Ranchi, Latehar, Gumla, Pakur, Garhwa, Dumka and Khunti. The first district is located in Damin-i-Koh region

Table 4.2: Regional Patterns of Infant Deaths among Primitive Tribal Groups in Jharkhand

Component of Infant Deaths	Districts											
	Ranchi	Khunti	Seraikella-Kharsawan	Latehar	Gumla	Paschimi Singhbhum	Garhwa	Pakur	Godda	Sahibganj	Dumka	Total
Live Births and Still Births	134	15	29	691	172	230	262	317	166	95	180	2291
Still Births	3	1	1	15	4	6	5	6	4	5	2	52
SBR	22	67	34	22	23	26	19	19	24	53	11	23
Live Births	131	14	28	676	168	224	257	311	162	90	178	2239
Early Neonatal Deaths	15	1	4	75	18	26	24	29	21	15	13	241
ENMR	115	71	143	111	107	116	93	93	130	167	73	108
Still Births and Early Neonatal Deaths	18	2	5	90	22	32	29	35	25	20	15	293
PMR	134	133	172	130	128	139	111	110	151	211	83	128

(Contd.)

Component of Infant Deaths	Districts											
	Ranchi	Khunti	Seraikella-Kharsawan	Latehar	Gumla	Paschimi Singhbhum	Garhwa	Pakur	Godda	Sahibganj	Dumka	Total
Late Neonatal Deaths	2	1	1	16	4	5	4	6	4	3	3	49
LNMR	15	71	36	24	24	22	16	19	25	33	17	22
Post-Neonatal Deaths	13	2	3	76	18	25	22	25	13	10	17	224
PNMR	99	143	107	112	107	112	86	80	80	111	96	100
Neonatal Deaths	17	2	5	91	22	31	28	35	25	18	16	290
NMR	130	143	179	135	131	138	109	113	154	200	90	130
Infant Deaths	30	4	8	167	40	56	50	60	38	28	33	514
IMR	229	286	286	247	238	250	195	193	235	311	185	230

whereas the last district is located in the Central Highland, which are characterised by dissected rugged topography. Otherwise, there is no clear-cut pattern of ENMR and the districts are located in haphazard manner. It has already been discussed earlier that the district level analysis of ENMR does not produce emphatic picture of early child deaths as the survey did not consider uniform representation of the PTGs due to their sporadic kind of distribution.

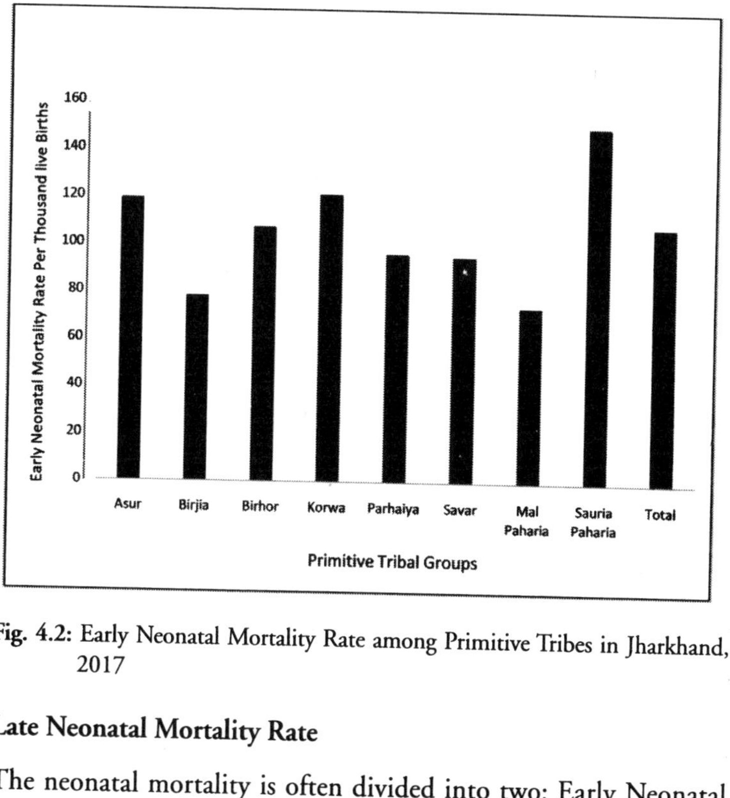

Fig. 4.2: Early Neonatal Mortality Rate among Primitive Tribes in Jharkhand, 2017

Late Neonatal Mortality Rate

The neonatal mortality is often divided into two: Early Neonatal Mortality Rate (ENMR) and Late Neonatal Mortality Rate (LNMR) and the later refer to a number of deaths, which occur at the age of 8 to 28 days against per thousand live births during the particular statistical year. It is manifested from Table 4.1 that on the whole there is a phenomenal decrease in late neonatal mortality rate, i.e. 22 per thousand live births in compare to early neonatal mortality rate among the primitive tribes in Jharkhand at the time survey. This is mainly due to their customary behaviour wherein there is universal practice of breastfeeding to the neonates after few days. That is why; there is a huge gap between ENMR and LNMR among the primitive tribes.

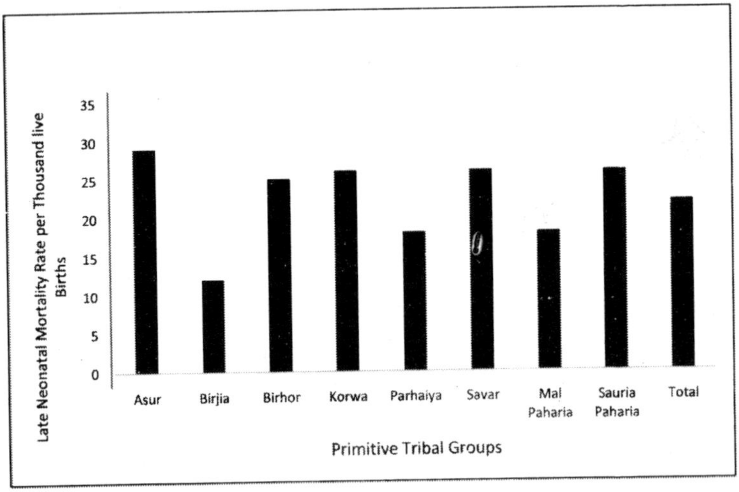

Fig. 4.3: Late Neonatal Mortality Rate among Primitive Tribes in Jharkhand, 2017

Tribe-wise analysis elucidates that the Asurs have the highest proportional share of Late Neonatal Mortality Rate (LNMR), i.e. 29 per thousand live births. The other tribes, viz. the Sauria Paharias, the Savars, the Korwas,the Birhors, the Parhaiyas the Mal Paharias, and the Birjias incorporate the possession of LNMR in descending order, which capitulate of LNMR at26, 26, 26, 25, 18, 17 and 12 per thousand live births, which is clearly portrayed in Fig. 4.3. It clearly manifests that there is a marginal difference of LNMR among the various communities of primitive tribes due to having same level of poverty and same pattern of child rearing. So far district level analysis of LNMR is concerned; the LNMR illustrates a little bit different picture owing to not taking consideration of the proportionate share of households for every district. Khunti takes lead in context of LNMR as the district is abode of a large agglomeration of the Birhors. However, the total cases of late neonate death were only one and the share of LNMR is high due to small selection of survey households in the district. On the other hand, Purbi Singhbhum has the lowest contribution of LNMR as the district incorporates a large section of the Savars and they take benefit from medical facilities of West Bengal. The other districts, namely Seraikella-Kharsawan, Sahibganj, Godda, Latehar, Gumla, Purbi Singhbhum, Pakur, Dumka and Garhwa fall in ascending order, which is explicitly reflected from Table 4.2. Nevertheless, the highest concentration of LNMR is situated in Damin-i-Koh region of Santhal Pargana, wherein the Sauria Paharias and the Mal Paharias live in abundance, where medical facility is of very poor quality.

Neonatal Mortality Rate

The Neonatal Mortality Rate (NMR) refers to the neonate deaths during the first 28 days of life in a year for thousand live births of the same year. It is the most vulnerable time for child's survival, while they face the highest risk of dying and the factors which affect neonatal mortality are mostly of endogenous nature. The endogenous factors are related to the formation of foetus in the mother's womb and are biological in nature. These include age of mother, birth order, period of spacing between births, pre-maturity, weight of the child at the time of birth (Raj, 2003). The common cause of neonatal deaths includes asphyxia, prematurity, tetanus, diarrhoea, malformation, jaundice and respiratory difficulties.

It is explicitly manifested from Table 4.1 that the Neo-Natal Mortality Rate (NMR) was as much high as 130 against the state average of 27 per thousand live births during the investigation year of 2017. Despite having the highest neonatal mortality among the localities of primitive tribes in the state, the neglected tribal areas are lacking with the problem of ill-equipped public health facilities. After a glance of tribe-wise distribution of NMR, it is perceived that the Sauria Paharias perform worse even in neonate deaths, which comprise 176 per thousand live births whereas the lowest rate of neonate deaths is found among the Birjias, which is 90 per thousand live births. The other primitive tribes, namely the Asurs, the Korwas, Birhors, the Savars, the Parhaiyas and the Mal Paharias contain 148, 147, 132, 121, 114 and 92 per thousand live births respectively. It is further observed from Fig. 4.4 that the highest concentration of NMR is found either in Pat region or Dami-i-Koh region. The former region is the abode of the Asurs, the Parhaiyas and Korwas, whereas the later region is endowed with the population of the Sauria Paharias and the Mal Paharias. Moreover, the Birjias have the lowest ENMR, which avails the facility of famous Netarhat school and they are spread around it. Lastly, the Savars have the lowest, which are primarily concentrated in Dhalbhum region and that particular primitive tribe takes the benefit of better endowed medical facilities of West Bengal.

In short, the same pattern of NMR is exhibited on district level analysis. The districts, namely Gumla, Garhwa and Latehar of Pat region have the highest share of NMR, which is followed by Godda, Dumka, Pakur and Sahibganj of Damin-i-Koh region. Furthermore, the lowest NMR is exclusively confined to Dhalbhum region of Purbi Singhbhum. WHO (2016) also reported in case of developing countries that many neonates (about 75%) die within the first week of life and 25 per cent to 45 per cent of those deaths which occur in the first 24 hours of the new-born's life. In fact, the preterm labour and low-birth-weight-neonates are direct manifestations of negligence of antenatal care, maternal defects and gestational complications. Besides this, the new born neonate can also become weak and ill due to infections of many kinds. These vulnerable new-born babies may have lifetime risk against their physical, mental and developmental defects.

It is universal truth that the developing countries have insufficient resources to take care of baby booms. Additionally, these countries have to confront with their unscientific traditional cultural beliefs about rearing of new born babies whereby the risk of their survivals are minimal. Poverty, social denial, superstition and abandonment results in insufficient low intake of nutritious food by the mother during gestation period. Thus, neonatal mortality is a major contributor of infant mortality, accounting for two-thirds of deaths in children under the age of one year. Nearly 5 million neonatal deaths have been estimated to occur around the world annually, 98 per cent of these being in developing countries. Moreover, around 57 per cent of infant deaths are engulfed by the NMR among the primitive tribes in the state. This is because of the fact that universal practice of breastfeeding curtails the late neonate deaths dramatically among the primitive tribes. Finally, there is a lack of accountability and supervision of the existent staff, which is unwilling to work in remote forested tribal areas. Above all, there is lack of care seeking behaviour and fatalistic attitude of the community due to illiteracy and socio-economic constraints.

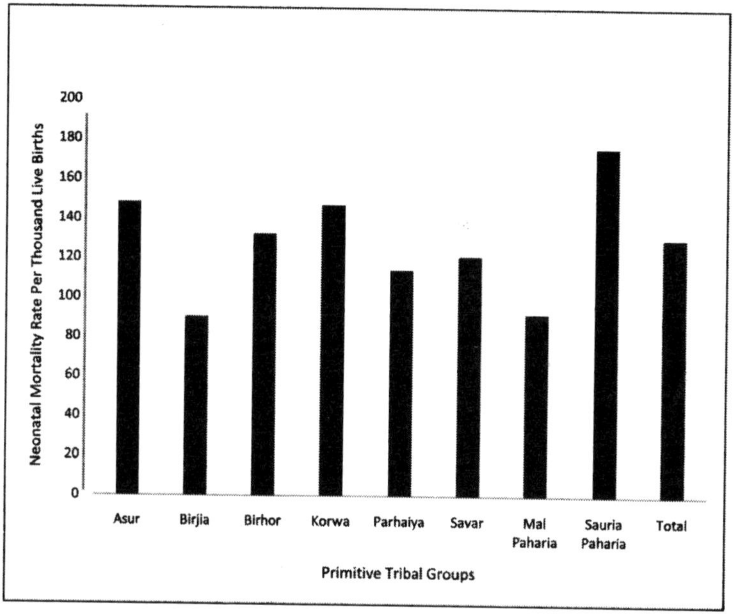

Fig. 4.4: Neonatal Mortality Rate among Primitive Tribes in Jharkhand, 2017

Perinatal Mortality Rate

Perinatal period commences at 20 completed of gestation and ends seven completed days after birth. Thus, Perinatal Mortality Rate (PMR) refers to the number of stillbirths and deaths in the first week of life against per thousand births in a year. Of course, perinatal mortality rate is a sensitive indicator of quality and quantity maternal and neonatal health services. The new born baby dies because of poor maternal health inadequate care during pregnancy, inappropriate management during delivery and first few hours of life and lack of new birth care. Nevertheless, still-birth mortality is induced by hypertension, antepartum, intrapartum, haemorrhage, asphyxia, infection and so on and so forth (Singh, 2010). It is exhibited in Table 4.1 that the perinatal mortality was very high, i.e. 128 per thousand births just like other measurement indices of infant mortality at the time of survey among the primitive tribes in Jharkhand. The Sauria Paharias contain the highest ratio of perinatal mortality, i.e. 150 per thousand births, which falls in Damin-i-Koh region of Santhal Pargana. It is succeeded by the Asurs and the Korwas, which have PMR at 144 and 140 per thousand births respectively and both tribes are conglomerated in Pat region, where there is rugged dissected terrain of the scarp forested zone. They are original inhabitants of the state but there is decline of population due to poverty, illiteracy, difficult transport amenity, harsh physical environment and so on and so forth. The next group of primitive communities in context of descending perinatal mortality belong to the Birhors, the Savars, the Parhaiyas, the Birjias, and the Mal Paharias and this primitive tribe's account for 129, 121, 115, 97 and 82 per thousand births for PMR and all these tribes have perinatal mortality ranging from 82 to 150 per thousand births.

The district level analysis of perinatal mortality does not repeat the proportional share of the primitive tribes as the same ratio of selection of households for every district has not been adopted in this survey. On the contrary, the main emphasis was placed for fair selection of tribal community.Regional analysis at district level from Table 4.2 manifests that Sahibganj stands at the top, i.e. 211 per thousand births whereas Dumka is placed at the bottom, i.e. 83 per thousand births in context of perinatal deaths. Other districts, namely Seraikella-Kharsawan, Godda, Purbi Singhbhum, Ranchi, Khunti, Latehar, Gumla, Garhwa, and Pakur are lying between the two extremes of perinatal mortality in ascending order. In short, the poor health and poor diet of mothers, abject poverty, home delivery through untrained nurses, addiction of alcoholic or *handia* drinks and unavailability of medical and transportation facilities are mainly responsible for high perinatal mortality among the primitive tribes in the state. Again, it is Damin-i-Koh region of Santhal Pargana, where the northern Damin-i-Koh, usual abode of the Sauria Paharia has the highest incidences of PMR whereas the southern Damin-i-Koh, natural home of the Mal Paharias has the lowest PMR, which is vividly portrayed in Fig. 4.5. That is why, the highest growth of population was observed among the Mal Paharias whereas the lowest increase in population was noticed for the Sauria Paharias in 2011 Census, which has already been discussed in second chapter.

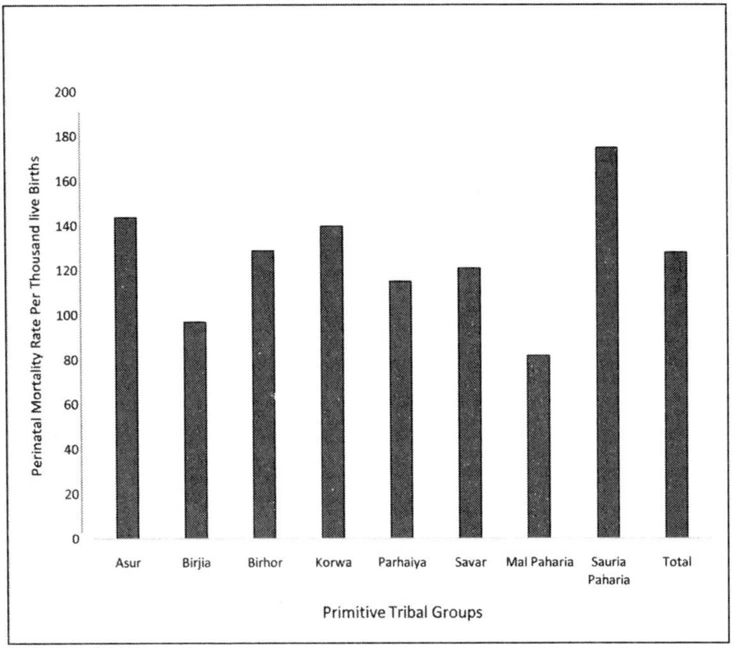

Fig. 4.5: Perinatal Mortality Rate among Primitive Tribes in Jharkhand, 2017

Post-Neonatal Mortality Rate

The Post-Neonatal Mortality Rate (PNMR) is death of babies from 29 days to the end of the first year per thousand live births. It is mainly affected by exogenous factors. Socio-economic, cultural and environmental factors are considered as exogenous factors, which are more responsible for mortality during post-neonatal period. The post-neonatal care that influences the chances of survival of babies includes both preventive and curative care. The former category includes immunization of children against diphtheria, pertussis, tetanus, polio, tuberculosis, hepatitis B, measles, mumps, rubella etc. diseases. The latter is related to prelection feeds, the timing of initiation of breast feeding, the duration of lactation, the timing of introduction of supplementary semi-solid food, hygiene, crowding and congestion, physical environment quality of water, nutrition of the mothers and the infants and socio-cultural practices of child rearing.

It is revealed from Table 4.1 that the average post-neonatal mortality was 100 per thousand live births in 2017 among the primitive tribes. The above high rate is definitely alarming predicament for the extinction of primitive communities in the state. If we dig up the reason behind such deplorable condition, we perceive that extreme poverty, addiction of alcohol drinking, smoking and chewing of narcotic, abode in small huts, inaccessibility of their villages, primitive method of living, illiteracy and drinking of polluted water are primarily responsible for the excessive mortality. Tribe-wise analysis from Fig. 4.6 reveals that the Birhors occupy the first ranking in context of high PNMR, i.e. 173 per thousand live births whereas the lowest PNMR of 56 per thousand live births is observed among the Savars. The remaining primitive tribes, viz. the Sauria Paharias, the Parhaiyas, the Korwas, the Asurs, the Birjias, and the Mal Paharias have the proportionate share of 127, 110, 103, 90, 87 and 80 per thousand live births respectively. They usually do not provide supplementary food to their children even in phase of post-neonatal period due to their poverty accompanied by their custom. The children are exclusively dependent upon breastfeeding. Again, the mothers are not given sufficient food during their lactation period. That is why, children are bereft of proper food, which invite various kind of diseases and finally, they are forced to leave this earthly life.

The district level analysis of PNMR illustrates that the districts, namely Sahibganj, Dumka, Pakur and Godda of Damin-i-Koh region command the hearth of post-neonate deaths. It is the region where the moneylenders have exploited them ruthlessly and mercilessly. Therefore, the first revolution against the moneylenders was started here during the British period. Latehar and Gumla of Pat region also experiences high PNMR due to complete dearth of medical facilities. The remaining districts also face high post-neonatal deaths owing to extreme poverty, drinking addiction and superstition regarding child rearing. Thus, it can be easily concluded that wherever the share of concentration of primitive tribes is more, there is high post-neonatal deaths in those districts of the regions in the state of Jharkhand.

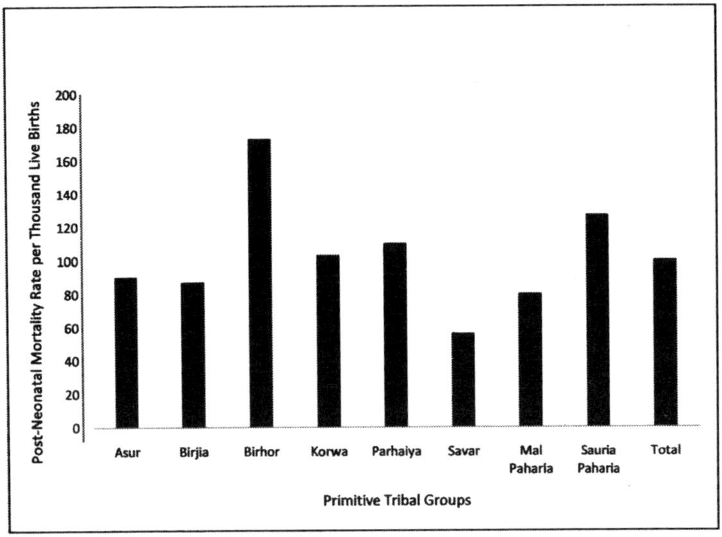

Fig. 4.6: Post-Neonatal Mortality Rate among Primitive Tribes in Jharkhand, 2017

Infant Mortality Rate

Infant mortality refers to deaths of children under the age of one year. It is measured by the Infant Mortality Rate (IMR), which is the total number of deaths of neonates under the age of one year for every thousand live births. It is an important indicator of the overall physical health of a community. Again, it reflects the effect of economic and social conditions on health of mothers and new born babies as well as the effectiveness of health systems in a region. The IMR is often broadly divided into two components relating to timing of death: neonatal and post-neonatal, which have already been discussed earlier. Table 4.1 explicitly reveals that the infant mortality among the primitive tribes stood at 230 per thousand live births at the time of survey against the state average of 29 per thousand live births, which was in fact below the national average of 34 per thousand in 2017. The hypothesis concerning with high infant mortality rate among the primitive tribal groups than the state average gets vindicated from the above analysis. It has already been described in Chapter 3 that unprecedented high level of infant deaths is due to their relatively poor socio-economic condition and social deprivation. Thus, it is a matter of great concern that the infant mortality among the primitive tribes is around eight times higher than the rest of population. This pitiable situation has risen over the absence of medical and transport facilities, complete illiteracy, thoroughly addiction of alcohol drinking, low weight of baby at birth and extreme poverty, where there is a question of their survival. The spread of naxalism in their areas has further deteriorated their well-being, which ultimately escalates the infant mortality because no doctor or health personal such as Sahias visit their localities due to fear psychosis.

Tribe-wise investigation reveals that almost all primitive tribes have infant mortality rate above 172 per thousand live births, which is found among the Mal Paharias whereas the highest infant mortality, i.e. 305 per thousand live births is noticed among the Birhors. The remaining tribes of the Sauria Paharias, the Korwas, the Asurs, the Parhaiyas, and the Birjias have the infant mortality rate at 302, 249, 238, 224, 177 and 177 per thousand live births respectively. It is further disclosed from Fig. 4.7 that there is a uniform high rate of infant deaths across all the communities of primitive tribes, which ranges from 172 to 305 per thousand live births.

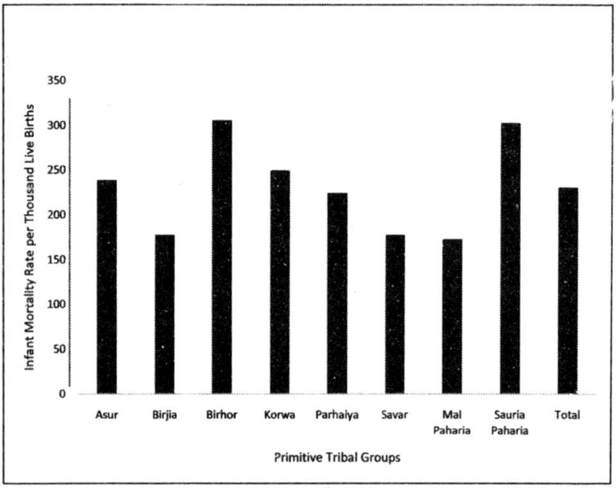

Fig. 4.7: Infant Mortality Rate among Primitive Tribes in Jharkhand, 2017

The district-wise analysis from Table 4.2 discloses that Sahibganj, Seraikella-Kharsawan, Khunti, Purbi Singhbhum, Latehar, Gumla, Godda, Ranchi, Garhwa, Pakur and Dumka with their infant mortality rate of 311, 286, 286, 250, 247, 238, 235, 229, 195, 193 and 185 per thousand live births stand in descending order of IMR. Minute investigation further manifests that it is the Damin-i-Koh region spreading over Dumka, Sahibganj, Godda and Pakur districts take lead in infant deaths, which was demarcated by the Britisher in 1832 for safeguarding the interests of the Sauria Paharias and the Mal Paharias. Unfortunately, even today they are the most exploited tribal groups by the moneylenders and they are suffering from various diseases and the average life expectancy is only 32 years among the Sauria Paharias. The next to this is Pat region extended over Latehar, Gumla and Garhwa districts face high mortality rate, where the Asurs, the Birjias, the Parhaiyas and the Korwas are concentrated in a large number. The lowest mortality is experienced in Dhalbhum region of Purbi Singhbhum district, which is inhabited by the Savars and they generally avail the medical facilities of West Bengal. In fact, the Savars are also inhabited in the neighbouring areas of West Bengal and that is why they enjoy medical facilities along with the local Savars of that state. The Infant mortality rate reflects a country's level of socio-economic development and is used for monitoring and evaluating population, health programmes and policies. It is an outcome rather than a cause and hence directly measures the results of the distribution and use of resources (Haines, 1995). In a nut shell, it can be easily perceived that lack of access to drinking water, basic health services, sanitation, proper nutrition, excessive boozing of alcohol and *hadia*, smoking and chewing of narcotic, shelter in closed small huts, spread of infection and communicable diseases, complete dearth of transport facilities are mainly responsible for unprecedented level of infant deaths, which accounts for more than one-third of total deaths. It was perceived during the survey that there is absence of young person and only either child and old people were seen in primitive tribal villages. This is mainly due to acute level of malnutrition among the people. Prevalence of alcohol and narcotic, strong faith in shamanism and bongaism etc. are mainly accountable for such alarming rate of infant deaths.

Summary

From the above analysis it can be easily perceived that still birth rate and late neonatal mortality rate inherit the state average pattern of infant deaths but early neonatal mortality is high among the primitive tribes, which is mainly due to universal home delivery of child in which the untrained old lady of the households or villagers take part. These former two components of infant deaths are purely biological in nature. It is, therefore, the mortality pattern follows the state average pattern in the above components. However, other components of infant deaths, namely early neonatal mortality rate, neonatal mortality rate, perinatal mortality rate, post-neonatal mortality rate, and infant mortality rate have by and large around eight times more mortality rate among the children of the primitive tribal groups than the state average of Jharkhand. The main factors behind this high rate of infant deaths are lack of access to drinking water, absence of basic health services, living in closed small huts, unscientific sanitation and hygiene habit, lack of proper nutrition in their meals, excessive boozing of hadia and alcohol, smoking and chewing of narcotic, spread of infection and communicable diseases, illiteracy among parents, delayed breastfeeding, extreme poverty, low weight of baby at birth, no antenatal check-ups, less consuming of food by the mother during gestation and lactation period, inaccessibility of their localities and complete dearth of medical and transport facilities.

Further, it is noticed that the Sauria Paharias have the most pathetic situation in all the aforesaid components of infant deaths. That is why, there is a sharp decline of their population in every census from the first census of 1872 to the census of 2001 but that reduction is stopped in current 2011 Census, when there is a slight increase of their population after carving out Jharkhand as a separate state on 15th November, 2000 and several welfare schemes were actually implemented for them. Since they eat both beef and pork simultaneously, they were hated by both the Hindus and the Muslims as well but due to spread of Christianity in their areas, a large number of schools and hospitals are opened in recent past, which have curtailed their mortality rate. On the contrary, the Mal Paharias have the lowest rate in all the aforesaid components of infant deaths and they have largely adopted the religion of Hinduism, which has removed their superstition of child rearing. Again, they also get maximum benefit from government scheme. That is why, the highest growth of population has been noticed among the Mal Paharias, which is already discussed in the previous chapter.

The other primitive tribal groups, namely the Birhors, the Korwas, the Asurs, the Parhiyas, the Birjias and the Savars have infant deaths between the two extremes but the primitive tribe of Parhaiyas has experienced decline in their population in 2001 Census in comparison to 1991 Census but there is marginal increase in 2011 Census. The spatial distribution of infant deaths also illustrates that Damin-i-Koh region in general and Sahibganj district in particular encompasses the highest infant mortality rate, which is as high as 311 per thousand live births whereas the district of Dumka contains the lowest rate of infant deaths, where the Mal Paharias are found in large numbers in which the IMR was only 172 per thousand live births in 2017. In spite of having low IMR in the Mal Paharias among the primitive tribes, it is as high as around six times higher than the state average.

So far policy is concerned, it is inferred that free distribution of 100 iron and folic acid tablets and free delivery kit to the pregnant mother through the Sahiyas, compulsory tetanus vaccination against the pregnant mother, free and compulsory training to the local untrained *Dais* with minimal remuneration by the state government can reduce the early neonatal mortality at satisfactory level within a short period of time. Similarly, vaccination drive against six preventable diseases, namely tuberculosis, diphtheria, pertussis, tetanus, polio and measles and free supplementary food to the children will curtail post-neonatal mortality at reasonable level among the children of primitive tribes and reduction in these two parameters will surely affect in reduction of other components of infant deaths. Over and above, delayed breastfeeding can be easily stopped through social awareness whereby there will be dramatic reduction in infant deaths.

REFERENCES

Arokiasamy, P. and A. Gautam (2008). "Neonatal mortality in the empowered action group states of India: Trends and determinants", *Journal of Biosocial Science*, *40*(2), 183-201, Retrieved from http://dx.doi.org/10.1017/S0021932007002623

Haines, R. Michael (1995). "Socio-economic Differentials in Infant and Child Mortality during mortality decline: England and Wales, 1890-1911", *Population Studies, 49*(2), pp. 193-223.

Raj, Hans (2003). *op. cit.,* pp. 1-43.

Singh, M. (2010). *op. cit.,* pp. 2-12.

Weinstein, J. and V.K. Pillai (2017). *Demography: The Science of Population* (2nd ed.), New Delhi: Rawat Publication, pp. 138-144.

WHO (2016). "Maternal mortality", Retrieved August 21, 2016, from http:// www.who.int/ media centre/factsheets/ fs348?

World Health Organization (1994). *Mother—Baby Package: Implementing Safe Motherhood in Countries,* Geneva, Switzerland: Maternal Health and Safe Motherhood Programme.

World Health Organization (1996). *Perinatal Mortality: A Listing of Available Information,* Geneva, Switzerland: World Health Organization.

5
Health, Hygiene, Sanitation and Morbidity among the Primitive Tribes in Jharkhand

Health involves complete spectrum of food habit, intake of nutrient, hygiene, sanitation and medical facility, which have kept the primitive tribes as the victims of marginalisation, neglect and exploitation. The parameters, namely health, hygiene, sanitationand morbidity of infant deaths are very closely interrelated for physical growth of children and their ailments and diseases leading very often too premature deaths. These parameters are critical for the survival of infants. In fact, the former capitulates entire spectrum of food habit, intake of nutrient and medical facility whereas hygiene relates to those conditions and practices, which are conducive for maintaining good health thereby preventing the spread of diseases. It improves the health of an individual human being and focuses on personal cleaning. So far it is concerned for the primitive tribes of Jharkhand, they do not lead healthy hygienic habit through not taking bath daily because they have mostly one set of cloth. However, they sweep their houses twice a day and the rubbish are thrown into the kitchen garden which according to them increase the fertility of the land. Furthermore, some of them use dry leaves or stones instead of water after evacuation of bowels. On the other hand, sanitation refers to do away with the waste we produce through public health conditions related to disposal of human excreta, sewage etc. However, the poor sanitation among the primitive tribes weakens the health of children leading to high rate of infant mortality. Further, morbidity denotes the state of being unhealthy for a particular disease or situation, which is generally understood to be outside the scope of a healthy person and it is designated to describe illness, impairment, or degradation of health. The children of PTGs are more prone to morbidity than adults since the widespread prevalence of diseases impedes infant's ability to absorb nutrients thereby stunting their growth.

Historical Perspective of Health Care Systems for Children

India is a glaring example of developing country in the world, which have adopted national policy for children since many decades. Moreover, it launched its first multispectral child health programme on a large scale in 1975 with the help of World Bank, popularly known as "the Integrated Child Development Service" (ICDS). Under the heading of the aforesaid programme, the services of supplementary nutrition, immunization, health check-up, referral services and pre-school health education etc., are provided to the children and the mothers as well. The prime responsibility for smooth functioning of the above programme lies on a chain of Anganwadi workers, Lady Supervisors, CDPOS, Medical Officers and Para Medical Staffs and the whole system is governed by respective state government. These services are provided through community based anganwadi centres. The approach gets further strengthened by the Alma Ata Declaration of 1978, which advocated the goal of "Health for All" by 2000 through primary health care services with full participation of individuals and families. Subsequently over the years, the two important programmes were further introduced for the promotion of health care of children and mothers, viz. (i) Universal Immunization Programme (UIP) in 1985 and (ii) integrated Child Survival and Safe Motherhood (CSSM) programme in 1992. The process of agglomeration of related programmes was initiated in 1994, when the International Conference on Population and Development took place in Cairo, which suggested that the participating countries should implement integrated programmes for reproductive and child health. That is why, the above two programmes were merged into one and retitled as Reproductive and Child Health (RCH) programme in 1997 wherein the IMR is considered as the key target. The above approach was also endorsed in the National Population Policy of 2000 wherein the immediate objective was to address the unmet needs for contraception, health care infrastructure, health personnel and to provide integrated service delivery for basic reproductive and child health care. Further, the medium-term objective was to bring the Total Fertility Rate (TFR) at replacement levels by 2010 whereas the long-term objective was to achieve a stable population by 2045.

India being the signatory to the Millennium Summit Declaration, 2000 targeted to acquire the Millennium Development Goals (MDGs) by the year 2015 and reduction in child and infant mortality rate had been focused as one of the eight MDGs by reducing two-third between 1990 and 2015. The country adopted National Rural Health Mission (NRHM) for striving the above goals and the above programme was launched by the Government of India in 2005. The Accredited Social Health Activists (ASHAs) known as Sahiyas in Jharkhand at village level executes the maximum work under the programme. The main objectives behind this programme are: (i) reduction in infant mortality rate and maternal mortality rate, (ii) universal access to integrated comprehensive public health services, (iii) child health, water, sanitation and hygiene, (iv) prevention and control of diseases. Another programme and namely, Janani Suraksha Yojana (JSY) also comes under the overall canopy of NRHM, which focused at reducing maternal and neonatal mortality rate through promoting institutional deliveries. In spite of launching of so many health-related programmes between 2005 to 2015, there was hardly any progress in reduction of maternal and infant mortality rate.But the launching of the National Rural Health Mission (NRHM) in 2005 was the real beginning, which incorporated all aspects of health in rural areas. A large number of programmes and initiatives were initiated under it with a vision to ameliorate the health status of the country. Almost all existing programmes were amalgamated under the heading of NRHM. Again, this programme was designated as National Health Mission (NHM) in 2013, which also consists of the urban counterpart of the programme. The above programme was limited to a few variables, namely mortality and disease prevalence. However, such selective focus and limited infrastructural development are not enough for overall development of rural societies. There are a lot hinderances in implementation of NRHM—limited availability of skilled health personnel, poor coverage in marginalized communities with low skilled staff posting, insufficient supportive supervision of front-line workers, poor training, lack of quality services and unsatisfactory Information Education and Communication (IEC) on key family practices. There is an emergent need of improving health systems but it requires high levels of investment. Again, states with better capability at base level could take advantage of financing from NRHM rapidly whereas the states with poor health infrastructure facilities will lag behind.

The differences in attainment were higher in BIMARU States where base line status was poorer. These differences were further aggravated due to less fund utilization and poor governance. In spite of strong economic growth in recent years, the total expenditure on health sector in 2018 for the country was only about 1.3 per cent of GDP. Global evidence suggests that, as long as a country does not spend more than 5 per cent of its GDP on health department, fundamental healthcare needs of people are hard to achieve. Although it is 3.8 per cent of total Government expenditure but it adds to 28.6 per cent of total health spending. The above proportion gets reduced for every child health care programme at bottom level. Therefore, a differentiated and more focused strategy is called for the new NHP 2017, has set stringent objectives for child health, viz. to reduce under-five mortality to at least 23 by 2025, infant mortality rate to at least 28 by 2019; neonatal mortality to at least 16 and still birth rate to "single digit" by 2025 (National Health Policy, 2017). The policy aims at universal health cover age with provision of comprehensive services to all while reducing out of pocket expenditures. The above challenge is now especially cumbersome for BIMARU states of Uttar Pradesh, Bihar, Madhya Pradesh, Rajasthan, Chhattisgarh and Jharkhand where the Integrated Child Development Services (ICDS) scheme, the problem of undernutrition still continues and the reduction in the prevalence is relatively unimpressive even after 45 years of its inauguration.

Further, the situation is quite pathetic in Jharkhand, wherein state-run healthcare infrastructure comprising Health Sub-Centres (HSC), Primary Health Centres (PHC), Community Healthcare Centres (CHC) and Sub-Divisional Hospitals (SDH) and District

Hospitals (DH) are very less than the required number as per the required number by the Indian Public Health Standards (IPHS). A state needs to have one HSC for every 5000 persons, one PHC for every 30000 people and one CHC for every 1.2 lakh population on the basis of IPHS criteria. However, Jharkhand has only188 sanctioned CHCs, of which 171 are functional. This is only 68 per cent of the total number required as per the population ratio. While the state requires a total of 1096 PHCs to cater to a population of over 3.29 crore, it has total strength of only 330 PHCs across the state, of which 291 are functional. Again, it has a total of 3958 HSCs, it requires 6580 as per IPHS standards. It is also battling a crisis of manpower with merely 2800 doctors employed with the state health services (Jharkhand Economic Survey, 2019). Even after inclusion of private practitioners the figure rises to around 10,000 doctors, there is still lack of 22,900 as WHO mandates one doctor per 1,000 persons.

Health among the Primitive Tribes

Health is very deeply related to natural and man-made factors, which have kept the primitive tribes along with their children as victims of marginalization, neglect and exploitation. They still believe that diseases are caused by evil spirits and witches. When they suffer from any disease, the traditional diviner of the village is consulted, who tries to ascertain through divination, the names of the evil spirits and witches. The local traditional medicine-man is also consulted who gives them herbs. No special arrangement has been made for them for the preventing and curative side of the diseases prevalent among them. They feel shy incoming to the hospitals and health centres for the treatment of their diseases. However, it is observed that the primitive tribes are ready to accept the hospital facilities if the doctor visits their settlements and give them medicine. The primary focus of health concerns here with the reproductively and its resultant effect on children, which have been studied under the sub-heading of antenatal care, food eaten by mother during pregnancy, delivery, family planning method, weight of baby at birth, medical check-up of children, breastfeeding, supplementary food, addiction, immunization of children and abortion.

Antenatal Care

Health check-up services denote Ante-Natal Care (ANC) of pregnant women. It is essential to ensure health-care during pregnancy. Its goal is to provide necessary and regular health check-ups to pregnant mother to prevent childbirth related health complications during the entire course of pregnancy and delivery. The health of mother is crucial for the survival of children as it is nexus between two generations. The intake of nutrition and performance by the mother during pregnancy and early childhood has strong impact upon the mental and physical health of infant. Generally, the impoverished mothers give birth to malnourished and underweight children and they are more susceptible to morbidity and infant mortality. If the essential nutrients are given to the children, the problem of malnutrition can be easily addressed thereby the chronic problem of retarded growth and poor physique among the children will be eliminated. It is easy to understand the growth of foetus after regular health check-up during pregnancy, further, if there is any problem with foetus, it can be easily identified by ultra sound technology. Two doses of anti-tetanus vaccine and 100 tablets of iron and folic acid and several other tablets supply essential micronutrients and minerals to mother and foetus (Singh, 2010). However, the primitive tribes in Jharkhand are unwilling to take the above doses of medicine due to extreme poverty, ignorance, low income and inaccessibility of health centres in their localities. The diseases are also caused by ignorance, respect for traditional dietary habits and scarcity of protective foods. Again, it is found that if the health centre is located near to the pregnant house, regular check-up can be done more frequently.

The pregnant woman does not observe any special rules and taboos. Neither any food taboos nor such other precautions are taken. The only precaution is to avoid being alone in the jungle or at the waterfall. Every pregnant woman should receive at least 3 antenatal health check-ups during pregnancy. The mother should consume additional 350-500 K calories and 20 g proteins by taking fresh green vegetables, pulses, milk and seasonal fruits. She should take at least 2.6 g of omega-3 fatty acids and 300 mg of docosahexaenoic acid to ensure adequate growth of brain. She should receive 100 tablets of iron and folic acid and two doses of tetanus toxoid and provision of rest during last trimester of pregnancy (Singh, 2010). It is noticed from Table 5.1 that medical check-up during pregnancy period is very uncommon among the primitive people due to extreme poverty and backwardness. Owing to ignorance and inaccessibility of health centres, they neither visit government hospital nor do they consult the private doctor. Sometimes, they are forced to visit health centres when there is severe complication in their abdominals. It is noticed that only 0.4 per cent of primitive tribal mother undergo medical check-up of abdominal, blood pressure, weight, urine and blood examination. As we know that two doses of anti-tetanus vaccine and 100 tablets of iron and folic acid lower the neo-natal mortality but only 0.1 per cent and 0.3 per cent of tribal mothers had taken the above doses of tetanus and iron and folic acid tablets. However, 99.2 per cent of tribal mothers do not undergo for any kind of medical check-up during pregnancy, which simply point out about high infant and maternal mortality rate among the primitive tribes. Again, more or less the same trend of medical check-up during pregnancy is found in all eight primitive tribes.

Table 5.1 illustrates the reason behind not caring of foetus when there is an urgent need to take care of them so that healthy and intelligent children can be delivered without any harm caused to the mother. It is found that awareness is the main hurdle behind not caring of foetus among the primitive tribes in Jharkhand, which capitulates 44.6 per cent share of negligence and people simply explain that the kind of medical check-up during gestation period is against their tribal customary laws. It is followed by poor quality infrastructural facilities, which engulfs around 29.8 per cent. It points out about complete negligence of government health infrastructural facilities and even if there is primary health centre but no doctor attends the hospital. It is already mentioned earlier that government hospitals and schools are not located in their localities and they are generally situated far away from their surroundings. That is why, only 14.9 per cent of pregnant women do go for medical check-up due to the above-mentioned factor. The cost incurred in medical check-up is high against the private doctors, who are available in the neighbouring town and 9.9 per cent of pregnant women do not undergo any check up behind their abject economic poverty. Overall, the situation behind not undergoing check-up during gestation is more or less the same among all primitive communities in Jharkhand. In spite of availability of cheap and good medical amenities in government primary health centres, they are complete failure in attracting primitive tribal population as they are located far away from their localities.

Food Eaten by Mother during Pregnancy

During pregnancy period, the need of rich food is more important since the growth of embryo depends on the quality of food consumed by the pregnant women. A pregnant woman has to take sufficient calories including carbohydrate, fat, mineral salt, protein and vitamin rich nutritious food so that she gives birth to a healthy child. The need of the above food is more during the last trimester of the pregnancy since the growth of embryo at that period is very rapid. In fact, nutritional level is directly linked to the availability of food and the purchasing power. The primitive tribal people in general and the female in particular depending upon food gathering and shifting cultivation suffer from malnutrition because of the poor nutritional content of their food more so because animal fat derived from hunting is also denied to them as a result of curtailment of forest rights. Further, they hardly consume pulses, vegetables, milk products, oil, sugar etc. during pregnancy period up to the recommended level of daily intake. It is obvious that those pregnant women, who do not take special food during pregnancy period, will have a greater number of neonatal deaths. The nutritious food eaten by mother during gestation period plays an important role in reducing the infant deaths.

Table 5.1 explains the type of availability of food among the pregnant primitive mothers in various primitive tribal communities. It is found that above 62 per cent of pregnant women narrated that they consumed insufficient diet during gestation period but they blamed poverty for the above factor. It is followed by that kind of mothers, who had consumed moderate kind of food and the share of the group is around 30 per cent. Only 8 per cent of primitive mothers did not have any kind of grudges regarding the availability of food and they used to eat sufficient food during gestation period. Again, these fortunate women have less share of infant deaths. Tribe-wise analysis manifests

Table 5.1: Health Condition of Mothers among the Primitive Tribes

Sl. No.	Health Condition of Pregnant Women	Number	% of Distribution
1.	Maternal Characteristics	2239	100.0
.	Antenatal Care	18	0.8
	Abdominal Examination	9	0.4
	T.T. Injection	2	0.1
	I.F.A. Tablet	7	0.3
	No Antenatal Caring	2221	99.2
	Cost Too Much	222	9.9
	Far Away	333	14.9
	Lack of Knowledge	999	44.6
	Poor Quality Service	667	29.8
2.	Food Eaten by Mother during Pregnancy		
	Sufficient	179	8.0
	Insufficient	1388	62.1
	Moderate	672	29.9
3.	Place of Delivery		
	Government Hospital	10	0.4
	Home	2229	99.6
4.	Attendant at Birth		
	Dai	2211	98.7
	Family Member	26	1.2
	None	2	0.1
5.	Type of Delivery		
	Normal	2234	99.8
	Caesarean	5	0.2
6.	Family Planning Method		
	Vasectomy and Tubectomy	550	24.6
	Copper T	62	2.8
	Pill	169	7.5

(Contd.)

Sl. No.	Health Condition of Pregnant Women	Number	% of Distribution
	Condom	203	9.1
	Herb	203	9.1
	No Family Planning	1052	46.9
7.	Weight of Baby at Birth		
	Below 2 kg	1051	46.9
	2-2.5 kg	586	26.2
	2.5-3 kg	233	10.4
	Above 3 kg	369	16.5
8.	Medical Check Up		
	Within 7 Days	78	3.5
	After 7 Days	123	5.5
	No Check Up	2038	91.0
9.	Immunization of Children		
	Yes	11	0.5
	No	2228	99.5
	Not Customary	1700	76.3
	Not Aware	246	11.1
	Far Away	225	10.0
	Fear of Side Effect	57	2.6
10.	Start of Breastfeeding		
	Within 1 Hour	157	7.0
	1-24 Hour	190	8.5
	2-3 Days	1478	66.0
	After 3 Days	322	14.4
	Never	92	4.1
11.	First Food Given to Child		
	Milk of Mother	347	15.5
	Honey, Ghee and Gutty	1650	73.7
	Sugar and Glucose	72	3.2
	Animal Milk	170	7.6

(*Contd.*)

Sl. No.	Health Condition of Pregnant Women	Number	% of Distribution
12.	Duration of Breastfeeding		
	Below 6 months	36	1.6
	6-12 Months	148	6.6
	1-2 Years	80	3.6
	Above 2 Years	1583	70.7
	No Breastfeeding	392	17.5
13.	Supplementary Food		
	Animal Milk	425	19.0
	Semi-Solid Smashed	994	44.4
	Solid	808	36.1
	Fruit	12	0.5
14.	Addiction		
	Alcohol	1043	46.6
	Narcotic	464	20.7
	Both	260	11.6
	None	472	21.1
15.	Abortion		
	Complication and Health Problem	33	1.5
	No Abortion	2206	98.5

that there is hardly any difference regarding the food consumed by the mothers during gestation period and almost all primitive tribes are living in the same level of abject poverty.

Delivery

During delivery time, place of delivery, attendant at delivery and type of delivery play important role on the health of baby and mother in primitive rural areas of Jharkhand, which ultimately lead to reduction in intrapartum death. It is observed that scientifically equipped hospital makes the infants survival more possible as compared to the children born in an average home as the hospitals provide the trained doctor and nurses, protection from infection and exemplary hygiene and sanitation facilities. A significant proportion of neonatal deaths is attributed to certain birth related practices among the tribes and that can be easily avoided. A majority of the rural tribal births take place at home and are attended by village *dais* or other family members. The training of dais in some basic minimum hygiene and safe delivery practices are essential key elements in the programme of improving maternal and infant health care. The *dais* play crucial role in the circumstances of intra-natal phase of delivery, which covers under the umbrella functions of delivering the neonate, cutting and tying the umbilical cord, burying the placenta and cleaning the new-born and the mother.

Place of Delivery: Table 5.1 manifests that almost all deliveries were performed in house itself as the tribal localities are situated far away from the urban areas, where there is a maternity home. Beside this, there is no means of transportation facilities through which they can reach to the government hospital. Further, they cannot afford the cost of private nursing home, where the exorbitant charge for executing delivery is demanded. It is, therefore, 99.6 per cent of deliveries were carried out in their houses by their relatives.That is why; perinatal mortality is very high among the various primitive tribes, which results in either decline or stagnant population. Moreover, there is exception in case of the Korwa tribe, where institution delivery was practised due to proximity of maternity home, which is located at Bhandaria Block and the above surveyed tribal villages are exclusively confined to the premises of block itself.

Attendant at Birth: Table 5.1 indicates that both untrained *dais* and family members were only available during pregnancy period among the primitive tribal mothers in Jharkhand. In few cases, none was present during the birth of child as the nuclear family is more common among them. However, the delivery conducted at home either by the doctor or the nurse was not noticed at all as they can not afford the fee charged by them. Thus, about 98.7 per cent and 1.2 per cent of tribal births were delivered at home by the untrained midwives and family members respectively. Just like other variables, there was no significant difference among the different primitive tribal communities in Jharkhand.

Type of Delivery: Whenever a woman delivers a child, it is considered as rebirth of women. That is why, type of delivery is a vital aspect for mothers' health and life. The result imbibed in Table 5.1 manifests that not even a single case of assisted child birth was found among the primitive tribal mothers, which clearly conveys that whenever there is a need of assisted delivery, they avoid that kind of delivery due to extreme poverty and finally results in as infant death. Barring few examples of caesarean delivery almost all, i.e. 99.8 per cent deliveries occur through normal procedure of delivery. Thus, majority of child births in primitive tribal locality are executed by the unskilled family members and midwives in an unhygienic situation, which are injurious for both baby and mother as well. That kind of risk increases for both the infant and maternal mortality as well. Therefore, it should be done in proper monitoring by the experts so that tribal birth could occur only in hygienic environment of health centres. However, the private doctors are not economically affordable to the primitive tribes. That is why; special mobile delivery van and trained local females ought to be employed by the government in a relatively inaccessible remote areas to avoid infant, child and mother's death. The disposable sterile delivery kits of blade, cotton, antiseptic lotion, soap and plastic sheet should be distributed to all pregnant women of the primitive tribes in last trimester.

Family Planning Method

Importance of family planning method as a device to control population explosion is now widely accepted in Jharkhand. It provides the ability to decide about the number of children and the spacing between them. People are offered all available methods of contraception and the decision of adopting of implementation of family planning method is left to them. It is observed that the various family planning methods vary with spatial and temporal scale as the country comprises a hub of culture and diversity in regional context as well. In this survey, the married women were asked whether they or their counterparts are using any contraceptive method of family planning so that spacing for children and the unwanted children can be worked out as unmet need for family. Levels of use of contraceptives provide the most obvious and widely accepted criterion for assessing the success of family planning programme. The family planning methods include both modern as well as traditional, which is more popular among the primitive tribes. Generally, the unmet need of children for the family is subject to be neglected and finally results in infant deaths.

Table 5.1 illustrates a detailed study of various planning processes adopted by the primitive tribal communities in Jharkhand. The prevalence of castration in the form of vasectomy for male and tubectomy for female is more popular, which accounts for around 24.6 per cent of total usage of family planning methods. It is followed by herb, abstinence and withdrawal, which include about 9.1 per cent of contraceptives. The use of condom, pills and copper T occupy 9.1 per cent, 7.5 per cent and 2.8 per cent respectively of the total contraceptive usages. They altogether comprise 53.1 per cent, who use at least one type of contraceptive for reducing fertility and growth rate, which is equivalent to state level contraceptive use in 2011 (Annual Health Survey, 2011). However, 46.9 per cent of families do not use any kind of family planning method. As we know that the use of contraceptive reduces the fertility rate, which finally controls the unmet need of family and reduces infant mortality indirectly. From the above analysis it can be easily concluded that they use only either government sponsored family planning method or they use Ayurvedic method of family planning, which are locally available in the forest. Since almost all the primitive tribes have adopted the similar pattern of family planning method on account of monetary benefit provided by the government. That is why, there is no need of tribe-wise analysis of adopting various family planning methods.

Weight of Baby at Birth

Low Birth Weight (LBW) is the single most significant characteristics associated with higher infant mortality. The biological characteristics of parents, mother's nutritional status and gestation period are the principal variables of weight of a baby at birth, which ultimately controls the rate of neonate deaths. The Indian women in general and the primitive tribes of Jharkhand in particular have low height, which also contributes to a low birth weight. That is why, it is felt that full term babies weighing between 2 and 2.5 kg can certainly survive with a minimum input of care and low birth weight is a weight less than 2 kg at birth in Indian perspective. The low birth weight of new born baby clearly demonstrates that the nutrition level of food consumed by the primitive tribal mother was of very poor calorie intake during gestation period.

Table 5.1 reveals that around 47 per cent of new born babies had weight less than 2 kg known as very low birth weight babies, which is not quite desirable according to medical science. There are minimum chances of survival of low weight babies. Even if they survive during the first few days, the probability of their survival beyond the first is very dim. It is followed by another category of babies whose weight was varying from 2 to 2.5 kg known as low-birth-weight babies and the share of the group is above 26 per cent and they also regarded as underweight by WHO. Thus, above 73 per cent of new born babies had weight less than 2.5 kg, which vividly reflects the grim situation for the new born babies among the primitive tribes and there is an urgent need of government intervention through supplying of nutritious food to the pregnant women. The babies whose weight varying from 2.5 to 3 kg at the time of child birth comprises 10.4 per cent and another group of babies weighing above 3 kg account for 16.5 per cent at the time of child birth. Thus, only about one-fourth children are born of standard weight, which clearly divulges the reason behind high neonatal mortality. Generally, the sick primitive tribal mother gives birth to an ill and weak child and the above child faces great possibility of death in infancy. The low birth babies are also delivered due to cultural impact, including early marriage and childbearing. Many of the women who are participating in early marriage but they are still adolescents (Hockenberry, Wilson and Rodgers, 2012). These adolescents are not capable of taking care of their infants as they are not mature enough. Although they reach very early sexual maturity due to hot and humid climatic factor, but they receive physical, cognitive, and emotional maturity later on. Delivery of low-birth-weight baby is also related with preterm labour when a baby is born before 9 months of gestation. It is usually observed that infants do not get sufficient time to develop in uterus in case of premature delivery and they do not gain weight in the uterus, as the majority of weight is gained during the last stage of the pregnancy. Another factor, related to LBW delivery is intrauterine growth restriction defined as foetal development less than the standard growth possible for an infant because of genetic or environmental factors (Murki & Sharma, 2014). That kind of situation arises when the infant does not develop well in the uterus because of less intake of nutritional food during gestation period, complications with the placenta, the mother's health, or sometimes birth-defects.

Medical Check Up of Children

Getting a post-partum check-up soon after the birth of baby is crucial for the health of the infant. It is generally believed that the mother of new born babies did not receive any medical check-up after delivery had a much higher mortality danger than whose mothers sought some post-natal care and the same is true in case of new born baby. It looks ridiculous to transpire from Table 5.1 that neither the mother nor their offspring undergo any kind of medical check-up during the first three days after delivery, which can protect both of them from infection. It is only after complication they go for medical treatment after 4 days of delivery. The new born babies, who undergo for medical check-up between 4 and 7 days comprises 3.5 per cent. The share of medical check-up rises to 5.5 per cent, when the children are examined after 7 days. However, the lion's share incorporates to those children, who do not undergo any kind of medical check-up and this category of children comprises 91 per cent of the total infants. A marginal variation in the above category of medical check-up is also observed among the primitive tribal communities. From the above analysis, it is now crystal clear that the medical negligence regarding the new born babies contribute to unprecedented level of infant mortality rate among the primitive communities.

Breastfeeding

Breast milk contains all sort of nutrients, which are essential requirement for the growth of infants. In fact, the resistance and immunity strength are enhanced among the children by breast milk thereby weakness, allergies and diseases are easily tackled by it. Different kinds of diseases and infections are also protected by it. From nutrition point of view, it is the best digestible food for the new-born neonate, which contains a large quantity of colostrum thereby enhancement of immunity and resistance power. Leela Visaria (1988) rightly remarked that "Breastfeeding enhances child survival by transmitting to the infant, along with nutrients for growth, certain immunity-raising elements which can help fight for the high infection load found in the environment, where the replacement foods are not ordinarily free from contamination. Breast feeding also tends to delay the resumption of menstruation and thereby elongates the birth interval, which in turn enhances child survival."

***Start of Breastfeeding*:** Most of the primitive rural tribal mothers get away their new-born neonates from immediate breastfeeding, which is the major reason behind alarming rate of neonatal mortality among the children.They consider that they are impure to feed their children immediately after giving birth to new-born. The situation gets further worsened when almost all mothers threw away dark yellowish milk, known as colostrum, which are essential for the new-borns as it contains white blood corpuscles thereby increase the immunity system against diseases. They usually start breastfeeding after some kind of ceremonial function. That particular trait of breastfeeding among the primitive tribal female mothers accelerates the rate of infant mortality.

Table 5.1 portrays the behaviour of tribal mothers regarding the commencement of breastfeeding to the new-born babies and it is found that only 7.0 per cent of mothers had started breastfeeding to the new-born babies within one hour after delivery. It is rightly highlighted by Singh (2010) that the new-born baby should be offered first breastfeeding within 1 hour after birth. The colostrum milk must never be discarded and all babies should invariably receive it because it is rich in energy, protein, protective antibodies and cellular elements. The next group of mothers used to start breastfeeding varying from 1 to 24 hours comprising 8.5 per cent. There are another dominant group of tribal mothers, who had started breastfeeding from 2 to 3 days consisting of 66.0 per cent and they had started a little late due to their health problems, which is very common as they start breastfeeding after purification. While 14.4 per cent of tribal mothers started breastfeeding after 3 days owing to their ill health. However, 4.1 per cent of tribal mothers are such that they can not breastfeed their children on account of their poor health. In fact, breastfeeding enhances immunity power and keep them away from diseases and infections. It increases the physical growth and development of children.

First Food Given to Child: During the first 3 days, when lactation is not fully established, the primitive tribal mother is often anxious that her baby is not getting adequate nourishment. It must be explained to her that the act of sucking establishes lactation and whatever little colostrum the baby receives during the first few days is enough to meet the nutritional needs of a baby. The babies do not require any complementary feeds. Hence, the first food should be breast milk and no prelacteal feeds should be offered. By virtue of its composition, colostrum is best suited to serve the nutritional and immunological needs of the baby which should not be denied. It is yellow and thick and contains more antibodies, higher proteins and white blood cells (Singh, 2010). Since in a large proportion of primitive tribal mothers, breastfeeding is not initiated for one to three days, the new-born is given some pre-lacteal feeds.

Table 5.1 indicates that around 74 per cent of the new-borns were given honey, ghee, animal milk diluted with boiled water, glucose, boiled water mixed with sugar or candy and gutty as the first food to children among the primitive tribes. Only 15.5 per cent of new-born babies were given first food as mother's milk within one day, which is not very common among the primitive tribal mothers. It is followed by those mothers who had used cow milk diluted with boiled water as first food to the children and it capitulates 7.6 per cent of first food. The corresponding figure for the use of sugar and glucose as first food inculcates around 3.2 per cent among the primitive tribal children. This feed of gutty is believed to cleanse the infant's system.

Duration of Breastfeeding: It is already discussed earlier that breastfeeding is a universal phenomenon among the primitive tribal mothers in Jharkhand. So far duration of breastfeeding is concerned, it is found that more than 70 per cent of tribal mothers feed their milk to the children of above 2 years and thus they believe in breastfeeding for prolonged period. The proportional share of breastfeeding of 1 to 2 years, 6-12 months and below 6 months are 3.6 per cent, 6.6 per cent and 1.6 per cent respectively. It is further noticed that these mothers exclusively breastfeed their babies up to 6 months and the above practice diminishes malnutrition among the infants to a certain extent. One peculiar habit of breastfeeding was noticed among the primitive tribal mothers that they generally breastfeed to their children after 6 to 8 hours during day time, when they work as labourers either in the forest or field outside their home and that long spell of breastfeeding is also responsible for high infant mortality rate.

Supplementary Food

After about six months, when breast milk cannot be adequate for the growing child, children are given supplementary milk and other foods which are essentially carbohydrates. Smashed solid food supports the physical growth of babies and keeps them away from different infections and malnutrition. Staples of rice, wheat, fruit etc. are believed to be light and easily digested by the infants. In primitive tribal areas of Jharkhand mothers work hard as farm labourers hence they are not able to provide such food to their children. The infants are generally taken care of by their relatives. That is why even though they are given supplementary food but they are not given on time. According to Ghosh (2004), there are two main causes of malnutrition: The poor living condition among the primitive tribes is the foremost reason behind it. Secondly, it is associated with lack of awareness among parents about the need of child's food. Five elements of supplementary food, namely water, animal milk, semi-solid mashed, solid food and fruits are analysed in case of the primitive tribal mothers. The supplementary food is generally started after 6 months among the primitive tribal society in Jharkhand. The semi-solid mashed of rice and pulses are given to the children on large scale. Around 19 per cent of children are also given animal milk, which is quite nutritive but they are not given on time by their relatives and neighbours, while mothers are engaged in agricultural or forestry activities outside their home. The highest proportion of children are given smashed solid food, which account for 44.4 per cent and it is followed by another group of children, who take solid food as their supplementary food. Only in certain cases, solid food in the form fruits was given to the children, which were locally available fruits either in their orchard or forest.

Addiction

Both sexes of primitive tribes use *biri*, *khaini*, *ganza*, *hukka* and *chutti* as narcotic whereas they usually consume wine, toddy, *handia*, *mahua* wine and liquor as alcoholic drinks. They cannot think of any occasion or function without sumptuous supply of their drink and narcotics—in child birth, in daily life, in marriages, in worshipping of spirits, in curing diseases, in receiving the guest and gift to the dead. It also has a social and religious value as it is taken especially during folk dances, village meetings and ceremonial festivals. In fact, fermented beverage is an important part of their life and culture because of its social and religious indispensability. It is also reflected from Table 5.1 that around 47 per cent of primitive tribal females are indulged in alcohol drinking. Another 21 per cent of primitive tribal females were in the habit of *biri* and *chutti* kind of narcotic smoking and chewing of tobacco. The next around 12 per cent of tribal females used to take both kinds of addiction—smoking and chewing of narcotics and alcohol drinking. However, 21 per cent of primitive tribal females never used to take any kind of narcotics and basically, they were teetotallers. That is why, Lakshmi Narayan (1998) had highlighted on their culture that one of major cause of the poor economic condition of tribes is their excessive consumption of liquor. The heavy consumption of liquor and narcotics by the poor people lead to poverty, which ultimately reduces purchasing power and causes food insecurity, poor health and insufficiency. Further, the malnutrition and ill health result in decreasing work efficiency. Less efficiency results in to low production and small profit. Low earning in family leads to further addiction. Thus, a vicious circle of addiction completes through the path of malnutrition and infant deaths in primitive tribal people of Jharkhand.

Immunization of Children

Immunization is another essential process for the good health of children whereby a child is made immune to an infectious disease typically by the administration of a vaccine. The vaccine stimulates the body's own immune system to protect the person against subsequent disease. According to WHO guidelines full immunization coverage is defined as a child has received a BCG vaccination against tuberculosis, three doses of DPT to prevent diphtheria, pertussis and tetanus, at least three doses of polio drops and one dose of measles vaccine. However, the universal immunization programme was rolled out in India in 1985 extending the expanded programme for immunization, which had attempted to provide recommended vaccine against tuberculosis, polio, diphtheria, tetanus, pertussis, hepatitis and pneumococcal disease. Vaccination protects children from serious illness and complication of preventable disease and it increases the immunity system in the body. Immunization of children is essential for protecting the children through the following national vaccination programme of BCG vaccine against tuberculosis, oral polio drops against polio, DTP vaccine against diphtherias, tetanus and pertussis, MMR vaccine against measles, mumps and rubella, HBV vaccine against hepatitis B, Typhoid vaccine against typhoid, PPV vaccine against pneumonia, Hib vaccine against influenzae (Singh, 2010).

Unfortunately, the primitive tribal people are not aware of their positive outcome of vaccination. That is why, only 0.5 per cent of children were vaccinated at the appropriate time, which is almost negligible figure. The rest, i.e. 99.5 per cent of children were not vaccinated. Now when we further investigate the reasons behind the no vaccination, the result indicates towards their backwardness. More than three-fourth of the respondents reported that they were not aware about the government sponsored programme of vaccination for children. Again, that kind of scheme goes against their customary laws of amelioration and their belief in *status quo* regarding their cultural practices. It is followed by another group of respondents who do not know the place of immunization, where the children are given free vaccination under the government scheme and around 11.1 per cent people fall in this category. There are another 10 per cent of such respondents that they believe in necessity of immunization but they found the distant location of immunization centres. Further, transportation creates a lot of hurdles in their movement under rugged and uneven topography. However, 2.6 per cent of people are scared from their side effects, which have been locally sponsored by the rumour mongers.

Abortion

Although abortion in Jharkhand is legally valid in certain circumstances, but it should be performed before the expiry period of conceiving of 20 weeks of pregnancy on certain legal health grounds. Sometimes, women prefer induced abortion, when that particular woman gets a pregnancy terminated voluntarily due to various social stigmas and situations. However, abortion is the third leading cause of maternal deaths in India. It is usually restricted in primitive tribal society due to various social, economic, unavailability of medical facility and logistical barrier. Stigma also performs a major factor behind not adopting abortion for limiting the size of household as approved local medical centres are located far away from their usual places of residence. Further cheap and safe abortion is a rare phenomenon in Jharkhand especially for the primitive tribes who are living in abject poverty. Moreover, it is considered a proper method for terminating unwanted pregnancy. So far, the abortion is concerned, the primitive tribal female never uses it as a means of unmet need for limiting the size of family. They use abortion only in case of complication in pregnancy, which creates inconvenience in their health and only 1.5 per cent females had adopted abortion during their pregnancy. Therefore, large scale abortions are not noticed in majority of tribal females and above 98 per cent of females had not experienced any kind of abortion during their reproductivity. Further, a lot of amount has to be spent on abortion, which they cannot afford at any cost due to their economic hardship. Simultaneously, the children are not considered as burden for the family. The reason behind it is simple that they do not spend money on children's education, rather the children become helping hand in the family at the time of cultivating the land in the locality of the primitive tribes.

Hygienic Conditions among Primitive Tribes

Healthy hygienic condition is essential for maintaining good health and preventing disease away from the household and it is mainly associated with individual approach. It requires availability of cleanliness of house, bathing and treatment of water in houses where people live in. Unfortunately, the primitive tribes by and large do not maintain healthy hygienic situations whereby the children should not fall ill.

Cleanliness of House

Home provides safer place to take rest on, when people are tired of daily economic activities. It not only protects us from wild beasts, insects, enemies, unhygienic environment and so on but the safer house also, produces healthy conducive environment so that people in general and children in particular do not fall ill. The primitive tribal people generally live-in condition of poor drainage and sewerage facilities. The drainage system is completely absent in the tribal localities. The waste water of home and rainy water is usually accumulated in nearby small ditch during rainy season which generates an awesome smell within the premises of house itself. The dung of animal, stool of small children and urinal of animals are also stored in the ditch. That kind of ditch becomes the breeding ground for various insects, germs and bacteria including 'anopheles' mosquito for malaria. They also keep cattle and pigs within the four walls of their houses, where they themselves sleep at night. They do not take care of hygienic situation around their houses because of lack of any efficient drainage system. The drainage is naturally developed, which is not cleaned at regular intervals. During the rainy season, the hygienic condition in and around the settlement become awfully nuisance.

Table 5.2 reveals the scenario of hygienic condition found in the houses of primitive people in Jharkhand during the investigation year of 2017. There were 254 households where animal wastes were spread within the house during the period of survey and bad smell was coming out from them. Ironically the small children were playing adjacent to them and that might have affected the health of those children. Again, around one-third households do not have any drainage system and water poured in the house get dried up naturally in the sunlight. It is believed that diseases are driven away from the family when proper cleaning of house and floor takes place at regular intervals. That kind of cleanliness habit provides additional security to their children since they are more vulnerable to infection and therefore, they become easy victims of various kinds of morbidities. Around 40 per cent of households keep their pet animals within the premises of houses on account of fear of wild beast. An outsider cannot stay for a long period of time in their houses due to bad smell of urinal and waste of animal. Only 9.2 per cent of households had separate provision of room for their animals to keep them away from their houses, which was somehow conducive with respect to cleanliness of houses. It is further noticed that the infant mortality was of meagre amount in the above households. Lastly, there were 11 per cent of households having neat and clean system of cleanliness of their houses and these houses had good drainage system and no trace of animal waste. Again, the practise of washing hands with soap before eating and after passing stool was not found at all. Sinha (1986) also observed that availability of cooking space and fuel consumption patterns in the household can also influence morbidity among the tribes in Jharkhand. In fact, they wash their hands with local soils after passing stool.

Table 5.2: Hygienic Situations of Households among the Primitive Tribes

	Kinds of Awareness	**Number**	**% of Distribution**
1.	Cleanliness of House	2209	100.0
	Spreading of Animal Waste	254	11.5
	Lack of Drainage System	643	29.1
	Animals Residing within House	865	39.2
	Separate House for Animals	204	9.2
	Neat and Clean	243	11.0
2.	Bathing	11051	100
	Daily	2545	23
	2 and 3 Times in a Week	2761	25
	Weekly	5526	50
	Occasional	219	2
3.	Treatment of Water	2209	100
	Add Bleach, Chlorine, Alum	5	0.2
	Cloth	80	3.6
	Boiling Water	187	8.5
	No Treatment	1937	87.7

Bathing

The bathing is considered as a part of routine life to keep body fit and it also provides mental pleasure. It is an essential requirement to keep the skin of human body free from dust as the pores are of large size and of outer origin of body. Perspiration takes place through these pores of skin for keeping constant temperature of body. Bacteria and germs are not allowed to enter into the body of human as the skin act as shiver. Bathing as a major constituent of hygiene provides refreshens feeling to the body since scrubbing removes dusts of body, bacteria and dead cells of body. That is why, a man needs regular and punctual bath for cleanliness of body, which ultimately results in good health Thus, regular and punctual bath keeps skin free from skin diseases. Unfortunately, the primitive people do not take bath daily due to limited set of clothes and scarcity of fresh water. The tribal people in general and the tribal children in particular were observed that they were wearing old, dirty, torn and unwashed clothes at the time of survey. The women were found more conscious about washing their clothes and they also used to take regular baths in compare to their men folk. They are usually indulged in physical and manual work and that sort of activities brings forth a lot of perspiration. The skin as an outer organ of body has to fight with bacteria and germs of environment wherein dust particles and filthy items settle on their skin. Bathing with soap is the only alternative to get rid of the unwanted said dust particles and toxic elements. People feel refreshes and relaxed after taking bath as the pore of skins open after that. The primitive tribes are not very conscious of their hygienic habits and cleanliness of body. They usually take bath only two to three times in a week and sometime even go without taking bath for more than a week or so particularly during the winter season.

Table 5.2 discloses the frequency of bathing among the primitive tribal population in Jharkhand on sex-wise distribution. It is noticed that 21 per cent of females used to take bath regularly whereas only 7 per cent of males had regular bath at the time of survey. The trend of more bathing of females continues even in the group of 2 and 3 times in in a week, which accounts for 29 per cent. On the contrary, the representation of males in this group comprises of 21 per cent. In fact, the people who take bath only once in a week comprises the highest share, which are 49 per cent and 51 per cent for females and males respectively. Further, 21 per cent of males and 1 per cent of female go for occasional bathing. Thus, a large proportion of tribal population do not take regular bath. That is why, skin diseases are found among the primitive tribal people in general and in the children in particular.

Even the children are not bathed regularly due to scarcity of fresh water. That is why, leprosy and jaundice are common among them.

Animals and Humans take baths in the same contaminated Pond in Birjias' Villages

Treatment of Water

The water is considered to be drinkable when it is free from biological and chemical contamination. The presence of bacteria and excessive presence of fluoride, arsenic, nitrate and iron in water lead to serious health hazards. The use of contaminated water not only take a heavy toll of around 80 per cent of all diseases and over one-third of deaths in developing countries but it also spoils on an average as much one-tenth of each person's productive time (UNCED). That is why; the safe drinking is the key factor in achieving the ultimate goal of health for all. Hence, without adequate supply of safe drinking water to the primitive tribal communities, promotion of health and prevention of diseases are not possible. However, the native people do not use any modern means of water purifier, which makes water free from contamination. Only a limited portion of people use traditional method of water filtration, viz. cloth and boiling of water. It is found during the survey that almost all primitive tribal people were ignorant about the fact that water borne diseases play a decisive role for large chunk of infant deaths.

About 87.7 per cent of households do not use any kind of filter for purification of water, which is clearly exhibited in Table 5.3. The primitive people usually store water in earthen pots for keeping cold in summer and warm in winter and the said practice also save them from harmful effect of insects and ants. In fact, the people generally believe in traditional methods of water filteration. Around 8.5 per cent of households used to adopt the method of boiling water for removing impurities from water and annihilation of germs present in water so that it can be used for drinking purpose. Another 3.6 per cent of households use clothes for removing sediments from water so that even with full of turbidity can be used as drinking purpose. It hold backs dust and dirty material of water in the clothes. The use of bleach, chlorine and alum for water purification is found only in certain areas and only 0.2 per cent of households had adopted the above method for purification of water. However, not even a single household had adopted modern means of electronic purifier for purification of water.

Sanitation Conditions among Primitive Tribes

Sanitation emphasizes on the health of all the people in a community in which neighbourhood is more important for maintaining good health and preventing diseases away from the households. Basically, the whole process of disposal of human excreta, disposal of garbage, animal excreta, environmental degradation and handling of waste water comes under the gamut of sanitation. The PTGs do not take care of sanitation around their houses because of lack of any efficient drainage system. The drainage is naturally developed which is not cleaned at regular interval. During the rainy season the sanitation condition in and around the PTG settlements become awfully nuisance. Further, the children go out for clearing their bowels in front of their houses thus creating a very unhygienic. It is rightly observed by UNICEF (1991) that 90 per cent of the deaths among the very young children in developing countries were caused by the combined factors of malnutrition, inadequate sanitation and lack of immunization. The sanitation conditions, which lead to the child deaths have been studied here under the topics of sources of water, treatment of water, type of house, and kitchen facility.

Sources of Water

Water is primarily used by the primitive tribal people for daily activities of washing, bathing, drinking, cooking of food, and cleaning. Not only the localities of primitive have insufficient availability of water but there is limited accessibility of safe drinking water. The primitive tribal people prefer to drink stream water by their habits and traditions but most of the streams are seasonal, slow running and small hill rivulets. These rivulets contain contaminated water and they are extremely poor in quality with high degree of bacterial contamination thereby not satisfying their needs. The problem of drinking water is further accentuated among the primitive tribes, who reside either on the hill top or scarp land in Jharkhand. Basically, they depend upon four sources of water: handpump, well, pond and stream and *chua*. Handpumps and running tapes are hygienic whereas wells, ponds, streams and chuas are stagnant and have become abode of parasites, viruses and larva of mosquitoes. The evaluation and contribution of safe drinking water for curtailment of infant mortality rate need to be examined. It is to be mentioned here that water-borne diseases play a significant role in enhancement of infant and child deaths. That is why, provision of safe drinking water by the Government may bring down alarming rate of infant mortality to noteworthy reasonable extent. Drinking water facility in the household is one of the sources of diseases in the post-neonatal stage. Dehydration, chronic diarrhoea and infectious diseases are mainly caused due to unsafe and contaminated water. The diseases that occur due to unsafe water are major causes for high infant mortality in Jharkhand.

Table 5.3 divulges that there are mainly four sources of water in areas of rugged and undulating topography, where the primitive tribal people reside on: handpump, well, pond and stream and *chua*. The contribution of hand pump and running tap as a major source of water encompasses around 52 per cent of households, which is mainly possible through government sponsored boring system and they easily drill even in hard gneiss and schist rock. As information collected in investigation manifests that 26.3 per cent of households relied on open well, which occupy second position after handpump and that particular provision is also possible through government sponsored

Table 5.3: Sanitation Conditions among the Primitive Tribes

Sl. No.	Sanitation	Number	% of Distribution
1.	Source of Water	2209	100.0
	Handpump and Running Tap	1140	51.6
	Well	580	26.3
	Pond and Stream	226	10.2
	Chua	263	11.9
2.	Type of House	2209	100
	Kutcha	2019	91.4
	Semi-*pucca*	186	8.4
	Pucca	4	0.2
3.	Toilet Facility	2209	100
	Open Defecation with Water	641	28.9
	Open Defecation with Dry Leaves	862	39
	No Toilet Facility	706	32.1

Drinking source of water for Asurs while working in the Forest

scheme. It is further observed that the poor tribal people still depend upon pond and stream water, which are full of bacterial contamination. Even animals drink and bath in these open sources of water and people wash their dirty clothes in the above sources of water. Especially the environmental condition of the Sauria Paharias and the Savars is very pathetic regarding the above provision and more than 10 per cent families get their drinking water from the above source. Lastly, 11.6 per cent of households acquire water from *chuas*, which are confined to certain locality only. Thus, water supply in primitive tribal hamlets is quite irregular and the tribal females have to fetch water from long distances as stated earlier.

Type of Houses

The *kutcha* houses with defective design are more susceptible for the spread of diseases. The impoverished primitive tribal people usually live in dilapidated kutcha houses and hence they are having more risk of respiratory illness due to mud-built floor, poor ventilation and lower ceiling height. The houses are usually dark and damp even during day time since windows are absent in their houses. The houses are further located in a haphazard style, which are constructed by thatched ceiling and mud-built thatched walls. In most cases, the houses consist of either one or two rooms, which manifest their economic conditions and size of the households as well. The houses in general and floor in particular remain dirty, where dungs of animals can be easily visualised. On the one hand, the houses are not only deprived of windows but there is no means of sunlight and ventilation. The inner side of a house always remains dark and stuffy even during day time due to non-availability of electricity and no provision of ventilation through windows. Even, the main gates are made up of small sizes. Further, cooking space within the house and consumption of wood as fuel aggravates the situation. The above said construction of houses are prone to chronic cough, chest infection and bronchitis, which are mainly caused by unscientific poor ventilation in the kitchen and bed room thereby enhance the temperature and smoke within the premises of houses.

It is evident from Table 5.3 that more than 91 per cent of primitive tribal people dwell in *kutcha* houses, which clearly denote their deplorable economic condition. They are primarily of four types: vegetative walled house with thatched roofs of grasses and paddy straws, vegetative walled houses with tile roofs, mud walled houses with thatched roofs of paddy straws and mud walled houses with tile roofs. It is succeeded by semi-pucca houses, which takes into account of 8.4 per cent of houses, which are recently constructed by the help of government.

House of Savar

It is also noteworthy to notice that few pucca houses are also built by the government help in Birjia's locality, which are situated near the famous Netarhat School. They generally live in such a house, which is made of either one or two rooms with fenced gardens without a central courtyard. Generally, the kitchen is demarcated by a partition wall of smaller height within the house itself. The absence of window is common to all the houses. The rooms are ill-ventilated and are partially dark even during day. The flimsy nature of walls, which are made of bamboos, unfinished logs and unshaped twigs are really sanitary. The vegetation walled houses are more popular among the Sauria Paharias, the Mal Paharias, the Birhors and the Parhiyas as the abundance of white ants precludes the use of mud. On the contrary the mud walled houses are prevalent among the Savars, the Asurs, the Birjias and the Korwas. The thatched materials are more widespread for roofing by the deprived section of the society whereas tiles are practised as roof material by the slightly economic well-off people.

Kitchen Facility

The infant mortality rate is also influenced by the availability of space, cleanliness and type of utensils and consumption pattern of fuels in the kitchens. It is the most essential ingredient of a house as all family members eat foods prepared in the kitchen and nurture them. That is why, kitchen is considered as the largest growth engine of the world for having sound health. In fact, fresh and clean raw materials of food, cleanliness of utensils, proper cooked food, cleanliness of kitchen floor and so on are vital elements for keeping good health. However, when rotten raw materials and stale cooked food fall upon the floor of kitchen, they attract a variety of insects and bacteria, which may spread various kinds of diseases. The diseases, namely chronic cough, chest infection and bronchitis are spread due to having unscientific ventilation facility in the kitchen, thereby increase a high degree of heat and smoke in the premises of house. In fact, the houses with pathetic ventilation facility and the burning of traditional firewood fuel enhance the risk of respiratory problems, which include cough, breathlessness, wheezing and blood in sputum. Simultaneously, such unwanted circumstances also lead to termination of pregnancy outcomes. The situation gets further aggravated when the smoke produced from the hearths remain within the premises of four walls of houses and the children feel difficulty in respiration. The dirty mud-built floor, *kutcha* house with poor ventilation and low ceiling height are not conducive for amenities of kitchen room. That kind of kitchen is injurious for the health of people in general and the children in particular. It is a matter of great concern that not even a single house had separate kitchen room among the dwelling of the primitive tribes in Jharkhand. Thus, almost 100 per cent of houses did not have provision of separate kitchen among the primitive tribes in the state of Jharkhand, which reflects their deplorable sanitation condition. They usually cook within the premises of house, which are bifurcated with small wall in the corner of house.

Toilet Facility

It is general notion among the people of primitive tribes that open defecation is a natural process of passing stools and natural ecosystem covert these human excreta into organic fertilizer. That is why, there is no need of disposal of human excreta as it is managed nature itself. However, they are completely ignorant about the fact that a variety of infectious diseases may be spread through various causative organisms, as they are usually grown upon human excreta. Therefore, a proper method of demolition of human excreta should be applied so that the said diseases may be prevented. Even though the toilet rooms are constructed by the government at free of cost but they hardly use them. However, in few primitive tribal households they use them as store rooms. In their routine life, almost all the primitive tribal people have adopted the habit of passing stools in the field rather than using the toilet room since they have no awareness about its positive effects. They usually prefer nearby open fields for excretion with washing bowels by water, which increases worms among the children. Moreover, some of them especially among the Sauria Paharias also use dry leaves and stones instead of water after evacuation of bowels during the summer season, when there is scarcity of water. Many times, flies are usual carriers of diseases as they sit on human excreta and filthy rotten materials. Which are ultimately responsible for the death of infants. Due to ignorance and unawareness in hygienic aspects, skin disease is common among them. On the one hand, the state of Jharkhand is boasting for the largest number of constructions of Swachh Public Toilets in urban areas. On the other hand, not even a single community toilet facility was available at the time of survey in the locality of the primitive tribes. Unfortunately, 89 per cent of households go for open defecation with water whereas 11 per cent of households go for open defecation with dry leaves and stones. The later kind of practice is more common among the Sauria Paharias in the summer season. Thus, the change in behaviour is the first and foremost precondition before the construction of public toilet facility. Otherwise, they will use them as the store rooms.

Morbidity

The native concept of disease for the primitive tribes in the state of Jharkhand is as varied as their culture. It is usually believed that the diseases are spread through the breach of some established sacrosanct traditions or by hostile spirits, the ghosts, or the dead souls of their ancestors in the society. Morbidity is the natural punishment for their lapses and crimes meted out against them by the above mentioned spirits and the souls of their ancestors. In fact, it is considered that disease is related with their sacrosanct social value system and natural phenomena of the world. That is why, they have different approaches and method of salvations to get rid of their diseases. They have blind faith upon the village priest that the diseases will be cured by them by acting as a mediator between the people and the hostile spirits. By propitiations and prayers, the primitive people try to maintain good relationship between the people on one hand and the mystical powers on the other, which intervene on human affairs (Gupta, 1976). They feel shy in coming to the hospitals and health centres for the treatment

Table 5.4: Important Causes of Infant Deaths among the Primitive Tribes

Disease	No. of Neonatal Deaths	% of Neonatal Deaths	No. of Post-Neonatal Deaths	% of Post-Neonatal Deaths	No. of Infant Deaths	% of Infant Deaths
Diarrhoea	56	19.3	50	22.5	106	20.6
Measles	18	6.2	46	20.4	64	12.5
Low Weight	25	8.6	7	3.1	32	6.2
Malaria	15	5.2	30	13.5	45	8.8
Tetanus	10	3.4	7	3.1	17	3.3
A.R.I. and Pneumonia	33	11.4	28	12.6	61	11.9
Jaundice	18	6.2	0	0	18	3.5
Typhoid	28	9.7	23	10.3	51	9.9
Fever and U.D.	87	30.0	33	14.5	120	23.3
Total	**290**	**100.0**	**224**	**100.0**	**514**	**100.0**

of their diseases. As a result, the highest infant mortality, i.e. 230 per thousand live births have been taken into account among the primitive tribes of Jharkhand and a detailed analysis of infant deaths under the heading of various diseases have been carried out here in Table 5.4.

Diarrhoea

The most common diseases among the infants of the primitive tribes in the state of Jharkhand is diarrhoea and it is to be noticed here that the dysentery has also been included under it. It is observed from Table 5.4 that 19.3 per cent of infant deaths were caused by diarrhoea among the neonates whereas 22.5 per cent of infant deaths were ascertained by the above disease in the post-neonatal stage at the time of survey. It is a matter of great concern that only diarrhoea accounted for 20.6 per cent of all infant deaths among the PTGs in the state of Jharkhand. Thus, diarrhoea is still the vital disease among the impoverished tribal people, which claims around one-fourth, i.e. 106 out of total 514 infant deaths. The symptom of dehydration is common in diarrhoea among the babies, which sometimes results in to deaths. This particular disease needs to be addressed at the household level to reduce the number of complicated and fatal cases. All families of the primitive tribes should be educated on the proper procedure for preparing and administrating the ORS, dietary and foods. Simultaneously, free ORS packets should be delivered in those families, who have the small children in their houses.

Measles

Measles is a highly contagious viral disease among the small children of the primitive tribes in the state. It is usually transmitted through the air by respiratory droplets produced from coughing or sneezing of a person. Its system comprises cough, runny nose, inflamed eyes, sore throat, fever and a red blotchy skin rash. It is further noticed that measles is more common among the infants after their survival of one month. Consequently, neonatal deaths by it were only 6.2 per cent whereas it was as high as 20.4 per cent in the later part of infant deaths at the time of survey. On the whole, that particular disease accounted for 12.5 per cent of infant deaths among the PTGs in the state.

However, the above disease can easily be cured by the vaccination but the innocent tribal people are completely ignorant about its treatment.

Low Weight

Although low weight is not itself a disease but the low-birth weight infants have 2.3 times higher risk of infant mortality rate. Whenever infections occur in low-weight children in compare to normal birth weight babies after controlling of all confounding variables, the chances of survival among the low-weight babies are dim. The weight of baby is generally the result of starvation by their respective tribal mothers during gestation period and these mothers do not take nutritious food due to their extreme poverty. The deaths due to low weight is more prevalent among the neonates of the primitive tribal people, which alone accounted 8.6 per cent of all neonate deaths in 2017. On the contrary, the share of post-neonatal deaths was only 3.1 per cent. Overall, the proportion of infant deaths due to having low weight encompassed around 6.2 per cent of all infant deaths among the PTGs in Jharkhand. Naturally, the low weight of baby is more dangerous in the initial phase of life, which turns into less severe in the later phase among the primitives owing to having universal habit of breastfeeding.

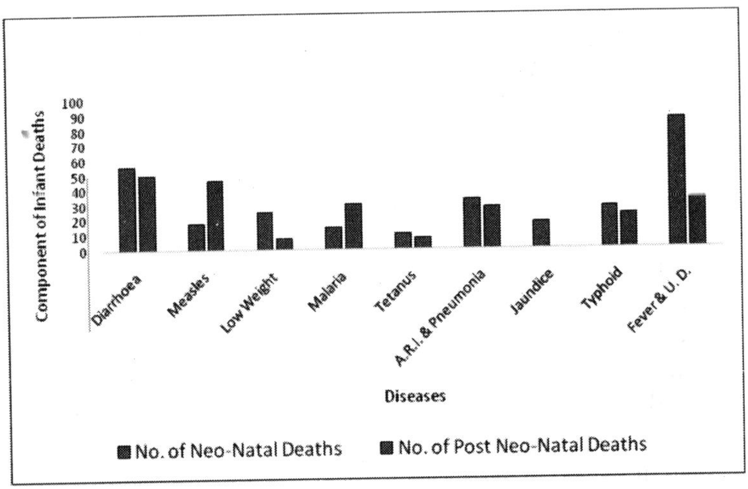

Fig. 5.1: Death of Neonates and Post-neonates among PTG through various Diseases, 2017

Malaria

Malaria is a unique disease among the primitive tribes in Jharkhand, which is not only transmitted through the bite of an infected 'anopheles' mosquito but by larvae of infected 'anopheles' mosquitoes are directly taken along with unhygienic water of springs and ponds. Symptoms of malaria fever start with sever chills, shivering fever lasts for few hours and settles down by itself; fever returns after one or two days with headache and muscle pain. It is such a disease among the tribes that all age groups of people are infected by it. More lives are lost in the age group of post-neonates, which claimed deaths of 13.5 per cent whereas the deaths caused under the heading of neonates taken into account of only 5.2 per cent at the time of survey. On the whole, the share of infant deaths was 8.8 per cent of all infant deaths owing to widespread prevalence of malaria in Jharkhand.

Neonatal Tetanus and Umbilical Stump Infection

Neonatal tetanus occurs among the children due to potent toxin generated by the tetanus bacillus. These bacilli are found in heavy concentration in tropical climate. That kind of infection is usually produced at the sight of umbilical stump among the infants of hot and humid region. The central nervous system of children is directly affected by the toxin of clostridium tetani and results in muscle spasms and seizures. The symptoms appear to 14 days after birth and death follows rapidly. Moreover, if the precautionary measures are taken by the pregnant woman through administering two doses of tetanus toxoid at the gap of at least one month and the another should be taken before one month prior to delivery. That kind of practice boosts the immunity among the neonates and guarantees cent-per-cent protection against neonatal titanium. Contamination and infection of the umbilical stump at the time of cutting the cord is an important cause of neonatal tetanus. The condition is limited to the untrained *dais* and the old ladies, who use unclear and unsterilized sharp weapons to cut the umbilical cord (Singh, 2010).

It is transpired from Fig. 5.1 that both tetanus and umbilical stump infection occur in early stage of new-born babies among the primitive tribes in Jharkhand. So far infant deaths are concerned, neonatal tetanus is exclusively responsible for neonatal deaths, which was 3.4 per cent at the time of survey. The above lives could have been saved if their mothers had been vaccinated with tetanus toxoids before the delivery of new-born babies. It is further noticed that 3.1 per cent of post-neonatal deaths were lost due to not caring of umbilical stump, which caused omphalitis disease and finally resulted in death of new born babies among the impoverished tribal people. So far, the percentage distribution of infant deaths is concerned, that particular disease took the toll of 3.3 per cent of all infant deaths. No antiseptic lotion and powder are used when the infant's umbilical cord got inflamed through bacterial infection. Sometimes, substances like ash of cow dung, butter or ghee are applied at the site of infected umbilical stump, which ultimately lead to omphalitis. In fact, white pus with foul smelling was oozing from the infected site of the children but no medical treatment was given due to complete isolation and destitute economic condition.

Acute Respiratory Infection and Pneumonia

Acute Respiratory Infection (ARC) constitutes the commonest cause of morbidity in new-born babies and pulmonary pathology is the most frequent autopsy finding in the neonates. When the respiratory rate is more than 60 per minute in a quite resting baby, it needs clinical treatment. Again, pneumonia accounts for more than 50 per cent cases of respiratory distress in the new-born and approximately 30 per cent of the ARI related deaths are due to measles, pertussis and diphtheria. It usually begins as a viral infection in the nose, trachea or lungs. It is vividly clear from Table 5.4 that neonatal deaths were 11.4 per cent, whereas post-neonatal deaths were observed 12.6 per cent but on the whole the infant deaths were recorded 11.9 per cent by the ARI at the time of survey among the PTGs in the state of Jharkhand. The non-availability of doctors in their localities is mainly accountable for such kind of alarming rate of child deaths. Thus, the ARI are the leading causes of morbidity and mortality in under one-year children among the primitive tribes in Jharkhand.

Jaundice

Jaundice is the commonest abnormal disease of new-born babies during first week of life. A large number of new-born babies also fall prey of jaundice when they have a high level of bilirubin, a yellow pigment produced during normal breakdown of red blood cells. Babies with jaundice have a yellow colouring of the skin and eyes. Just after a glance of Table 5.4, it is revealed that this particular disease of jaundice had taken death toll of 6.2 per cent in neonatal stage at the time of survey whereas its share in post-neonatal deaths was not observed at all. It is common practice among the PTGs that the new-borns are given bath immediately after delivery of child, which enhances the occurrences of the disease at neonatal stage. Nevertheless, overall jaundice accounted for death toll of 3.5 per cent for the infants of the primitive tribes in Jharkhand. The low infant mortality by Jaundice in post-neonatal stage may be traced for universalization of breast feeding and application of herbs for its treatment.

Typhoid

Typhoid is an extremely bacterial disease, which is generally spread through contaminated food and water, stools and wine. It has the characteristics of high fever, uneasiness, persistent vomiting and diarrhoea and swollen tummy in the new-born baby. It is reported from Table 5.4 that the above disease is a major cause of neonatal deaths and around 9.7 per cent of lives were lost due to the above disease before the reaching the age of one month among the primitive tribes in the survey year of 2017. That very disease also claimed the life of 10.3 per cent of post-neonatal deaths. Nevertheless, it is responsible for 9.9 per cent of lives in the stage of infancy among the primitive tribes in the state. First of all, drinking of unclean water and unhygienic living conditions are mainly responsible for such heavy toll of lives but universal breast-feeding habit of mother have marginally curtailed the infant morbidity.

Fever and Unknown Disease

It is difficult to identify the disease of infancy because many disorders that begin in childhood become clinically evident in childhood. Further, when the majority of respondents are uneducated, it is Herculean task to identify the disease of every infant death. That is why, all infant deaths due to fever, asphyxia, accident and unknown reasons have been clubbed under the heading of fever and unknown disease shown in Fig. 5.2. A large number of infant deaths are also occurred due to witchcraft, which is mingled with this group. Consequently 30 per cent of neonatal deaths were incorporated under the above group, whereas 14.5 per cent of infant deaths were encompassed under post-neonatal stage by the above-mentioned disease. On the whole, the above diseases have taken the death toll of 23.3 per cent of infant morbidity at the time of survey among the primitive tribes in Jharkhand. Thus, the maximum number of infants became the victims of fever and unknown reasons. In fact, fever itself is not a disease and its response of body to combat sickness. The above finding is also endorsed by Joshi (2013) that another major cause of infant morbidity and mortality in developing nations is the prevalence of infection.

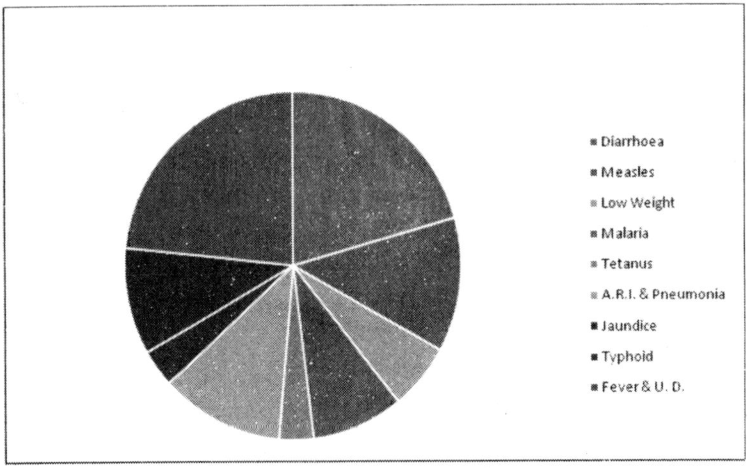

Fig. 5.2: Percentage of Infant Deaths among P.T.G. through various Diseases, 2017

The diseases namely diarrhoea, malaria, pneumonia, and tetanus take heavy toll of around 35 per cent of neonatal deaths, which are the results of an infection and that can be easily cured with medical intervention. According to the United Nations Children's Fund, although infant morbidity and mortality in some areas of developing nations is decreasing, Sub-Saharan Africa and Southern Asia's infant morbidity and mortality rates remain high, mainly due to infections (You, Hug, Ejdemyr and Beise, 2015). The rationale for the existence of consistent infection rates could include a number of reasons, some dependent upon cultural practices, unavailable resources, lack of healthcare providers or education, insufficient sanitary practices, and more. However, Mission Indradhanush has been introduced in India for the eradication of aforesaid diseases through gradual routine programme of immunization against seven vaccines—preventable diseases in the year 2015. Further, newer vaccines namely pentavalent vaccine, rotavirus vaccine and injectable polio virus vaccine have been introduced under the umbrella of national immunization schedule. The National Health Policy (NHP), 2017 aims at more than 90 per cent immunization coverage in the age of one year by year 2025 (National Health Policy, 2017). The above-mentioned goal can be achieved through proper provisioning of better infrastructural facilities with scientific logistic vision, which should definitely include universal vaccination, a team of dedicated local health workers and overall health awareness among all sections of the primitive tribes with special emphasis upon the targeted individuals.

Indigenous medicines are very popular compared to allopathy among the primitive tribes. It is, therefore, desirable to promote and develop the indigenous system of medicines in the primitive tribal localities for getting rid of diseases.

Summary

From the above discussion, it can be easily inferred that more than 99 per cent of primitive tribal mothers had not taken any kind of antenatal care in term of medical intervention during their gestation period. Further, around two-third mothers had taken insufficient food during the above period. Majority of child births in primitive tribal localities were executed by the unskilled family members and midwives in an unhygienic environment, which usually lead to infection to the new born babies. Further, one-quarter of mothers had adopted female sterilization only after they had completed their desired family size but around 50 per cent of mothers did not accept any form of family planning method. Simultaneously, majority of mothers did not adopt abortion for addressing the unmet need for contraception. Around

47 per cent of new born babies had weight less than 2 kg, which clearly divulges that the chances of their survival were dim. Again, no medical check was carried out in case of 91 per cent of new born babies. Immunization of children against sixserious diseases were not completed due to unawareness of mothers. Simultaneously, awareness regarding stopping of delayed breastfeeding and immediate bath to the new-borns among the primitive mothers can drastically curtail neonatal mortality rate. Although breastfeeding was universal among the tribal mothers but majority of them did not start it as their initial feeding. So far supplementary food is concerned, it was started very late. Around three-fourth of mothers were addicted of alcohol and narcotic.

A majority of houses had the provision of animals residing within the houses, which naturally create unhygienic condition for the small children. Again, more than 75.5 per cent of primitive tribal people along with their children do not take bath daily due to limited set of clothes and scarcity of water. Almost all of them prefer open field for excretion with washing bowels by water but the Sauria Paharias also use dry leaves and stones in place of water during summer season. The unhygienic habits of primitive tribal people augment high children mortality. They still use contaminated stream and spring water for drinking purpose by their habit and tradition. Further more than 87 per cent of households do not use any kind filter for purification of water. More than 91 per cent of primitive tribal people inhabit in a small kutcha house, which are generally made up of one or two rooms and these rooms are ill ventilated and dark even during day time. Generally, they do not have separate kitchen room and a small place is usually encircled in the corner of dwelling room itself, where traditional firewood is used for cooking purpose.

Now it can be easily summarized that the dogmas and superstitions of the primitive tribal groups regarding delayed start of breastfeeding by the mothers to the new-borns after throwing away colostrum, immediate bath to the new-borns, addiction of drinking and smoking, inculcation of unhygienic habits and insanitation, complete faith for remedy of diseases upon traditional diviner through evil spirits and witches etc. enhance the infant mortality rate. Thus, high infant mortality rate among the primitive tribes is largely contributed by poor sanitation and hygiene. Since they are living in such isolated inaccessible areas where modern well-equipped health amenities are unavailable. Hence, there is a definite decline of these tribal groups, which is not related with low fertility rate but high mortality is largely responsible for this unprecedented situation.

The poor health with the unhygienic habits and unscientific sanitation leads to victims of various kinds of diseases among the children and finally takes a heavy loss of infant lives. Diarrhoea and dysentery still account for the largest number of infant deaths. It is followed by mysterious disease, measles, acute respiratory infection, typhoid, malaria, low weight, tetanus and jaundice. It is further observed that mysterious disease, diarrhoea and dysentery, ARI, typhoid, low weight, measles and jaundice play an important role in case of neonatal mortality whereas the disease behind post-neonatal deaths are diarrhoea and dysentery, measles, malaria and low weight among the primitive tribes in the state. In fact, Jharkhand should adopt the health policy of Tamil Nâdu wherein, a trained qualified Auxiliary Nurse Midwives/Village Health Nurses is deputed for taking care of 5,000 rural people whereas it is one for 3,000 people in tribal areas for antenatal care and other services. The government also attracted medical officers to rural areas through incentives such as reserved places for post-graduate study (Padmanaban, 2009).

REFERENCES

Ghosh, S. (2004). "Child Malnutrition", *Economic and Political Weekly,* New Delhi: Samiksha Trust, p. 413.

Government of India. National Health Policy (2017). pp. 1-31, Retrieved from http://www. mohfw.nic.in/showfile.*php? lid=4275.* Accessed July 27, 2017.

Gupta, S.P. (1976). *op. cit.*, p. 112.

Hockenberry, M.J., Wilson, D. and Rodgers, C.C. (2012). *Wong's Essentials of Paediatric Nursing.* St. Louis, MO: Elsevier.

Jharkhand Economic Survey (2018-19). *op. cit.,* pp. 205-208.

Joshi, R., Sharma, S., and Van Teijlingen, E. (2013). *op. cit.,* pp. 247-257.

Lakshmi Narayan (1998). "Implication of Excise (liquor) and Bonded Labour Policy in Tribal Areas of Maharashtra State", Pune: Tribal Research and Training Institute, p. 58.

Murki, S. and Sharma, D. (2014). "Intrauterine Growth Retardation: A Review Article", *Journal of Neonatal Biology, 3*(135), 55-60, doi: 10.4172/2167-0897.1000135.

Padmanaban, P., P.S. Raman, D.V. Mavalankar (2009). *op. cit.,* 27:2021219.

Singh, M. (2010). *op. cit.,* pp. 34-35, 231-33.

Sinha, A.K. (1986). "Problems of Health and Hygiene in Bishanpur Block with Special Reference to Serka Village", *Man and Life*, Vol. 12, Nos. 3 and 4, pp. 181-192.

Visaria, L. (1988). "Determinants of Regional Variations in Infant Mortality in Rural India", pp. 85-86, in A.K. Jain and P. Visaria (eds.), *Infant Mortality in India: Differentials and Determinants*, New Delhi: Sage Publication.

You, D., L. Hug, S. Ejdemyr., and J. Beise (2015). Levels and trends in child mortality, Retrieved from https://data.unicef.org/wp-content/uploads/2015/12/IGME-report-2015-child-mortality-final_236.pdf.

6
Determinants of Infant Mortality

Explanatory variables of infant mortality vary from country to country and also within the country. They vary depending on the socio-economic, demographic and cultural factors. It occurs in response to wide range of factors, which affect different children in different ways and to which children do not necessarily respond in an identical fashion. Abject poverty with low income, unequal distribution of land, low productivity of land, inaccessibility of primitive tribal villages, location of villages in forested scarp land and hill tops, prevailing superstition regarding morbidity and its cure, inculcation of unhygienic habit, insanitation, complete dearth of medical facility, misconception regarding reproductivity, unmet need, low level of immunization, unavailability of transportation amenity, illiteracy, addiction of alcohol drinking and narcotic smoking, unavailability of safe drinking water, dilapidated housing condition, malnutrition, insufficient intake of food by the mothers during gestation and lactation period, home delivery by the untrained *dais* and old woman in place of institutional delivery, no implementation of any welfare scheme on the ground regarding the health of children, delayed breastfeeding and immediate bathing after delivery, higher order of births, early marriage etc., are the main factors behind unprecedented level of infant mortality, which have put the whole communities in the group of endangered primitive tribes in Jharkhand. However, the inclusion of explanatory and dependent variables depends on their importance and the availability of their measurement. Different models and techniques have been evolved to study the effect of various factors associated with infant deaths but the present study is limited to only zero order correlation matrix, stepwise regression and binary logistic regression analysis for examining the determinants of infant deaths.

Zero Order Correlation Matrix

The well-being and quality of life of infants are influenced by a large number of variables, which are essential for their good health and basic instinct of their survival hood. The study aims at finding out the likely determinants of the deceased babies and their intense relationship. More specifically, the focus is on six interrelated questions based on the objectives of the study: (a) Do the familial characteristics exert any influence on health and chances of survival of infants? (b) Do the maternal characteristics have any effect on reduction of infant deaths? (c) Do the perceptions of mothers have any role for good health among the children? (d) Do the biological characteristics of infants affect the major role in reduction of infant deaths? (e) Do the socio-economic profiles of the households have major say in curtailing of infant deaths? and (f) Does the availability of infrastructural facilities plays a major role in declination of child deaths? Using a correlation matrix, an analysis of neonatal mortality, post-neonatal mortality and infant mortality rates have been carried out with several variables of infrastructure, health, demography and socio-economic conditions here. The likelihood of neonatal mortality rate, post-neonatal mortality rate and infant mortality rate depend upon various social, economic, demographic, infrastructural and sanitary factors.

However, the present study is limited to only 16 explanatory variables, which have been examined to seek the relationship between infant deaths and these predictor variables, which are presented in correlation matrix table of 6.1. The explanatory variables are less in number due to multicollinearity problem. In this exercise neonatal mortality rate (Y_1), post-neonatal mortality rate (Y_2) and infant mortality rate (Y_3) are considered as dependent variables whereas mother's literacy (X_1), share of infants with fourth and higher order of births (X_2), share of mother's age between 20 and 30 years (X_3), share of mothers with breastfeeding within one day (X_4), share of working mothers (X_5), proportion of mothers received antenatal care (X_6), percentage of addicted mothers (X_7), child-woman ratio (X_8), share of immunized infant deaths (X_9), percentage of households having handpump and tap facilities (X_{10}), percentage of households having house with one room provision (X_{11}), percentage of landless households (X_{12}), per capita income in rupees (X_{13}), distance of bus-stand facility from village (X_{14}), distance of medical centre from village (X_{15}), and productivity per acre (X_{16}) are included under the heading of independent variables.

Mother's Literacy (X_1)

Indeed, mother's education is a decisive factor for social development approach, which finally reduces infant deaths. It raises the opportunity cost of women's time and generally opens up greater opportunities for women that often conflict with repeated child bearing. These educated women may be more receptive to modern social norms and family planning campaigns, which ultimately reduces child deaths. Again, infant feeding, clothing and treatment of common ailments are generally carried out scientifically by the educated mother. That kind of infant care reduces child deaths. Moreover, in primitive tribal society of Jharkhand knowledge about bearing and rearing child is also derived from folklore, traditionally handed down from mother to daughter.

The above notion is also corroborated in the present finding, where mother's literacy among the primitive tribes is negatively correlated with Neonatal Mortality Rate (NMR), Post-Neonatal Mortality Rate (PNMR) and Infant Mortality Rate (IMR) and the values of correlation coefficients are -.10, -.11 and -.14 respectively. Moreover, the relationships among them are not significant, which leads to manifest that only simple mother's literacy is not solely responsible for curtailing infant deaths among the children of PTGs in the state. Thus, the above finding supports our hypothesis partially that mother's education plays an important role in the decline of infant mortality among the PTGs in Jharkhand.

Share of Infants with Fourth and Higher Order of Births (X_2)

The prevalence of higher infant mortality rate among the late born siblings has been well documented and provided the basis for the classical approach to the planned parenthood movement. It is generally perceived that reduction in fertility imply reduction in unmet need of higher-order births, which would ultimately lead to a lowering of the overall infant mortality rate. It has already been discussed earlier that the primitive people have abject level of poverty and endowment of limited resources. Hence, whenever they have a large number of children, they are not properly taken care of. That is why, infant deaths are found more in number while the family consists of fourth and higher order of births. It is also evident in case of primitive tribes in Jharkhand and the value of correlation coefficient between neonatal mortality and share of fourth and higher order of infant births is .18. The relationship between the above birth order and PNMR is further accentuated, which is substantiated by the value of correlation coefficient, i.e., 32 and it is significant at 1 per cent level of confidence. The above relationship between IMR and higher order of birth is further substantiated by the value of correlation coefficient, which is .32 and it is also significant at 1 per cent level of confidence. From the above results, it can easily sum up that the higher the share of 4th and higher order of births among the primitive tribes in Jharkhand have higher the proportion of infant deaths. Thus, the hypothesis that the risk of infant death is very high for fourth and higher order of child births holds completely true in context of the primitive tribes in Jharkhand.

Share of mother's age between 20 and 30 years (X_3)

It is an established fact that the infant mortality is found at the lowest level, while the age of mother in case of child bearing is between 20 and 30 years among the primitive tribes in the state, which has been discussed in the previous chapter. As the mothers of primitive tribes generally do not take sufficient and nutritious food, their reproducing capacity of healthy child last very early period of youthfulness. This poor nutrition starts in uterus and extends throughout the life cycle. This not only amplifies the risks to the individual's health but also increases the likelihood of damage to future generations through further foetal growth, retardation and a limited ability to cope with stresses within the family and in the provision of child care. This particular variable has negative bearing upon neonatal mortality and

Table 6.1: Zero Order Correlation Matrix between Infant Deaths of the PTGs & Variables of Rural Development in Jharkhand

	Y_1	Y_2	Y_3	X_1	X_2	X_3	X_4	X_5	X_6	X_7	X_8	X_9	X_{10}	X_{11}	X_{12}	X_{13}	X_{14}	X_{15}	X_{16}
Y_1	1																		
Y_2	.21*	1																	
Y_3	.81**	.74**	1																
X_1	-.10	-.11	-.14	1															
X_2	.18	.32**	.32**	-.04	1														
X_3	-.06	.06	-.01	.23*	-.25*	1													
X_4	-.41**	1.00	-.54**	.47**	-.18	.34**	1												
X_5	-.41**	-.43**	-.54**	.29*	-.50**	.27**	.55**	1											
X_6	-.34**	-.26*	-.39**	.47**	-.14	.41**	.89**	.49**	1										
X_7	.16	-.13	.04	-.21*	.03	-.14	-.02	-.20	-.26**	1									
X_8	-.09	-.15	-.15	.28*	.29*	.23*	.55**	-.06	.45**	.19	1								
X_9	-.34**	.23*	-.30**	.08	.09	.01	.01	.02	.07	-.24*	-.13	1							
X_{10}	-.18	-.19	-.25*	-.14	-.12	-.23*	.06	.13	.03	.14	-.18	.10	1						
X_{11}	-.10	.14	.01	.01	-.06	.01	-.06	-.12	.06	-.34**	-.01	.24*	.11	1					
X_{12}	.15	-.03	.08	-.19	-.11	-.15	-.11	-.05	-.17	.39**	-.30**	-.04	.28**	-.26**	1				
X_{13}	-.13	-.12	-.16	.46**	.45**	-.23*	.26**	.12	.27**	-.20	.10	.13	.07	-.12	-.15	1			
X_{14}	.10	.02	.09	-.13	-.06	.15	-.13	-.12	-.07	-.01	-.05	-.21*	.01	.10	-.09	-.17	1		
X_{15}	.26*	.05	.21*	-.01	.17	.14	-.08	-.23*	-.01	.01	.08	-.08	-.13	.19	-.06	-.13	.42**	1	
X_{16}	-.24*	-.10	-.11	.19	.04	.18	.10	.16	.21*	-.60**	.16	.15	-.23*	.29**	-.91**	.17	.11	-.02	1

infant mortality rate and the values of correlation coefficients are -.06 and -.01 but both of them are not statistically significant. However, mothers having the age of 20 to 30 years is positively correlated (r= .06) with post-neonatal rate but it is also not significant. From the above relationship, it may infer that the age of mother does not play an important role for diminishing in curtailing of child deaths. Moreover, the above finding partially accepts that infant mortality in general and neonatal mortality in particular are lower in the age group of 20 to 30 years of age at the time of child births but the values of correlation coefficients are not significant at any level.

Share of Mothers with Breastfeeding within One Day (X_4)

Although breastfeeding is nearly universal among the primitive tribes in Jharkhand but almost all infants are deprived of first nutritious milk, i.e. colostrum and antibodies it contains and more than 99 per cent of children are given animal milk, honey, *gutty*, *ghee*, sugar, glucose, boiled water etc. as their first food among the primitive tribes other than breast milk during that initial period. It is recommended that nothing should be given to children other than breast milk in the first three days of life when the milk has not begun to flow regularly. However, mothers breastfeed for an average of 33 months in the state, which is longer than the minimum of 24 months recommended by WHO for most children. It is a scientific fact that women who intensively breastfeed their babies, do experience a longer interval before next menstruation. Breastfeeding is likely to lengthen birth intervals by an average of five to eight months. It is nature's way of helping to space children. It is further observed that those mothers who started breastfeeding within one day, their chances of survival among such children increase many more times than their counterparts.

That kind of relationship is also established in correlation matrix Table 6.1 that neonatal mortality, post-neonatal mortality and infant mortality rate are strongly negatively associated with the share of mothers, who started breastfeeding within one day. The values of correlation coefficients of the above three parameters of infant deaths with early breastfeeding are -.41, -.43 and -.54 and all of them are significant at 1 per cent level of confidence. Thus, it is crystal cut clear that so many lives of infants can be saved through mass campaign for early start of breastfeeding and alarming situation of infant deaths among the primitive tribes can be easily reduced through social awareness. The above finding clearly substantiates our hypothesis that the immediate breastfeeding within one day curtails in neonatal mortality rate among the PTGs in Jharkhand. The above result further indicates that the immediate breastfeeding reduces child deaths even in post-neonatal and infant mortality rate as well.

Share of Working Mothers (X_5)

It is preconceived notion that babies of working mothers face a higher risk of infant mortality than babies born to non-working mothers among the general society. The situation is completely contrary for the primitive people where females are the principal bread earner of the family. It is also pointed by Vidyarthi (1969) that the percentage of women earners is higher among the tribal people. It has already been discussed earlier that the primitive people are half-fed and half-dressed people where severe economic hardships are observed among almost all families of the state. It is remarkable to note that the primitive tribal females earn for the livelihood of the family whereas males spend major of their income on liquor consumption. Simultaneously, the females are more laborious than their counterparts. As a matter of fact, that the occupation of mother is more fruitful for the survival of their children. That is why; occupation of mother is negatively related with all three variables of infant deaths, viz. neonatal, post-neonatal and infant mortality rate. The values of correlation coefficients among them are -.41, -.43 and -.54 and all are significant at 1 per cent level of significance. Thus, the creation of more avenues of job for the females will curtail in reduction of child deaths. The above discussion completely refutes our hypothesis that infant mortality is high for the working mothers than the non-working mothers among the PTGs in Jharkhand.

Proportion of Mothers Received Antenatal Care (X_6)

No concern about antenatal care is still a reality in PTGs and pregnancy is considered as a natural state and not a state of illness requiring medical attention, taking rest and other precautions. Jejeebhoy (1997) had remarked that very few women have access to antenatal care and untrained attendants conduct a number of deliveries in unhygienic conditions. The awareness of eligible couples regarding four different aspects of maternal health care such as (i) tetanus toxoid injection to pregnant women, (ii) at least three check-ups of antenatal mother, (iii) healthy and nutritious food during gestation and lactation period, and (iv) consumption of IFA and calcium tablets during pregnancy are completely cypher about the above health precautions. Again, the lower immunization coverage is due to the lack of awareness, poverty and neglect by the system. As a matter of fact, only negligible portion of pregnant women among the PTGs is taken care of the above concerns during the gestation period but the result is very much promising and all three components of child deaths get weakened through proper care of mothers.

The result is also substantiated from Table 6.1 that the proportion of antenatal cared mothers are strongly negatively related with neonatal, post-neonatal and infant mortality rate and the values of correlation coefficients are -.34, -.26 and -.39 respectively. The result clearly adds to the fact that there will be a dramatic decline in child deaths if the primitive tribal females are properly taken care of during their gestation period. The women who enjoyed superior physical conditions and good diets during pregnancy brought forth babies in excellent health condition.The above finding clearly approves the hypothesis that antenatal care of mother creates a healthy environment for her offspring whereby there is reduction in neonate deaths.

Proportion of Addicted Mothers (X_7)

Drinking is a part of social milieu among the primitive tribes in Jharkhand from the times immemorial. The indigenous beverage prepared by fermentation of rice has been the favourite liquor of the primitive tribes in general and the females in particular. This is the traditional liquor of the tribes, which is prepared within the four walls of home and this indigenous beverage apart from fulfilling some of their religious and ritualistic needs, also supplements some of their nutritional deficiency. However, the primitive mothers also consume local distilled liquor these days along with their male counterparts, which is really intoxicant and carries little food value. Consequently, the share of liquor addicted mothers is positively associated with the neonatal and infant mortality. The values of correlation coefficients of proportion of addicted mothers with NMR, PNMR and IMR among them are -.16, -.13 and .04 and all of them are not significant at any level, which explicitly manifest that all three components of infant deaths are not largely responsible for ill health of children through the habit of drinking among the primitive females in the state.

Child-Woman Ratio (X_8)

Child-woman ratio is a better indicator of fertility, which measure the ratio between the number of children below the age of 5 years and the women aging between 15-49 years per thousand of reproductive age group. It is very high, i.e. 4.48 among the primitive tribes in Jharkhand because of uncertainty of their survival in absence of medical facilities. A large number of children involve for spreading the available meagre income into very thin and the children almost invariably receive a smaller share of food and medical care. This situation often leads to forced neglect, infantile ailments and even death in the absence of medical care, which are located far away from their localities. Again, the parents are not able to afford economic cost. Many parents look upon children as a kind of social insurance for their old age. In the absence of social security and old-age benefits parents tend to have many children so that a few may survive. It is further investigated that the higher number of children are born in those families which are comparatively well-off from the rest. Consequently, the inverse relationship is established between child-woman ratio and infant deaths. All three components of infant deaths, viz. neonatal, post-neonatal and infant mortality rate are inversely related with child-woman ratio among the primitive tribes in Jharkhand and the values of correlation coefficients are -.09, -.15 and -.15 respectively but they are not significant at any level. Thus, any scientific association between child-woman ratio and infant mortality cannot be established among the PTGs in the state.

Share of Immunized Infant Deaths (X_9)

The child survival programme has not received considerable attention and this is particularly true with the primitive tribes of Jharkhand. Immunization of children against seven serious but preventable diseases: tuberculosis, diphtheria, pertussis, tetanus, polio, measles and hepatitis B constitutes the cornerstone of preventive health care services in the state. These services are delivered in rural children through a chain of health care centres, viz. sub-centre, primary health centre and community health centres in the rural areas but its damn failure in implementation of immunization among the primitive tribal children, which is only 0.5 per cent. In fact, it is the low level of immunization, which has created dim situation of IMR. It is therefore, a UNICEF (1991) study has pointed out that 90 per cent of the deaths among young children in the developing countries are caused by the combined factors of malnutrition, unsafe drinking water, inadequate sanitation and lack of immunization.

It is evident from Table 6.1 that there is negative relationship between IMR and ratio of immunized children and this relationship is further established in case of NMR ($r = -.34$), which explicitly reveals that had the maximum number of children been immunized, the infant deaths would have been at lower rate but this is not the storey with PNMR, where it is positively associated ($r = .23$) with the proportion of immunized children. Moreover, the value of correlation coefficient between infant mortality rate and share of immunized infant deaths is -.30, which points out that immunization drive among the PTGs can lead to sudden decrease in infant deaths. Thus, the above verification through correlation matrix and step-wise regression analysis upholds the hypothesis that higher the share of immunization among the children of PTG; lower the proportion of infant deaths. This is also due to external factor wherein children are not provided with nutritious diet and safe drinking water.

Percentage of Households having Handpump and Tap Facilities (X_{10})

Provision of safe drinking water is a basic necessity of human being. The role of safe drinking water in declining the infant mortality among the PTGs in Jharkhand needs to be examined. A significant portion of infant and child deaths is attributed to water-borne diseases and provision of potable water through spring wells, handpump and tap can bring down infant mortality to a noteworthy extent. Since electronic water purifier is non-existent in their localities, the proportion of handpump and tap is considered as means of safe drinking water. In fact, the primitive tribal children suffer from many chronic diseases but the most prevalent taking heavy toll them are water-borne. This is mainly due to the very poor drinking water supply. Even when it is available in plenty, it is mostly dirty and contaminated and consequently the children are easily susceptible to intestinal and skin diseases (Hasnain, 2013).

Table 6.1 clearly manifests that NMR and PNMR are negatively associated with the proportion of households having handpump and tap facilities and the values of correlation coefficients are -.18 and -.19 in the survey year of 2017. That kind of negative relationship is further established between the share of households having safe drinking water provision and IMR and the value of correlation coefficient is -.25, which is significant at 5 per cent level of confidence. The above analysis explicitly demonstrates that there will be unprecedented decline in child deaths when the provision of safe drinking water through handpump and tap is supplied in their villages. On the basis of above exercise, the hypothesis relating to availability of safe drinking water reduces the mortality rate of children among the PTGs seem to be justified.

Percentage of Households having House with one Room Provision (X_{11})

Housing is one of the essential needs of human being. It is one of the vital determinants of the standard of living and the quality of life. Sewage treatment and waste disposal should form part of housing design. Housing design should have in built mechanism for harvesting sun and rain. Unfortunately, around 68 per cent of households dwell in *kutcha* houses with only one room provision among the PTGs in Jharkhand. In fact, these houses are constructed with thatched walls and thatched roofs and ground floors are built up of earthen mud. These houses have no provision of ventilation and usually houses have no window at all. The ceiling height of houses are lower, which are generally lower than 8 feet height and people can enter into these through crawling. Even during mid-day, the houses remain dark. Again, pigs, cattle, hen etc., are also kept in the same room and their waste materials are spread in the room. It is very difficult for an outsider to live in their houses as these waste materials stink too much but the small children play with them. There is provision of kitchen in the corner of same room, which is generally surrounded by three feet thatched mud wall. Further, there is no drainage system in their houses and the houses become hells in the rainy season. As a result, NMR is negatively related with the proportion of households with one room facility and the value of correlation coefficient is -.10 at the time of survey. Other components of infant deaths, i.e. PNMR (r= .14) and IMR (r=.01) are positively associated with the above variable but they are not significant at any level. Thus, even after living in healthy natural and unpolluted environment; poor ventilation increased heat and smoke during cooking; spreading of waste materials on the floor of houses have increased the PNMR among the children of primitive tribes in the state.

Percentage of Landless Households (X_{12})

The primitive tribes of Jharkhand have great emotional attachment with their lands. Land ownership is one of the basic measures of economic status in a village. In an economy where most people earn their living from the land, land ownership is relevant in determining the rate of infant mortality. Besides agriculture, the primitive people have also adopted artisan and fourth grade government job on a large scale. Since almost all primitive people get along in the midst of forest, they subsist on forest and some of them also work as labourers in the forest department. As a result, the share of landless households does not control the infant deaths in a persuasive manner. The percentage of landless households is positively associated with NMR (r= .15) and IMR (r= .08) whereas it is negatively related with PNMR (r= -.03). Nevertheless, all the values correlation coefficients are insignificant at any level. On the whole, no definite conclusion can be ascertained between the above variables.

Per Capita Income in Rupees (X_{13})

Income plays a crucial role in the curtailment of infant mortality among the primitive tribes in Jharkhand because a number of factors like food, hygiene, sanitation, housing, affordability of medical aid and so on and so forth are related with there economic status. All three components of infant deaths, viz. NMR, PNMR and IMR are negatively related with per capita income in rupees and the values of correlation coefficients are -.13, -.12 and -.16 respectively. From the above correlation, it may be inferred that higher the income level of primitive people would bring a positive change in the survival rate of livelihood among the children. In fact, income generated malnutrition; insanitation and unhygienic condition are primarily responsible for large scale ill health and death of children among the primitive tribes in Jharkhand. Indeed, the primitive tribes have become synonymous with lowest level income group, chronic and mass poverty in the state and almost all are living below the poverty line. Thus, the above discourse partially ratifies our hypothesis that the higher the share of low-income group among the primitive tribal groups has the higher share of infant mortality. Extreme poverty, indebtedness and high level of mother's illiteracy have been responsible for their backwardness and infant deaths.

Distance of Bus-stand Facility from Village (X_{14})

Roads are the only means of transportation as far as the primitive tribal localities are concerned in Jharkhand. The average length of roads per thousand square kms in the above areas is very poor and distance of bus-stand facility is further aggravated in these far-flung areas where inaccessibility and difficult terrain create a lot of problems in transfer of child patients, who are forced to walk here as no mobile medical unit and ambulances are traced in their localities. Therefore, all components of infant deaths, viz. NMR, PNMR and IMR are positively related with the villages located at the distance of above 5 kms from the bus-stand and the values of correlation coefficients are .10, .02 and .09. Thus, the primitive tribal villages located away from bus-stand amenity increase infant deaths among the primitive people. Moreover, the above relationship is not statistically significant at any level. From the above discussion, it cannot be established the credibility of hypothesis that the inaccessibility of villages from *pucca* road always enhances the infant mortality.

Distance of Medical Centre from Village (X_{15})

Over the years the state of Jharkhand has expanded its Primary Health Centre (PHC) up to 330 in 2018 but none is noticed in the areas where the primitive tribes are inhabited. It is, therefore, primitive tribal villages located more than 5 kms from the primary health centre is considered as an important variable for measuring infant deaths, viz. NMR, PNMR and IMR are positively related with the villages situated beyond 5 kms from PHC and the values of correlation coefficients are .26, .05 and .21. The first and last component of infant deaths are significant at 5 per cent level of confidence, which clearly transpires that the location of sub-centre and PHC is an important determinant for the child's survival rate and powerful force for improving the life of the child. A majority of men and women of the medical profession are very reluctant to offer their services in their villages, which are usually situated in rugged, hilly terrain covered with thick forests and dissected in all directions by numerous streams and rivulets. That is why, efforts must be made to train local people. Besides this, the use of Ayurvedic and tribal herbal medicine should be encouraged because of the fact that the primitive tribal people are already used to herbal remedies and hence there will be little problem of acceptability. Thus, the hypothesis that the longer distance of medical centre from the village, the larger the share of infant deaths holds completely true in context of the PTG in Jharkhand.

Productivity Per Acre (X_{16})

The primitive tribal region is undulating marked by isolated peaks and interspersed by numerous streams and rivers. The soil in all categories of land is poor, badly leached, acidic, and deficient in organic material, nitrogen and lime. The rain water because of undulating terrain is quickly lost from the fields. Again, inadequate water availability during the crop growth coupled with the inherent infertility are the principal factors for low productivity. The principal livelihood of the primitive people in the region is cultivation and productivity of land is considered as the chief determinant of well-being of people. Since most of the people consume those products what they produce from the field. That is why, productivity per acre in rupees is negatively related with NMR, PNMR and IMR and the correlation coefficients among them are -.24, -.10 and -.11 respectively. Thus, high productivity of land diminishes all components of deaths as female during gestation period and children during their early stage of life get proper food in those households, whose productivity of land is more for socio-economic sustenance. Moreover, the provision of assured irrigation may enhance the productivity of land whereby there will be reduction in infant deaths.

Stepwise Regression Analysis

After identifying major factors responsible for the operation of inter-regional differentials of infant deaths among the primitive tribes in Jharkhand, stepwise regression analysis has been employed here to ascertain the relative importance of these factors under the headings of neonatal, post-neonatal and infant mortality rate. The simple correlation gives us an idea of the relationship existing among the variables. But the crux of the problem remains to be solved that how much explaining variables influence the dependent variables under the study. Its procedure is adopted to obtain an optimum set of independent variables which could explain maximum possible variation in the dependent variables. It enables us to assess the extent of impact of each explaining independent variables upon dependent variables. Nonetheless, stepwise regression technique is also weakened by the tendency for highly intercorrelated variables to eliminate one another. Only when, there are prior guidelines and the number of variables is small, the stepwise procedure is used effectively. "Such a procedure tells us about the contribution of an added variable in explaining the dependent variables. Secondly, it helps to see whether the new variable is worth including in the model or not. Furthermore, it also helps us in keeping watch over the changes in the value of the regression coefficient and their standard errors. The contribution of independent variables has been tested by means of standard t-test. To test the goodness of fit, F-ratio is also computed. Here adjusted R^2 or R^2 is the square of multiple correlation coefficient adjusted to the degree of freedom that indicates the proportion of total variance accounted for by the equation" (Kumar, 2020).

Neonatal Mortality Rate of the PTG and Socio-Economic, Infrastructural and Demographic Variables

The explanatory variables of neonatal mortality among the PTG in step 1 of Table 6.2 is the share of mothers, who introduced breastfeeding within one day. It is a convention among the primitive mothers that they generally do not start immediate breastfeeding and they generally throw away the colostrum and new-born babies are given animal milk, honey, sugar, *ghee*, *ghutti*, glucose water etc. They generally start breastfeeding after three days of arrival of children. They have misconception about yellowish milk known as colostrum, containing antibodies in abundant quantity that it is waste product after remaining for nine months in breast. They generally threw away the valuable white blood corpuscles after making certain ceremony and the tribal mothers introduce breastfeeding later on to their babies which make the new-borns weak or sometimes kill the babies. It is, therefore, this particular variable explains 17 per cent variation in NMR among the primitive tribes in Jharkhand. It is significant at 1 per cent level of confidence and F-value is also significant on that very level.

The inclusion of share immunized infant deaths in step 2 improves the overall fitness of the equation considerable as the value of R^2 increases from .170 to .284 and $\bar{R}^2$ from .161 to .269. Thus, he contribution of immunized infant deaths is itself around 11.4 per cent in explanation of NMR, F-value and regression coefficient are also significant at 1 per cent level of confidence. It has already been discussed earlier that the level of immunization is very low among the children. That is why; its importance is exhibited here. The same process is repeated in 3rd step, wherein breastfeeding, immunized infant deaths and working mothers together interpret 32.8 per cent variation in NMR. Moreover, the contribution of working mothers alone accounts for 4.4 per cent in NMR and regression coefficient for the above variables are -.274, -.334 and -.251 respectively. Now it is an established fact that female work participation has a positive role in elimination of infant deaths among the primitive tribes as they are the main bread earners in their society. In step 4 the value of coefficient of determination (R^2) again raises to .371, which implies that the share of medical centre encompasses 2.5 per cent variation in NMR. Its importance is further aggravated for ENMR when the utility of medical centres for natality and delivery of new-born is well established. In step 5, the value of coefficient of determination is noticed as .371, which implies that 1.8 per cent variation in NMR is elucidated by literacy of mother.

The next explanatory variable for NMR is productivity of land, which takes into account of 2.1 per cent as the value of R^2 changes into .392 in step 6. The next variable, i.e. proportion of mothers received antenatal care upholds 1.6 per cent variation in NMR as the value of R^2 enhances to .408 in step 7. The contribution of safe drinking water in NMR is only 1.0 per cent as R^2 acquires the value of .418 in step 8 and both regression coefficient and F are significant at 1 per cent level of significance. The next variable in stepwise regression analysis enters as accessibility of bus-stand facility from their villages in step 9, which embodies only 0.4 per cent variation in NMR and both regression coefficient and F are significant at 1 per cent level of confidence. Another variable is enlisted as household with one room provision in step 10, which incorporates 0.3 per cent variation in NMR and it can be easily visualized through the value of coefficient of determination, which is .425. The next explanatory variable of NMR is the percentage of landless households in step 11, which predicts only 0.4 per cent variation in NMR and regression coefficient and F are significant at 1 per cent level of confidence. In step 12, the next variable enters as the share of mothers having the age between 20 and 30 years old, which explains 0.2 per cent variation in NMR as the value of R^2 increases to .431 and regression coefficient and F are significant at 1 per cent of confidence. Even in step 13, the value of R^2 remains the same value of step 12, i.e. .431, whereas the value of $\bar{R}^2$ has declined from .353 to .345. It simply means that the next variable of mother's age is not a dominant factor in explaining neonatal deaths. It also further reveals that share of mothers with breastfeeding within one day (X_4), share of immunized infant deaths (X_9), share of working mothers (X_5), productivity per acre (X_{16}), percentage of households having handpump and tap facilities (X_{10}), distance of bus-stand facility from village (X_{14}), percentage of households having house with one room provision (X_{11}) and percentage of landless households (X_{12}) are positively related with neonatal mortality rate whereas distance of medical centre from village (X_{15}), mother's literacy (X_1), proportion of mothers received antenatal care (X_6) and share of mother's age between 20 and 30 years (X_3) are positively associated with neonatal mortality rate among the PTGs in Jharkhand. These twelve variables taken together explain only 43.1 per cent variation in neonatal deaths

Table 6.2: Step-wise Regression between Neonatal Mortality Rate and Variables of Rural Development among the PTGs in Jharkhand

Variables	Intercept	R	t	R^2	$\bar{R}^2$	Increase in R^2	F	SE
Step 1								
X_4	232.19	-2.503	-4.478**	0.170	0.161		20.052**	0.559
Step 2								
X_4		-2.493	-4.777**					0.522
X_9	272.255	-0.795	3.927**	0.284	0.269	0.114	19.211**	0.202
Step 3								
X_4		-1.663	-2.744**					0.606
X_9		-0.787	-3.993**					0.197
X_5	352.057	-1.606	-2.517**	0.328	0.307	0.044	15.623**	0.638
Step 4								
X_4		-1.726	-2.883**					0.599
X_9		-0.76	-3.896**					0.195
X_5		-1.337	-2.074**					0.645
X_{15}	317.924	1.589	1.903**	0.353	0.325	0.025	12.943**	0.835

(Contd.)

Variables	Intercept	R	t	R^2	$\bar{R}^2$	Increase in R^2	F	SE
Step 5								
X_4		-2.135	-3.315**					0.644
X_9		-788	-4.06**					0.194
X_5		-1.393	-2.176**					0.64
X_{15}		1.53	1.847**					0.829
X_1	341.459	0.612	1.635*	0.371	0.337	0.018	11.072**	0.375
Step 6								
X_4		-2.178	-3.421**					0.637
X_9		-0.74	-3.827**					0.194
X_5		-1.253	-1.966**					0.637
X_{15}		1.563	1.909**					0.819
X_1		0.707	1.892**					0.374
X_{16}	346.911	-0.003	-1.821**	0.392	0.353	0.021	10.006**	0.002
Step 7								
X_4		-3.742	-3.167**					1.182
X_9		-0.779	-4.025**					0.194

(*Contd.*)

Variables	Intercept	R	t	R^2	$\bar{R}^2$	Increase in R^2	F	SE
X_5		-1.246	-1.97**					0.632
X_{15}		1.388	1.692**					0.82
X_1		0.663	1.782**					0.372
X_{16}		-0.004	-2.156**					0.002
X_6	366.42	1.47	1.567*	0.408	0.363	0.016	9.062**	0.938
Step 8								
X_4		-3.712	-3.151**					1.178
X_9		-0.743	-3.8**					0.195
X_5		-1.141	-1.794**					0.636
X_{15}		1.293	1.575*					0.821
X_1		0.58	1.54*					0.377
X_{16}		-0.005	-2.407**					0.002
X_6		1.494	1.597*					0.935
X_{10}	364.796	-0.165	-1.246*	0.418	0.367	0.01	8.171**	0.133
Step 9								
X_4		-3.793	-3.203**					1.186

(Contd.)

Variables	Intercept	R	t	R^2	$\bar{R}^2$	Increase in R^2	F	SE
X_9		-0.782	-3.88**					0.202
X_5		-1.14	-1.789**					0.637
X_{15}		1.593	1.758**					0.906
X_1		0.553	1.458*					0.379
X_{16}		-0.004	-2.201**					0.002
X_6		1.54	1.64*					0.939
X_{10}		-0.15	-1.122*					0.134
X_{14}	371.294	-0.443	-0.79*	0.422	0.364	0.004	7.302**	0.561
Step 10								
X_4		-3.897	-3.257**					1.196
X_9		0.755	-3.678**					0.205
X_5		-1.206	-1.869**					0.645
X_{15}		1.722	1.86**					0.925
X_1		0.551	1.45*					0.38
X_{16}		-0.004	-1.863**					0.002
X_6		1.63	1.717**					0.949

(*Contd.*)

Variables	Intercept	R	t	R^2	$\bar{R}^2$	Increase in R^2	F	SE
X_{10}		-0.123	-0.927*					0.138
X_{14}		-0.448	-0.797*					0.562
X_{11}	381.9	-0.15	-0.731*	0.425	0.361	0.003	6.592**	0.205
Step 11								
X_4		-4.146	-3.307**					1.254
X_9		-0.722	-3.414**					0.211
X_5		-1.076	-1.595*					0.674
X_{15}		1.602	1.696**					0.944
X_1		0.537	1.407*					0.382
X_{16}		-0.007	-1.381*					0.005
X_6		1.792	1.826**					0.981
X_{10}		-0.123	-0.885*					0.139
X_{14}		-0.395	-0.695*					0.569
X_{11}		-0.152	-0.739*					0.206
X_{12}	405.627	-0.329	-0.686*	0.429	0.357	0.004	5.999**	0.48

(Contd.)

Variables	Intercept	R	t	R^2	$\bar{R}^2$	Increase in R^2	F	SE
Step 12								
X_4		-4.114	-3.267**					1.259
X_9		-0.729	-3.43**					0.213
X_5		-1.146	-1.67**					0.686
X_{15}		1.555	1.636*					0.951
X_1		0.534	1.394*					0.383
X_{16}		-0.007	-1.373*					0.005
X_6		1.673	1.667**					1.003
X_{10}		-0.099	-0.688*					0.144
X_{14}		-0.456	-0.786*					0.58
X_{11}		-0.15	-0.727*					0.207
X_{12}		-0.329	-0.684*					0.482
X_3	405.159	0.34	0.614	0.431	0.353	0.002	5.492**	0.553

* Significant at 5 per cent level of significance.
** Significant at 1 per cent level of significance.

due to multicollinearity in explanatory variables among the primitive tribes in Jharkhand.

Post-Neonatal Mortality Rate of the PTG and Demographic, Infrastructural and Socio-Economic Variables

Table 6.3 illustrates all the details of demographic, infrastructural and socio-economic variables as predictor variables which influence the post-neonatal rate (PNMR) among the primitive tribes in Jharkhand through analytic results of stepwise regression. It is evident that the share of working mothers is the most important variable in determination of PNMR among the primitive tribes. This single variable explains 18.8 per cent variation in PNMR as the value of R^2 is .188. Both regression coefficient and F value are significant at 1 per cent level of confidence. The next variable is the share of immunized infant deaths, which explains 5.5 per cent variation in PNMR and the regression coefficient (β) is positively related with infant deaths. Both R^2 and $\bar{R}^2$ have increased from .188 and .179 to .243 and .227 respectively in 2nd step. The importance of the above variable is also enhanced because β and F are significant at 1 per cent level of confidence. It is followed by the share of mothers with early breastfeeding within one day, which contributes 5.4 per cent variation in PNMR but its regression is negatively related with the above variable and both the values of β and F are significant at 1 per cent level of confidence. The next variable lying in 4th step is the proportion of mothers having the age between 20 and 30 years, which adds up to 6.0 per cent variation in PNMR as the value of R^2 raises from .297 to .357 in this step. It is already described earlier that the infants of the primitive mothers aged less than 20 years are exposed to a higher-than-average risk of dying during the neonate period of their life whereas the infants of older mother are exposed to a higher-than-average risk of dying during the post-neonatal period.

The next variable enters in step 5 is the proportion of mothers received antenatal care, which alone accounts for 3.3 per cent variation in PNMR as the value of coefficient of determination swells to .390. Both the values of β and F are significant at 1 per cent level of confidence. It is further observed that poor nutrition during gestation period and unawareness of maternal health care led to bring forth a

Table 6.3: Step-wise Regression between Post-Neonatal Mortality Rate and Variables of Rural Development among the PTGs in Jharkhand

Variables	Intercept	R	t	R^2	$\bar{R}^2$	Increase in R^2	F	SE
Step 1								
X_5	261.736	-2.403	-4.757**	0.188	0.179		22.631**	0.505
Step 2								
X_5		-2.423	-4.944**					0.49
X_9	238.877	0.48	2.657**	0.243	0.227	0.055	15.544**	0.181
Step 3								
X_5		-1.584	-2.798**					0.566
X_9		0.478	2.731**					0.175
X_4	262.001	-1.464	-2.724**	0.297	0.275	0.054	13.522**	0.538
Step 4								
X_5		-1.761	-3.216**					0.547
X_9		0.474	2.819**					0.168
X_4		-1.839	-3.457**					0.532
X_3	254.782	1.314	2.974**	0.357	0.33	0.06	13.181**	0.442

(Contd.)

Variables	Intercept	R	t	R^2	$\bar{R}^2$	Increase in R^2	F	SE
Step 5								
X_5		-1.723	-3.214**					0.536
X_9		0.415	2.487**					0.167
X_4		-3.764	-3.779**					0.996
X_3		1.064	2.384**					0.446
X_6	277.035	1.827	2.267**	0.39	0.358	0.033	12.032**	0.806
Step 6								
X_5		-1.157	-1.931**					0.599
X_9		0.381	2.308**					0.165
X_4		-3.78	-3.854**					0.981
X_3		1.237	2.762**					0.448
X_6		1.683	2.112**					0.797
X_2	219.024	0.78	1.992**	0.415	0.377	0.025	11.005**	0.392
Step 7								
X_5		-1.291	-2.132**					0.605
X_9		0.359	2.17**					0.165

(*Contd.*)

Variables	Intercept	R	t	R^2	$\overline{R}^2$	Increase in R^2	F	SE
X_4		-3.883	-3.963**					0.98
X_3		1.357	2.981**					0.455
X_6		1.772	2.226**					0.796
X_2		0.836	2.131**					0.392
X_{15}	235.759	-0.948	-1.324*	0.426	0.382	0.011	9.759**	0.716
Step 8								
X_5		-1.058	-1.677**					0.631
X_9		0.372	2.252**					0.165
X_4		-3.842	-3.931**					0.977
X_3		1.171	2.453**					0.477
X_6		1.922	2.395**					0.803
X_2		1.172	2.476**					0.473
X_{15}		-1.079	-1.496*					0.721
X_{13}	209.936	-0.008	-1.26*	0.436	0.386	0.01	8.792**	0.006
Step 9								
X_5		-0.983	-1.561**					0.63

(Contd.)

Variables	Intercept	R	t	R^2	$\bar{R}^2$	Increase in R^2	F	SE
X_9		0.363	2.211**					0.164
X_4		-4.017	-4.102**					0.979
X_3		1.001	2.047**					0.489
X_6		1.904	2.386**					0.798
X_2		1.335	2.759**					0.484
X_{15}		-1.174	-1.63*					0.72
X_{13}		-0.013	-1.812**					0.007
X_1	215.221	0.52	1.444*	0.449	0.394	0.013	8.14**	0.36
Step 10								
X_5		-1.218	-1.865**					0.653
X_9		0.316	1.885**					0.168
X_4		-3.182	-2.721**					1.169
X_3		1.076	2.193**					0.491
X_6		1.738	2.158**					0.805
X_2		1.686	3.048**					0.553
X_{15}		-1.264	-1.753**					0.721

(Contd.)

Variables	Intercept	R	t	R^2	$\bar{R}^2$	Increase in R^2	F	SE
X_{13}		-0.016	-2.146**					0.007
X_1		0.623	1.695**					0.367
X_8	235.488	-20.095	-1.294*	0.459	0.398	0.01	7.548**	15.529
Step 11								
X_5		-1.366	-2.051**					0.666
X_9		0.288	1.702**					0.169
X_4		-2.729	-2.203**					1.239
X_3		1.022	2.075**					0.492
X_6		1.511	1.819**					0.83
X_2		1.742	3.14**					0.555
X_{15}		-1.265	-1.757**					0.72
X_{13}		-0.017	-2.306**					0.007
X_1		0.627	1.709**					0.367
X_8		-25.085	-1.552*					16.161
X_{16}	237.68	0.002	1.1*	0.466	0.4	0.007	6.988**	0.002

(Contd.)

Variables	Intercept	R	t	R^2	$\bar{R}^2$	Increase in R^2	F	SE
Step 12								
X_5		-1.431	-2.23**					0.664
X_9		0.245	1.441*					0.17
X_4		-2.516	-2.038**					1.235
X_3		0.98	2.006**					0.489
X_6		1.261	1.505*					0.838
X_2		1.737	3.157**					0.55
X_{15}		-1.092	-1.512*					0.722
X_{13}		-0.017	-2.355**					0.007
X_1		0.667	1.828**					0.365
X_8		-18.686	-1.132*					16.512
X_{16}		0.008	1.906**					0.004
X_{12}	176.592	0.656	1.599*	0.481	0.41	0.015	6.732**	0.41
Step 13								
X_5		-1.448	-2.181**					0.664
X_9		0.248	1.462*					0.17

(Contd.)

Variables	Intercept	R	t	R^2	$\bar{R}^2$	Increase in R^2	F	SE
X_4		-2.946	-2.283**					1.291
X_3		0.964	1.974**					0.488
X_6		1.686	1.838**					0.918
X_2		1.787	3.242**					0.551
X_{15}		-1.062	-1.473*					0.721
X_{13}		-0.017	-2.382**					0.007
X_1		0.739	1.999**					0.37
X_8		-22.762	-1.349*					16.878
X_{16}		0.011	2.217**					0.005
X_{12}		0.818	1.885**					0.434
X_7	151.417	0.33	1.128*	0.489	0.412	0.008	6.332**	0.293
Step 14								
X_5		-1.42	-2.134**					0.665
X_9		0.267	1.56*					0.171
X_4		-2.934	-2.27**					1.292
X_3		0.876	1.755**					0.499

(Contd.)

Variables	Intercept	R	t	R^2	$\bar{R}^2$	Increase in R^2	F	SE
X_6		1.752	1.901**					0.922
X_2		1.736	3.129**					0.555
X_{15}		-1.067	-1.477*					0.722
X_{13}		-0.017	-2.271**					0.007
X_1		0.682	1.815**					0.376
X_8		-23.72	-1.401*					16.935
X_{16}		0.011	2.228**					0.005
X_{12}		0.847	1.944**					0.436
X_7		0.359	1.215*					0.295
X_{10}	152.27	-0.103	0.88*	0.494	0.41	0.005	5.919**	0.117
Step 15								
X_5		-1.343	-1.978**					0.679
X_9		0.243	1.38*					0.176
X_4		-2.909	-2.241**					1.298
X_3		0.913	1.811**					0.504
X_6		1.726	1.863**					0.926

(Contd.)

Variables	Intercept	R	t	R^2	$\bar{R}^2$	Increase in R^2	F	SE
X_2		1.7882	3.173**					0.562
X_{15}		-1.161	-1.568*					0.74
X_{13}		-0.016	-2.155**					0.007
X_1		0.673	1.783**					0.377
X_8		-24.606	-1.443*					17.056
X_{16}		0.011	2.233**					0.005
X_{12}		0.874	1.989**					0.44
X_7		0.407	1.329*					0.306
X_{10}		-0.122	-1.004*					0.122
X_{11}	137.742	0.115	0.621	0.496	0.406	0.002	5.51**	0.185
Step 16								
X_5		-1.376	-2.004**					0.686
X_9		0.223	1.223*					0.183
X_4		-2.948	-2.255**					1.307
X_3		0.945	1.846**					0.512
X_6		1.748	1.876**					0.932

(*Contd.*)

Variables	Intercept	R	t	R^2	$\bar{R}^2$	Increase in R^2	F	SE
X_2		1.757	3.1**					0.567
X_{15}		-1.009	-1.231*					0.82
X_{13}		-0.016	-2.124**					0.008
X_1		0.661	1.739**					0.38
X_8		-24.897	-1.452*					17.151
X_{16}		0.012	2.263**					0.005
X_{12}		0.905	2.024**					0.447
X_7		0.425	1.37*					0.31
X_{10}		-0.115	0.932*					0.123
X_{11}		0.115	0.62					0.186
X_{14}	139.735	-0.217	-0.44	0.497	0.4	0.001	5.129**	0.493

** Significant at 1 per cent level of significance.
* Significant at 5 per cent level of significance.

weak baby, who is susceptible to die after sometime. The next variable in step 6 is the share of infant deaths with fourth and higher order of births, which captures 1 per cent variation in PNMR. It further substantiates that high level of unmet need of the children culminate into high level of post-neonate deaths. Even during survey, we came to notice from several mothers that unwanted pregnancies are common problem to all primitive tribe mothers.

This process is followed up to 16th step but when we enter from step 15 to step 16, there is a decline in $\bar{R}^2$. This indicates that the variables included till step 15 influence variations in PNMR. Further, the other variables, namely distance of medical centre, per capita income, mother's literacy, child-woman ratio, productivity of land, percentage of landless households, proportion of addicted mothers and percentage of households having handpump and tap facilities enter into 7th step, 8th step, 9th step, 10th step, 11th step, 12th step, 13th step and 14th step respectively in stepwise regression analysis and the above enlisted variables explain 1.1 per cent, 1.2 per cent, 1.3 per cent, 1,0 per cent, 0.7 per cent, 1.5 per cent, 0.8 per cent and 0.5 per cent respectively variation in PNMR. The last variable enters in step 15 is the percentage of households having house with one room provision, which positively related with PNMR. At this particular juncture, the values of R^2 and $\bar{R}^2$ are .496 and .406 and F is significant at 1 per cent whereas regression coefficient is significant at 5 per cent level of confidence. In sum, share of mother's age between 20 and 30 years, proportion of mothers received antenatal care, literacy of mother, productivity of land, percentage of landless households, proportion of addicted mothers and percentage of households with one room provision are positively associated with PNMR among the primitive tribes. On the contrary, share of working mothers, share of mothers with early breastfeed within one day, higher per capita income, child-woman ratio and households with safe drinking water are negatively associated with PNMR. Moreover, all these fifteen variables together explain only 49.6 per cent variation in PNMR due to multicollinearity in explanatory variables among the primitive tribes.

Infant Mortality Rate of the PTG and Demographic, Infrastructural and Socio-Economic Variables

Table 6.4 brings out details of analytic relationship between infant mortality rate (IMR) and various variables of rural development through step-wise regression analysis. The share of mothers with early breastfeeding within one day is the first and foremost variable in step 1, which also accounts for 29.1 per cent variation in IMR. Both regression coefficient and F are significant at 1 per cent level of confidence and β is negatively related with IMR. It confirms that the higher the share of mothers with early breastfeeding is the lower the share of infant mortality. This is particularly true with the primitive tribes that they usually give animal milk diluted with contaminated water to the new born babiesas first food for the first three days and they usually start breastfeeding after three days after performing certain ceremony. Thus, those new born babies are fortunate enough who get fist food as their mother's milk and they generally have low infant deaths. The inclusion of next variable is the share of working mother in step 2, which improves the overall fitness of equation considerably as the value of R^2 increases from .291 to .377 and $\bar{R}^2$ from .284 to .364. Both values of β and F of the above variable are significant at 1 per cent level of significance. It alone explains 8.6 per cent variation in IMR and its regression coefficient is negatively related with IMR. It is usually observed that females are actively engaged in economic activity among the primitive tribes and their participation emancipate the family from acute shortage of food and thereby reducing infant deaths.

Another variable, i.e. the share of mothers having age between 20 and 30 years enters into 3rd step of regression analysis as the value of R^2 and $\bar{R}^2$ increases from .337 to .426 and .364 to .408 respectively. It alone explains 4.9 per cent variation in IMR and its regression coefficient and F are significant at 1 per cent level of significance and it is also negatively associated with IMR. It clearly demonstrates that the reproductive age group for the primitive tribal female is quite reasonable between 20 and 30 years in context of lower child mortality. Again, the value of coefficient of determination enhances to .450 in 4th step for the mothers received antenatal care, which vividly illustrates that it alone encloses 2.4 per cent variation in IMR. Both the values

Table 6.4: Step-wise Regression between Infant Mortality Rate and Variables of Rural Development among the PTGs in Jharkhand

Variables	Intercept	R	t	R^2	$\bar{R}^2$	Increase in R^2	F	SE
Step 1								
X_4	437.654	-4.766	-6.35**	0.291	0.284		40.32**	0.751
Step 2								
X_4		-3.092	-3.665**					0.844
X_5	599.292	-3.236	-3.644**	0.377	0.364	0.086	29.323**	0.888
Step 3								
X_4		-3.662	-4.372**					0.838
X_5		-3.505	-4.067**					0.862
X_3	588.047	1.998	2.872**	0.426	0.408	0.049	23.759**	0.696
Step 4								
X_4		-6.368	-4.079**					1.561
X_5		-3.457	-4.075**					0.848
X_3		1.645	2.33**					0.706
X_6	615.358	2.57	2.041**	0.45	0.427	0.024	19.447**	1.259

(Contd.)

Variables	Intercept	R	t	R^2	$\bar{R}^2$	Increase in R^2	F	SE
Step 5								
X_4		-6.312	-4.079**					1.547
X_5		-3.249	-3.824**					0.85
X_3		1.305	1.791**					0.728
X_6		2.595	2.08**					1.248
X_{10}	617.141	-0.296	-1.667**	0.466	0.438	0.016	16.405**	0.178
Step 6								
X_4		-6.865	-4.369**					1.571
X_5		-3.03	-3.552**					0.853
X_3		1.316	1.823**					0.722
X_6		3.12	2.44**					1.279
X_{10}		-0.366	-2.021**					0.181
X_{16}	628.639	-0.004	-1.623*	0.481	0.447	0.015	14.348**	0.003
Step 7								
X_4		-6.918	-4.436**					1.56
X_5		-2.327	-2.431**					0.957

(*Contd.*)

Variables	Intercept	R	t	R^2	$\bar{R}^2$	Increase in R^2	F	SE
X_3		1.578	2.145**					0.736
X_6		2.964	2.329**					1.272
X_{10}		-0.339	-1.877**					0.181
X_{16}		-0.005	-1.807**					0.003
X_2	555.018	0.973	1.571*	0.494	0.456	0.013	12.845**	0.619
Step 8								
X_4		-7.169	-4.596**					1.56
X_5		-2.284	-2.399**					0.952
X_3		1.601	2.188**					0.731
X_6		3.168	2.489**					1.273
X_{10}		-0.3	-1.652*					0.182
X_{16}		-0.004	-1.613*					0.003
X_2		1.065	1.722**					0.619
X_9	567.562	-0.38	-1.454*	0.506	0.462	0.012	11.639**	0.261
Step 9								
X_4		-7.48	-4.771**					1.568

(Contd.)

Variables	Intercept	R	t	R^2	$\bar{R}^2$	Increase in R^2	F	SE
X_5		-2.381	-2.507**					0.95
X_3		1.589	2.184**					0.728
X_6		3.034	2.39**					1.27
X_{10}		-0.258	-1.407*					0.183
X_{16}		-0.004	-1.704**					0.003
X_2		1.022	1.659*					0.616
X_9		-0.407	-1.563*					0.26
X_1	595.143	0.7	1.393*	0.516	0.468	0.01	10.669**	0.502
Step 10								
X_4		-7.481	-4.775**					1.567
X_5		-2.073	-2.09**					0.992
X_3		1.278	1.63*					0.784
X_6		3.138	2.466**					1.273
X_{10}		-0.23	-1.244*					0.185
X_{16}		-0.004	-1.57*					0.003
X_2		1.489	1.968**					0.757

(Contd.)

Variables	Intercept	R	t	R^2	$\bar{R}^2$	Increase in R^2	F	SE
X_9		-0.401	-1.539*					0.26
X_1		1	1.736**					0.576
X_{13}	564.448	-0.012	-1.062*	0.522	0.469	0.006	9.728**	0.011
Step 11								
X_4		-6.473	-3.309**					1.956
X_5		-2.35	-2.251**					1.044
X_3		1.32	1.678**					0.787
X_6		2.886	2.206**					1.308
X_{10}		-0.238	-1.285*					0.185
X_{16}		-0.003	-1.285*					0.003
X_2		1.845	2.138**					0.863
X_9		-0.454	-1.694**					0.268
X_1		1.096	1.865**					0.588
X_{13}		-0.015	-1.293*					0.012
X_8	584.622	-21.916	-0.862*	0.526	0.467	0.004	8.886**	25.433

(Contd.)

Variables	Intercept	R	t	R^2	$\bar{R}^2$	Increase in R^2	F	SE
Step 12								
X_4		-6.95	-3.368**					2.063
X_5		-2.283	-2.173**					1.051
X_3		1.303	1.651*					0.789
X_6		3.375	2.301**					1.467
X_{10}		-0.251	-1.342*					0.187
X_{16}		-0.002	-0.638*					0.003
X_2		1.887	2.177**					0.867
X_9		-0.437	-1.622*					0.27
X_1		1.15	1.937**					0.594
X_{13}		-0.015	-1.29*					0.012
X_8		-27.629	-1.038*					26.629
X_7	574.876	0.33	0.744*	0.529	0.464	0.003	8.15**	0.433
Step 13								
X_4		-6.955	-3.363**					2.068
X_5		-2.366	-2.235**					1.059

(Contd.)

Variables	Intercept	R	t	R^2	$\bar{R}^2$	Increase in R^2	F	SE
X_3		1.269	1.602*					0.792
X_6		3.369	2.292**					1.47
X_{10}		-0.262	-1.395*					0.188
X_{16}		0.003	0.433*					0.008
X_2		1.917	2.203**					0.87
X_9		-0.468	-1.715**					0.273
X_1		1.205	2.011**					0.599
X_{13}		-0.015	-1.32*					0.012
X_8		-24.909	-0.925*					26.926
X_7		0.452	0.957*					0.472
X_{12}	524.418	0.529	0.768*	0.532	0.462	0.003	7.533**	0.689
Step 14								
X_4		-7.066	-3.4**					2.078
X_5		-2.486	-2.317**					1.073
X_3		1.381	1.71**					0.807
X_6		3.467	2.343**					1.479

(Contd.)

Variables	Intercept	R	t	R^2	$\bar{R}^2$	Increase in R^2	F	SE
								0.19
X_{10}		-0.244	-1.289*					0.008
X_{16}		0.004	0.545					0.872
X_{2}		1.914	2.195**					0.284
X_{9}		0.525	-1.851**					0.601
X_{1}		1.193	1.986**					0.012
X_{13}		-0.016	-1.347*					27.087
X_{8}		-26.652	-0.984*					0.476
X_{7}		0.492	1.033*					0.693
X_{12}		0.57	0.823*					0.709
X_{14}	538.661	-0.542	-0.765*	0.536	0.459	0.004	7.003**	
Step 15								
X_{4}		-7.078	-3.389**					2.088
X_{5}		-2.46	-2.28**					1.079
X_{3}		1.36	1.675**					0.812
X_{6}		3.431	2.306**					1.488

(Contd.)

Variables	Intercept	R	t	R^2	$\bar{R}^2$	Increase in R^2	F	SE
X_{10}		-0.239	-1.25*					0.191
X_{16}		0.005	0.629					0.008
X_{2}		1.823	2.029**					0.899
X_{9}		-0.53	-1.856**					0.285
X_{1}		1.163	1.915**					0.607
X_{13}		-0.015	-1.235*					0.012
X_{8}		-25.56	-0.936*					27.319
X_{7}		0.512	1.066*					0.48
X_{12}		0.636	0.895*					0.711
X_{14}		-0.696	-0.883*					0.788
X_{15}	528.452	0.588	0.457	0.537	0.454	0.001	6.489**	1.288

** Significant at 1 per cent level of significance.
* Significant at 5 per cent level of significance.

of β and F are significant at 1 per cent level of confidence. The next variable in explanation of IMR is the percentage of households with safe drinking water facility, which alone contributes 1.6 per cent variation in IMR as the value of R^2 raises up to .466 in step 5. Safe drinking water is burning problem of primitive tribes and even new-born babies are given contaminated water of either ponds or streams. Both the values β and F are significant at this juncture. It is followed by productivity of land in step 6 wherein it safely incorporates 1.5 per cent variation in IMR as the value of coefficient of determination raises to .481. At this juncture the values of β and F are also significant at 1 per cent level of significance. In fact, productivity of land is the lowest in their territories due to heavy dependence on rainfed crops wherein primitive method of cultivation is carried out as there is no provision of irrigation in their lands.

Again, in step 7, the prevailing condition is more or less the same wherein the share of infant deaths with fourth and higher order of births contributes 1.3 per cent variation in IMR separately as the value of R^2 increases from .481 to .494. The subsequent variable enters in step 8 is the share of immunized infant deaths, which contains 1.2 per cent variation in IMR independently as the value of R^2 increases from .494 to .506. It is followed by literacy, which explains 1 per cent variation in IMR as the value of R^2 acquires .516 in step 9. The value of β is significant at 5 per cent level of confidence. The remaining variables from step 10 to step 14 contribute less than 1 per cent variation in IMR. Simultaneously, regression coefficients and F values are also significant at various levels. The variables, namely per capita income, child-woman ratio, proportion of addicted mothers, percentage of landless households, distance of village from bus-stand explains 0.6 per cent, 0.4 per cent, 0.3 per cent, 0.3 per cent, 0.4 per cent variation in IMR, which are vividly depicted in the table. The first two and the last variable are negatively related with IMR, on the contrary other two variables are positively associated with IMR. The last variable namely distance of village from medical centre amenity contributes only 0.1 per cent variation in IMR as the value of R^2 has increased from .536 to .530 in 15th step. The regression coefficient is significant at 5 per cent whereas F is significant at 1 per cent level of confidence. In step 16, the value of $\bar{R}^2$ get decline from .454 to .447 whereas the value of R^2 remains constant, i.e. .537. It clearly divulges that the role of households with one room provision is negligible in explanation of IMR.

In a nutshell, the variables, namely share of mothers with breastfeeding within one day (X_4), share of working mothers (X_5), child-woman ratio (X_8), share of immunized infant deaths (X_9), percentage of households having handpump and tap facilities (X_{10}), Productivity per acre (X_{16}), per capita income in rupees (X_{13}), distance of bus-stand facility from village (X_{14}) reduce infant mortality rate. On the contrary, the variables, namely share of mother's age between 20 and 30 years (X_3), proportion of mothers received antenatal care (X_6), share of infants with fourth and higher order of births (X_2), mother's literacy (X_1), percentage of addicted mothers (X_7), percentage of landless households (X_{12}), and distance of medical centre from village (X_{15}) accelerate the quantity of child demise. However, all these 15 variables taken together explain only 53.7 per cent variation in IMR among the primitive tribes in the state due to multi-collinearity.

Explanatory Variables under Binary Logistic Regression Analysis

Explanatory variables of infant mortality vary from region to region and also within the region. They vary depending on the socio-economic, infrastructural, demographic and cultural factors. Infant death occurs in response to a wide range of factors, which affect different children in different ways, and to which people do not necessarily respond in an identical fashion. The inclusion of an explanatory variable depends on its importance and the availability of its measurement. The selection of independent variables used in the present study is the product of the scale of investigation, the availability of data and results of similar studies in the past as gleaned from the existing literature, which explains the alarming rate of very high demise of the primitive tribal children in the state. Different needs and techniques have been evolved to study the quality of infant deaths among the primitive tribal groups in Jharkhand but the present study is limited to only binary logistic regression analysis for explaining the determinants of infant deaths

(Kumar, 2005). The binary logistic regression technique facilities in eliciting the effects of several predictor variables, which may be qualitative, categorical or mixture of the two on the response variable, which has only two categories.

The dependent variable (response variable) used in the regression model in this chapter being qualitative in nature are dummy variable (also called dichotomous variable, binary variable or contrast variable). The qualitative variables, called dummy variables are a device of incorporating into the regression model variables, which cannot be quantified and which are used to represent yes-no-type response. In a logistic regression model, we assume that P (probability of occurrence of events) is related to the independent variables in the form of logistic function instead of a linear function. It is used to access the net effect of socio-economic, infrastructural, demographic and cultural factors on infant mortality. P is the estimated probability of child deaths. The quantity P/(1-P) is called the odds, hence the quantifying log {P/(1-P)} is called the log odds or the logit of P. The logit regression coefficient for a category of variable is interpreted in relation to the reference category and exp (β) gives the 'odd ratio' ratio of the odds for the specified category to the odds of the reference category. This technique has been used to determine the predictors for the infant mortality, which are dichotomous dependent variables. Probability of infant mortality is estimated with a dichotomous dependent variable taking on the value of 1 for inclusive group, if there is an infant death or 0 for control group, if there is no infant death. The sample for infant deaths among the primitive tribal groups are composed 514 children whereas those who survived consist of 1725 children in Jharkhand at the time of survey. All the selected independent variables explain 49.3 in infant deaths among the PTG in the state through Nagelkerk R Square logistic regression technique. The important independent variables explaining the dependent variables of infant mortality rate among the PTG in Jharkhand are given in Table 6.5. All independent variables are in categorical form whereas dependent variables are of dichotomous nature.

Table 6.5: Result of Logistic Regression for IMR among the PTGs in Jharkhand

	Variable	Coefficient	S.E.	Odd Ratio
A.	Birth Order of Child			
	4th and Higher Order of Birth			**
	1st Order of Birth	-0.041	0.305	0.96*
	2nd Order of Birth	-1.151	0.329	0.316**
	3rd Order of Birth	-1.98	0.337	0.138**
B.	Mother's Age at Child Birth			
	Below 20 Years			**
	20-30 Years	-1.282	0.328	0.277**
	Above 30 Years	1.085	0.391	2.958**
C.	Attendant at Birth			
	Husband and Children (None)			**
	Dais	-2.307	0.735	0.1**
	Lady Family Member	-0.405	0.77	0.667*
D.	Breastfeeding			
	Breastfeeding within 1 Day			**
	Breastfeeding after 1 Day	1.052	0.486	2.864**
E.	Food Sufficiency during Gestation Period			
	Sufficient			**
	Moderate	0.357	0.493	1.43*
	Insufficient	1.326	0.479	3.766**
F.	Size of Households			
	Small (< 4 Persons)			**
	Medium (5-7 Persons)	2.171	0.293	8.766**
	Large (8-10 Persons)	2.321	0.344	10.186**

(*Contd.*)

	Variable	Coefficient	S.E.	Odd Ratio
G.	Sources of Drinking Water			
	Handpump and Running Tap			**
	Well	0.155	0.223	1.168*
	Pond, Stream and *Chua*	0.463	0.214	1.589**
H.	Mother's Education			
	Illiterate			**
	Literate	-0.139	0.29	0.87*
I.	Income			
	Middle Income Group (> 800 Rupees)			**
	Lower Income Group (400-800 Rupees)	0.396	0.26	1.486*
	Lowest Income Group (< 400 Rupees)	0.711	0.422	2.036**
	N	514		
	Constant	-0.215		
	2 Log Likelihood Ratio	825.827		
	Nagelkerke R Square	0.493		

Significance level **P < .001.

Significance level *P < .005.

Birth Order of Child

The prevalence of high infant mortality rate among the later born has already been well documented earlier and provided the basis for the classical approach to the planned parenthood movement. In a general sense a reduction in child-woman ratio, implying a reduction in higher order births would lead to a lowering of the overall infant mortality rate. It was observed that women who gave a smaller number of births, their children were healthier than the mother who gave more births and this means that children at fourth and higher orders are at disadvantageous position as almost all mothers are half fed. Most of them are the results of unwanted pregnancies. The fourth and higher order of births among the PTGs in Jharkhand have been considered as reference category. The odd ratio of infant mortality for all other birth order, viz. second and third are significant at 1 per cent level of significance. The children in the first order of births have 4 per cent less likely to die in compare to fourth and higher order of births among the PTGs in Jharkhand.The situation gets further ameliorated in case of the children born in second order of birth, who have 68 per cent less likely to depart their lives than the higher order of births. Lastly, the chances of survival rate are very high in case of third order of children, who are 86 per cent less likely to cut down their lives in compare to high order of births. Thus, it is crystal cut clear that the level of infant mortality is at lower risk for second and third order of births among the children of PTG. Nevertheless, it also refutes that the first order of child is at the greatest risk, which is universally observed in almost all the cultures.

Mother's Age at Child Birth

The next influential parameter for infant mortality among the PTGs in Jharkhand has been examined here as mother's age at child birth considered of those mothers, who are found below the age of 20 years. The odd ratio is significant at 1 per cent in all three categories of mother's age at child birth, viz. below 20, 20-30 and above 30 years. The value of regression coefficient is negative for those mothers, who have in age between 20 and 30 years whereas it is positively related with the mothers having the age above 30 years. It is found that the children born to mothers in the age group between 20 and 30 years are 72 per cent less likely to die than the children born to mothers aged less than 20 years. Nevertheless, the children of the mothers aged above 30 years are around 3 times more likely to die than the children of under-aged mothers.

The above analysis explicitly manifests that the children are at high risk of deaths when they are born from the mothers aged above 30 years. As a result, it is an accepted part of received wisdom that the IMR shows a U-shaped relationship with the age of mother among PTG in Jharkhand. A very young mother is biologically not fully mature so that the probability of pregnancy-related complications is high. On the other hand, beyond the age of 30 years, the risk of pregnancy complications apparently increases because of the increasing inflexibility of the female reproductive organ due to their ill fed and starvation. Simultaneously, they have to take care of more what existing children in this age group. and the new born babies are neglected in the quality of infant care by the parents due to their limited resources. That is why, a slightly high proportion of small children die during their infancy among the PTGs in the states.

Attendant at Birth

Child births in rural areas of primitive society in Jharkhand are attended to mostly by the untrained dais. In some cases, the family members assist the pregnant women during the deliveries. However, when the houses are located far away from the village in the midst of dense forest, no one except husband remains in the house during the period of delivery, the children are brought forth without any help from other ladies and that kind of deliveries are recognised as the reference category. All three categories of attendants are significant at 5 per cent level of confidence and regression coefficients of the above variables are negatively associated with the infant mortality. So far odd ratio is concerned, it illustrates that whenever the deliveries are conducted by the dais, there are 90 per cent of less chances of infant deaths than the circumstances when no one except husband remains during the delivery period. In another situation, the children have 33 per cent less likely to die, while some experienced female members are available during that crucial period of deliveries than none. It is, therefore, our objective should be to recruit local untrained dais for the training purposes so that such measures of reorientation and training will help them for rendering better service in these isolated and remote villages usually found in the midst of tribal dominated rural parts of the state. Again, every pregnant woman should be given delivery kit so that they should not force to bring forth the new-born in unhygienic condition. Jejeebhoy (1997) has rightly remarked that very few women have access to antenatal care and untrained attendants conduct a majority of deliveries in unhygienic condition.

Breastfeeding

Breast milk constitutes the principal source of nutrition and anti-infective defence for infants. It acts as a protection against common childhood diseases like diarrhoea and pneumonia and may also have long-term health benefits such as reducing the risk of overweight and obesity in childhood and adolescence. Therefore, WHO recommends initiation of breastfeeding as soon as possible after childbirth within the first hour after delivery? Unfortunately, majority of infants among the PTGs in Jharkhand are deprived of the highly nutritious first milk, viz. colostrum and antibodies it contains. The new born babies are generally offered animal milk mixed with contaminated water and honey as their first prelacteal feed and they generally introduce breastfeeding after throwing away colostrum within few days.

That is why, only two categories have been constructed for breastfeeding. The first group comprise those children who were given mother's milk as their first food within one day and another group consist of those unfortunate babies, who were deprived of it within the stipulated period of time. The former group is taken as reference category and odd ratio is significant at 5 per cent level of confidence. It is further noticed that infant mortality rate is 2.9 times higher among those primitive children, who were given mother's milk after one day in comparison to the children who were offered mother's milk within one day. Thus, delayed practice of introducing mother's milk and offering animal milk and honey diluted with contaminated water are mainly responsible for very high infant mortality among the primitive tribes in Jharkhand. It is rightly said that breastfeeding including early start of breastfeeding with colostrum feeding is the right of children.

Food Sufficiency

It is generally understood that the women should eat healthier and sufficient food during lactation and gestation period and poor nutritious will have an adverse effect on the physical condition and development of the foetus and is largely responsible for the high incidence of infant mortality rate. Again, it is observed that those who enjoyed superior physical condition and good diets during pregnancy brought forth babies in excellent conditions. In fact, access to good nutrition is a necessary condition for mothers to produce a healthy child. As a matter of fact, that food sufficiency for mother is also an essential requirement for a healthy child during lactation period. That is why, the sufficient food eaten by the mother during gestation period is considered as the reference category. The odd ratios are significant for both kinds of mothers, who had taken either moderate or insufficient food during gestation period. At the same time regression coefficients of the above two types of mothers are also positively associated with IMR. It explicitly manifests that the mothers who are consuming moderate kind of food during their gestation period, the chances of their offspring to pass away are 1.4 times higher than the mothers with sufficient food among the PTGs in Jharkhand. That kind of relationship is further established in case of those children who were born from such unfortunate mothers who were half fed and half dressed. The probability of infant deaths is increased to 3.8 times higher among the off springs of ill-fed mothers. Thus, consumption of sufficient food by the mothers during gestation period is the first and foremost requirement for antenatal care.

Size of Households

The next important parameter for determining the intensity of IMR is considered as the size of households. It is usually conceived that the small size of household plays a deterrent to IMR. It is owing to the fact that almost all primitive tribal people live in nuclear kind of family with extremely limited resources. That is why, infant deaths with small size of households are considered as reference category and odd ratios are observed to be significant at 1 per cent level of confidence. The regression coefficients of medium and large size of households are 8.8 and 10.2 times more likely to end their lives than children with small size of household. Thus, it can be easily concluded that the children of primitive tribal people with 5 to 10 members in a household have the maximum potentiality of IMR. It simply implies that the poor PTG can not afford a large family since most of them have limited land and resource. Low return from land is further aggravated through their poor quality of soil, poor techniques of cultivation and the ever-increasing burden of indebtedness.

Sources of Drinking Water

Safe drinking water and its continuous supply in the localities of primitive tribes is a big challenge due to its geo-climatic position. Here, there is a lack of perennial rivers and very poor stock of underground water. Again, the high concentration of iron, fluoride and arsenic in water has an adverse impact on the water quality and children health in their localities. Water for drinking must be safe and clean. The polluted water causes many diseases like diarrhoea, jaundice, gastro intestinal disorder etc. The children are especially susceptible to these diseases. Therefore, safe drinking water is crucial for the well-being of children. Water taken from uncovered pond or well is likely to be unsafe and may causes the diseases. In fact, safe drinking is a prerequisite for the eradication of water borne diseases among the children of primitive tribes.

There are mainly three sources of water in the localities of PTG in which hand pump and running tap, which are considered as the safest sources of drinking water have been considered as reference category so that its impact on IMR can be examined with other sources of water, i.e. well and natural water of pond, stream and *chua* are positively related with IMR. Again, odd ratio of former source of water is significant at 5 per cent level of confidence whereas odd ratio of later source is significant at 1 per cent level of confidence. The infant death rate among the children of PTG households have 1.2 times more probability of their departure from earthly lives than children of those households where people acquire drinking water from hand pump and running tap. It is further visualised that children consuming natural water of pond, stream and *chua* have 1.6 times higher mortality rate than children drinking from hand pump and running tap water. It has already been discussed earlier that natural water is usually contaminated with larvae of mosquitoes, which enhances IMR among the children of PTG in the state. Hasnain (2013) rightly remarked that the tribes suffer from many chronic diseases but the most prevalent taking heavy toll of them are water-borne. This is mainly due to the very poor drinking water supply. Even when it is available in plenty, it is mostly dirty and contaminated and consequently the children of tribes are easily susceptible to intestinal diseases. Water is further polluted as people bathe or wash their cloths or animal or defecate near the source of water. Some primitive families also do not know how to store it properly.

Mother's Education

Mother's education is the most crucial determinant in social development approach, which finally reduces infant mortality. It is a tool, which helps them to break some of the traditional norms and makes them more independent in taking decisions within the family situation. It raises the opportunity cost of women's time and generally opens up greater opportunities for women that often conflict with repeated child bearing. Subsequently, infant feeding, clothing and treatment of common ailments are generally carried out scientifically by the educated mother. Further, educated mother may be more receptive to modern social norms and family planning campaigns, which ultimately reduces infant mortality. That is why, primitive mothers belonging to illiterate category are considered as a reference category. The odd ratio is insignificant for literate primitive mothers and regression coefficient also bears negative relationship with IMR. It is further noticed that the children of educated mothers are 13 per cent less likely to die than the children of illiterate mothers. Hussain (1970) rightly remarked that a host of studies have shown negative relationship between female education and IMR. The relationship is created by education affecting the life style and value system, contraceptive knowledge and use and economic activity. As a matter of fact, this is one most important variable, which creates chain effect on all desirable components of economic, social and demographic development.

Per Capita Annual Income

Several economic indices are devised to measure individual's needs. In this regard, per capita income is considered more a telling index than its absolute because it is dirctly associated with public health and standard of living. It plays a crucial rate because a number of factors like food, hygiene, sanitation affordability of medical aid and son and so forth influences infant mortality among the PTGs in Jharkhand, where people often suffer from want of money. Per capita yearly income level of PTG has been classified here into three groups: the middle-income group (above 800 rupees monthly), lower income group (between 400 and 800 rupees) and very low-income group (below 400 rupees). It is a widespread notion that the middle-income group people can hire private medical facility. Consequently, IMR is generally found low in this category of people. That is why, people with middle income group are considered as reference category. The regression coefficients with later two groups are positively associated with IMR. The odd ratios of both lower income group and very lower income group are significant at 1 per cent level of confidence. It is conceived that IMR in lower income group households is 1.5 times higher than the middle-income group households. That kind of predicament is further deteriorated in very lower income households where IMR is 2 times bigger than the middle-income group of households. It clearly elucidates that income level of households among the PTGs in Jharkhand is the main deterrent for high infant deaths.

Summary

The relationship between infant deaths and various variables of rural development have been established through correlation matrix, step-wise regression and binary logistic analysis. On the one hand, neonatal mortality is negatively influenced by early breastfeeding of babies, economic participation of mother, antenatal care, immunization of children and productivity of land whereas it is positively associated with the distance of medical centres from their villages. The variables namely breastfeeding within one day, mother's economic participation, antenatal care is responsible for high PNMR among the PTGs. However, infant deaths with fourth and higher order of births and immunized infant deaths largely contribute for high PNMR. Simultaneously, IMR is negatively affected with early breastfeeding, economic participation of mother, antenatal care, and safe drinking water but it is positively correlated with higher order of birth.

The regression analysis illustrates that early breastfeeding, immunized infant deaths, mother's economic participation, distance of medical centre, mother's education and productivity of land etc. explain 43.1 per cent variation in neonatal deaths among the primitive tribes in Jharkhand. Simultaneously, around 50 per cent variation in PNMR is accounted for by the proportion of young mothers, proportion of mothers received antenatal care, literacy of mother, productivity of land, percentage of landless households, share of working mothers, early breastfeeding, higher per capita income, child-woman ratio and households with safe drinking water and so on and so forth. In addition to above mentioned variables of PNMR, safe drinking water, share of immunized children, availability of transport and medical facility, higher order of births, mother's literacy etc.

explain more than 53 per cent variation in IMR among the children of PTGs in Jharkhand.

It is evident from the preceding discussion that children at fourth and higher orders have highest incidences of infant deaths as they are at disadvantageous position as almost all mothers are half-fed among the PTGs in Jharkhand. With regard to mother's age at child birth it is found that the children born to mothers in the age group between 20 and 30 years are 72 per cent less likely to die than the children born to mothers aged less than 20 years. In case of attendant at birth it is observed that whenever the deliveries are conducted by the *dais*, there are 90 per cent of less chances of infant deaths than the circumstances when no one except husband remains during the delivery period since no doctor remains present during that crucial period of time. So far, the role of breastfeeding is noticed that infant mortality rate is 2.9 times higher among those primitive children, who were given mother's milk after one day in comparison to the children who were offered mother's milk within one day. The determination of sufficient intake during gestation period reveals that the probability of infant deaths is increased to 3.8 times higher among the off springs of ill-fed mothers. The next parameter, namely size of household manifests that children of medium and large size of households are 8.8 and10.2 times more likely to end their lives than children with small size of household. Another parameter, namely sources of drinking water exhibit that children consuming natural water of pond, stream and *chua* have 1.6 times higher mortality rate than children drinking from hand pump and running tap water. The subsequent parameter of mother's education points out that the children of educated mothers are 13 per cent less likely to die than the children of illiterate mothers. The last parameter of income suggests that the incidences of infant deaths are 2 times higher in poor income group than the middle-income group. Thus, immediate breastfeeding, safe drinking water, mother's age at child birth in the age group of 20 to 30 years, high per capita income, availability of nurses and *dais*, high proportion of educated mothers, small size of households, reduction in high order of child births and antenatal care of mothers may drastically reduce the infant mortality rate among the PTGs in Jharkhand.

REFERENCES

Hasnain, N. (2013). *Indian Society and Culture: Continuity and Change*, New Delhi: Jawahar Publishers and Distributions, pp. 63-64.

Hasnain, N. (2013). *op. cit.*, p. 314.

Hussain, I.Z. (1970). "Educational Status and Differentials Fertility in India", *Social Biology*, 17 (3), p. 133.

Jejeebhoy, J.S. (1997). "Addressing Women's Reproductive Health Needs Priorities for the Family Welfare Programme", *Economic and Political Weekly*, Bombay, pp. 475-474.

Kumar, S. (2005). *op. cit.*, pp. 216-222.

Kumar, S. (2020). "A Geographical Analysis of Rural Male Out-Migration: A Case Study of Bhagalpur District", in A. Banerjee, N.C. Jana and V.K. Mishra (eds.), Singapore: Springer, pp. 331-335.

UNICEF (1985). *The State of Asian Children: Pre-Congress Symposium on Social Paediatrics*, New Delhi: UNICEF.

UNICEF (1991). *Children and Women in India—A Situational Analysis*, India: UNICEF, p.14.

Vidyarthi, L.P. (1969). *Cultural Configuration of Ranchi*, Calcutta: J.N. Basu and Co., pp. 101-105.

7
Conclusion

The present study under its Head *Infant Mortality among Primitive Tribal Groups in Jharkhand* investigates the reasons and consequences behind unexpected and unnoticed very high death rate among the siblings of the primitive tribal groups in Jharkhand; thereby declining and stagnating the population of the above groups in the state on the basis of primary and secondary data. Under the present scheme of investigation, it addresses six basic issues related to the child deaths:

(i) Spatial distribution of scheduled tribes in general and primitive tribal groups in particular on the basis of secondary sources of data;
(ii) Demographic and socio-economic profile of infant deaths among the PTG;
(iii) Availability of infrastructural facilities;
(iv) Assessment and regional pattern of infant deaths;
(v) Health, hygiene, sanitation and diseases among the children of PTG; and
(vi) Determinants of infant mortality.

Although the detailed findings have been provided in the summary of every chapter, some of the major ones have been synthesized here to provide an overall view of the facts and arguments.

Summary

The first chapter analysis includes origin of the research problem, literature survey, objectives, hypotheses, sample design and database, research method, introduction to study areas, spatial distribution of scheduled tribes in Jharkhand, significance of the study and plan of the study so that scientific study can be carried out smoothly.

The second chapter deals with spatial distribution pattern, growth and concentration of the primitive tribes in the state on the basis of census data at district level whereas micro level study at block level is based upon the survey conducted by Ministry of Welfare, Government of Jharkhand. First of all, it deals with the physical characteristics and composition of scheduled tribes in general and primitive tribal groups in particular. Almost all primitive tribes belong to Proto-Australoid racial groups and by and large they speak languages of either Austro-Asiatic or Dravidian families. Its historical nomenclature has also been discussed. The physical traits, racial characteristics, linguistic composition and trend of growth of each primitive tribe, viz. the Asurs, the Birjias, the Korwas, the Parhaiyas, the Mal Pahaias, the Sauria Paharias, the Savars, the Birhors have been thoroughly investigated in the present-day context. It deals with separate and composite distribution of all eight primitive tribes in Jharkhand and it is found that every PTG is agglomerated in particular area of the state.

The district level analysis reveals that the Asurs and the Birjias are primarily found in Gumla and Latehar districts of the Pat region whereas the Korwas and the Parhaiyas are basically concentrated in Garhwa, Palamu and Latehar districts in the north-western part of the state. So far, the concentration of the Sauria Paharias and the Mal Paharias is concerned; they are exclusively confined to Damin-i-Koh of Santhal Pargana. Under the similar pattern of isolation, the Savars have their habitation in the Dhalbhum region of Purbi Singhbhum. However, the Birjias are noticed throughout the areas of Chotanagpur Plateau due to their nomadic habit but more than 50 per cent of population are agglomerated in Chatra, Hazaribagh and Kodarma of the Outer Plateau. The decadal growth of the PTGs manifests that barring the negative growth in 1901 and 1921 Censuses, the growth rate of PTGs remained either quite slow or stagnant up to 2001, but a phenomenal increase in their population was manifested in 2011 Census, which is the result of carving out Jharkhand as separate state in 2001. The geographical concentration of the above-mentioned tribes has been identified through the application of location quotient, which clearly demonstrates that the highest concentration of primitive tribes is exclusively confined to the Damin-i-Koh region, the Pat region, the North Koel-Kanhar Interfluvial Upland and the Dhalbhum Hills whereas the lowest level of concentration is mainly centred in and around the Damodar Basin and the Central Plateau Region, where mining, industrial and service sectors play an important role for the livelihood of people. Moreover, high concentration of the PTGs is confined to Damin-i-Koh and Pat region.

The third chapter is based on the primary data for the analysis of '**Demographic and Socio-Economic Profile and Infrastructural Facilities**' among the PTGs in Jharkhand. Mother's age at child birth, birth order of children and marriage age have been cross-examined by neonatal, post-neonatal and infant mortality rate. The noteworthy point which to our view is that it is not a welcome step to bring forth a new baby by the PTG mother after the age of 30 year old, when the infant mortality escalates to 300 per thousand live births. It may be due to the early start of child bearing accompanied with malnutrition. So far birth order is concerned, the highest IMR is found in fourth and higher order of birth and lowest in third order of birth. It must, however, be noted that the highest early neonate mortality is found in 1st order of birth. The female is considered as confounding variable, which clearly demonstrates that all three components of infant deaths decline with the increase in age of female marriage but early female marriage is a common practice among them. Under the social characteristics mother's education, size of household, type of family and religion have been incorporated for the evaluation of infant deaths. It is noteworthy to point that illiteracy, large size of households; single parent family and Sarna religion play a dominant role in augmenting the IMR among the PTGs in the state. The role of economic indicators, namely income and landholding status and occupation of mother and father have been examined in the context of infant deaths. It is observed that the high IMR is found among the primitive people of low income, landlessness, labourers as occupation of parents.

Further, it examines the prevalent situation of medical, communication, transportation, market, electricity, education and drinking water facilities, which cause alarming rate of infant deaths among the primitive people. So far, the availability of medical facility is concerned, it is observed that even ill-equipped primary health centre and sub-centre are not there around 10 kms from their residence. The existence of transportation and communication amenities is further deteriorated as approachable *pucca* road is beyond 15 km from their dwellings and there is almost no trace of post office in their habitation. Of all the infrastructural amenities, drinking water is considered as the basic amenity for the survival of children but one-third villages still rely on polluted spring and stream water. Even in case of location of schools, they are situated outside the territory of primitive tribal villages, where there is less feasibility of enrolling and attending schools in alien environment and almost all teachers do not know the local dialect of tribal people.

The chapter fourth, namely '**Assessment and Regional Patterns of Infant Deaths**' not only investigates the spatial and temporal dimensions of Infant Mortality Rate (IMR) among the primitive tribes in Jharkhand but it also takes into account of a detailed study of other components of infant deaths such as Early Neonatal Mortality Rate (ENMR), Late Neonatal Mortality Rate (LNMR), Neonatal Mortality Rate (NMR), Perinatal Mortality Rate (PMR), Post-Neonatal Mortality Rate (PNMR) and Still Birth Rate (SBR). The SBR and the LNMR exhibit the state average pattern of infant deaths but early neonatal mortality is high among the primitive tribes since almost all child births are attended by the untrained *dais* and family members. The first two components of infant deaths are purely biological in nature. It is, therefore, the mortality pattern follows the state average pattern in the above components. However, other components of infant deaths, namely early neonatal mortality rate, neonatal mortality rate, perinatal mortality rate, post-neonatal mortality rate, and infant mortality rate have by and large around eight times more mortality rate among the children of the primitive tribal groups than the state average of Jharkhand.

The main factors behind this high rate of infant deaths are lack of access to drinking water, absence of basic health services, living in closed small huts, unscientific sanitation and unhygienic habits, lack of proper nutrition in their meals, excessive boozing of *hadia* and liquor, smoking and chewing of narcotic, spread of infection and communicable diseases, illiteracy among mothers, delayed breastfeeding, extreme poverty, low weight of baby at birth, no antenatal check-ups, less consuming of food by the mother during gestation and lactation period, inaccessibility of their localities and complete dearth of medical and transport facilities. Further, it is noticed that the Sauria Paharias have the most pathetic situation in all the aforesaid components of infant deaths. That is why, there is a sharp decline of their population in every census from the first census of 1872 to the census of 2001 but that reduction is stopped in current 2011 Census, when there is a slight increase of their population after carving out Jharkhand as a separate state on 15th November, 2000 and several welfare schemes were actually implemented later on for them. Since they eat both beef and pork simultaneously, they were hated by both the Hindus and the Muslims as well but due to spread of Christianity in their areas, a large number of schools and hospitals are opened in recent past, which has curtailed their mortality rate.

It is noteworthy to mention that the Bansloi River in the Rajmahal Upland Region acts as a dividing line between the two extremes of infant deaths among the Sauria Paharias and the Mal Paharias. On the contrary, the Mal Paharias have the lowest rate in all the aforesaid components of infant deaths and they have largely adopted the religion of Hinduism, which has removed their superstition of child rearing. Again, they also get maximum benefit from government scheme. That is why, the highest growth of population has been noticed among the Mal Paharias. The other primitive tribal groups, namely the Birhors, the Korwas, the Asurs, the Parhaiyas, the Birjias and the Savars have infant deaths between the two extremes. The spatial distribution of infant deaths also illustrates that Damin-i-Koh region in general and Sahibganj district in particular encompasses the highest infant mortality rate, which is as high as 311 per thousand live births whereas the district of Dumka contains the lowest rate of infant deaths, where the Mal Paharias are found in large numbers in which the IMR was only 172 per thousand live births in 2017. In spite of having low IMR in the Mal Paharias among the primitive tribes it is as high as around six times higher than the state average.

The fifth chapter under the heading of '**Health, Hygiene, Sanitation and Morbidity among the Primitive Tribes in Jharkhand**' has examined the role of poor health of females, unhygienic condition and unscientific sanitation which have credited the wide-spread prevalence of diseases among the children of the primitive tribes in Jharkhand, thereby finally resulted in high neonatal, post-neonatal and infant mortality rate. One common thing that came to our notice is that the parameter related to the female and child precautions, namely antenatal care, food eaten by mother during pregnancy, home delivery through untrained *dais*, delayed start of breastfeeding and giving diluted animal milk in contaminated water to the new-borns as pre-lacteal food, drinking of *handia* and addiction of smoking, hesitant in adoption of female planning method, low weight of baby at birth, delayed start of supplementary food, rare medical check-up and immunization of children are not only pathetic but they are deplorable too.

More than 99 per cent of primitive tribal mothers had not taken any kind of antenatal care in term of medical intervention during their gestation period. Further, around two-third mothers had taken insufficient food during the above period. Majority of child births in primitive tribal localities were executed by the unskilled family members and midwives in an unhygienic environment, which usually lead to infection to the new born babies. However, one-quarter of mothers had adopted female sterilization only after they had completed their desired family size but around 50 per cent of mothers did not accept any form of family planning method. Simultaneously, majority of mothers did not adopt abortion for addressing the unmet need for contraception. Around 47 per cent of new born babies had weight less than 2 kg, which clearly divulges that the chances of their survival were dim. Again, no medical check-up was carried out in case of 91 per cent of new born babies. Immunization of children against seven serious diseases were not completed due to unawareness of mothers. The hygienic condition of the PTGs in context of cleanliness of house, bathing and toilet facility stand at bottom level in all the above indicators. A majority of houses had the provision of animals residing within the houses, which naturally create unhygienic conditions for the small children. Again, more than 75.5 per cent of primitive tribal people along with their children do not take bath daily due to limited set of clothes and scarcity of water.

The unhygienic habits of primitive tribal people augment high children mortality. Almost all of them prefer open field for excretion with washing bowels by water but the Sauria Paharias also use dry leaves and stones in place of water during summer season. The predicament of sanitation in terms of source of water, treatment of water, type of houses and kitchen facilities are quite pathetic in their localities. They still use contaminated stream, pond and spring water for drinking purposes habitually and traditionally. Further, more than 87 per cent of households do not use any kind of filter for purification of water. More than 91 per cent of primitive tribal people inhabit in a small *kutcha* houses, which are generally made of one or two rooms and these rooms are ill ventilated and dark even during day time. Generally, they do not have separate kitchen room and a small place is usually encircled in the corner of dwelling room itself, where traditional firewood is used for cooking purpose. Thus, the poor health with the unhygienic habits and unscientific sanitation lead to victims of various kinds of diseases among the children and finally lead to heavy loss of infant lives. That is why, diarrhoea and dysentery still account for the largest number of infant deaths. It is followed by mysterious disease, measles, acute respiratory infection, typhoid, malaria, low weight, tetanus and jaundice. It is further observed that mysterious disease, diarrhoea and dysentery, ARI, typhoid, low weight, measles and jaundice play an important role in case of neonatal mortality whereas the disease behind post-neonatal deaths are diarrhoea and dysentery, measles, malaria and low weight among the primitive tribes in the state.

The sixth chapter, namely '**Determinants of Infant Mortality**' is an investigation of the relationships of various socio-economic, demographic, and infrastructural variables with reference to neonatal mortality rate, post-neonatal mortality rate and infant mortality rate. It is observed under zero order correlation matrix that the variables, namely early breastfeeding of babies, economic participation of mother, antenatal care, immunization of children and productivity of land reduce neonatal mortality rate whereas it is positively associated with the distance of medical centres from their villages. The variables namely breastfeeding within one day, mother's economic participation, antenatal care led to the lowering PNMR among the PTGs. However, infant deaths with fourth and higher order of births and immunized infant deaths largely contribute to high PNMR. Simultaneously, IMR is negatively affected with early breastfeeding, economic participation of mother, antenatal care and safe drinking water but it is positively correlated with fourth and higher order of birth.

The step-wise regression analysis illustrates that early breastfeeding, immunized infant deaths, mother's economic participation, distance of medical centre, mother's education and productivity of land explain more than 40 per cent variations in NMR whereas other variables, namely mother's economic participations, immunized infant deaths, early breastfeeding, mother's ages between 20 and 30 years, antenatal care, high order of births and distance of medical centre, per capita income and mother's literacy influence 45 per cent variations in PNMR. In addition to the above-mentioned variables for PNMR, early breastfeeding, safe drinking water determines more than 50 per cent variation in IMR among the children of PTGs in Jharkhand. The similar result was drawn through binary logistic regression analysis wherein around fifty per cent variation in infant deaths are affected by birth order of child, mother's age at child birth, attendant at birth, breastfeeding, food availability, size of household, drinking water and per capita income.

The last chapter under the heading of 'Conclusion' a summing up of all the chapters critically includes summary, conclusion and policy implications. In a nutshell, the gist of every chapter is summed up the topic of summary. The analysis of all hypotheses in consideration of either approval or rejection has been made under the caption of conclusion. Further, the strategies for amelioration of the PTGs in reduction of infant deaths have been discussed under the title of policy implications so that the endangered communities cannot be wiped out from the state.

Conclusion

The first hypothesis relating to the very high infant mortality level among the PTGs has already been endorsed in previous chapter that the IMR is 230 per thousand live births more than the state average of 29 per thousand live births, which was in fact below the national average of 34 per thousand in 2017, which clearly indicates that it is around eight times higher than the state average. This kind of high mortality is also observed in neonatal and post-neonatal mortality, which were 130 and 100 per thousand respectively during the survey year of 2017. The other components of infant deaths such as still-birth, early neonatal mortality, perinatal mortality and late neonatal mortality rate uphold 22, 108, 128 and 22 per thousand live births, which are tremendously higher than the state and national average. This is mainly because of the fact that the socio-economic conditions and social deprivations in the context of education, size and type of family, religion, income status, landholding status and occupation are pitiable, which stimulate very high infant deaths among the primitive people. That is why, total population of the Sauria Paharias and the Parhaiyas have gone down even in 2001Census in comparison to 1991 Census whereas population of other tribes have substantially increased in the current census, which itself manifests the overall predicament of the PTG in Jharkhand.

The present study elucidates the second hypothesis, that the biological variables namely share of old age mothers, proportion of first and above fourth order of child births, ratio of low age of mothers at first time of child birth, very low weight, i.e. below 2 kg of the new-borns etc. enhance the neonatal mortality rate whereas post-neonatal mortality is controlled by environmental variables, namely percentage of illiterate mothers, share of large size family, quota of single parent family, portion of low per capita income and proportion of landless households. In context of prevailing situation, Still Birth Rate (SBR) and Late Neonatal Mortality (LNMR) are purely biological in nature among the PTGs in Jharkhand, which manifest the state average pattern of infant deaths. On the contrary, other components of infant deaths are also influenced by socio-economic conditions of the people. That is why, infant mortality is more than eight times high in these components. It is further observed that mysterious disease, diarrhoea and dysentery, ARI, typhoid, low weight, measles and jaundice play an important role in case of neonatal mortality whereas the disease behind post-neonatal deaths are diarrhoea and dysentery, measles, malaria and low weight among the primitive tribes in the state.

Income plays a decisive role in the survival of children as good housing, affordability of medical facility, nutritious food, transportation and communication facilities, mother's education, living standard etc. requiring for curtailing infant deaths are directly related to the income of household. Hence, the third hypothesis concerning higher the share of low-income group among the primitive tribal groups, higher the share of infant mortality upholds completely true for Jharkhand. The households with income level of above Rs. 800 per month are negatively related to NMR, PNMR and IMR. The above association is also established by step-wise regression analysis wherein per capita income explains 1 per cent and 0.6 per cent variation in PNMR and IMR respectively but it does not influence NMR, which is by and large biological in nature. The above relationship is further established through logistic regression analysis, which illustrates that the households with income level of between Rs. 400 and 800 per month and below Rs. 400 per month have infant mortality rate 1.5 and 2 times higher than the reference category of income above 800 rupees per month. The odd ratios of both lower income group and very lower income group are significant at 1 per cent level of confidence.

It has already been discussed that mother's literacy plays a minor role in reducing the IMR among the PTGs in Jharkhand. Moreover all three important components of infant deaths, viz. NMR, PNMR and IMR are negatively associated with mother's level of literacy. The above correlation establishes that women's literacy has a crucial role in the decline of infant mortality among the PTGs. It is a tool, which helps the mother in breaking some of the traditional norms and makes them more independent in taking decision within the family situation. Again, it enables the mother to understand her surroundings and environment and acts as a very strong catalyst force in the process of keeping good health, which ultimately reduces infant mortality. The educated mother brings forth only the wanted new-born babies, which creates such a healthy environment in the family whereby there is biological emancipation of frequent pregnancies. In fact, infant feeding, clothing and treatment of common ailment are generally carried out scientifically by the educated mother. The above relationship is also established through stepwise regression analysis, in which mother's literacy independently affects 1.8 per cent, 1.3 per cent and 1.0 per cent in NMR, PNMR and IMR respectively for the PTG in the state. That kind of relationship is further established through logistic regression analysis in which it is observed that there is 13 per cent less likely to get infant deceased among the literate mothers of PTG in comparison to the illiterate mothers. Thus, this is one of the most important variables, which creates chain effects on all desirable components of economic, social and demographic development for the PTG in Jharkhand.

In primitive tribal society of Jharkhand mothers play an important role in the process of earning a livelihood for the family. In a family-based agriculture and household industry, they are almost equal partner in the productive work. They do wide range of activities, which sustain the household. In addition to cooking food, household cleaning and child care, they spend several hours in fetching and carrying heavy loads of water and fuel. The animal rearing and active participation in food production are also their responsibilities. In fact, they are considered as main means of livelihood and they work together in every walk of life along with their counterparts. Thus, they, of course, do all sort of arduous work. Again, they also work as labourers either in the field or forest. Due to their hard work, their economic earning is very fruitful for the sustenance of family by which they and their children get proper and nutritious food. That is why, the hypothesis relating to high infant mortality rate among the working mothers is nullified in case of primitive mothers. All three components of infant deaths, viz. NMR, PNMR and IMR are negatively associated with mother's work participation rate and all are significant at 1 per cent level of confidence. The above relationship is also qualified by stepwise regression analysis in which mother's work participation rate control 4.4 per cent for NMR, 18.8 per cent for PNMR and 8.6 per cent for IMR among the primitive tribes in the state. In fact, women are considered as main means of livelihood and the main responsibility of sustenance lies on their shoulders of them. It explicitly manifests that the primitive tribes are half-fed and half-dressed but no government do pay heed to the wretched condition of poor tribes, who were once the land owner of the area.

The sixth hypothesis concerning the immediate breast-feeding within one day curtailing reduction in neonate mortality rate among the PTG is substantiated through correlation matrix, step-wise regression analysis and logistic regression analysis. It is observed that the value of correlation coefficient between the above two variables is -.41, which is significant at 1 per cent level of significance. The other components of infant deaths namely PNMR and IMR are also negatively associated with early start of breast-feeding and the values of correlation coefficients are -.43 and -.54 respectively and they are also significant at 1 per cent level of confidence. The logistic regression analysis also presents the similar scenario, which reveals that infant mortality rate is 2.9 times higher among the new-born babies, who were devoid of initial breastfeeding within one day in comparison to the children with early start of breastfeeding. The benefit of early invitation of breastfeeding is also reflected through step-wise regression analysis, which explains 17 per cent reduction in NMR, 5.4 per cent in PNMR and 29.1 per cent in IMR among the PTGs. In fact, breastfeeding has several benefits for the new-born babies. Initial breast milk contains different essential nutrients such as colostrum and antibodies, an infant need during the first six months of life. It acts as a protection against common childhood diseases. Therefore, WHO recommends initiation of breastfeeding as soon as possible after childbirth, within the first hour after delivery? However, almost all primitive mothers threw away initial breast milk and the new-born babies are given diluted animal milk, honey, gutty, ghee, sugar, glucose etc. with contaminated boiled water etc. as prelacteal food. They have misconception about initial breast milk that the milk remained nine months in the breast is injurious for their new-borns since they look yellowish in colour. Again, only small quantity of milk ekes out from their breasts and they have preconceived notion that that initial breast milk at each feed is small. That is why, these primitive tribal mothers have to be educated that colostrum, i.e. initial breast milk is not only harmless but it is richer in body-building nutrient than artificial prelacteal food and needed for the protection of baby against infection. The above exercise explicitly illustrates that if the new born be given mother's milk as prelacteal food; there would be reduction in one third of IMR.

Antenatal care includes curative and preventive health services for the women of reproductive ages. Maternal health during pregnancy is extremely crucial to ensure good health of new-born. Therefore, health check-ups and poor nutrition support during pregnancy are imperative. Antenatal care (ANC) is necessary to ensure health-care during pregnancy. Its goal is to provide necessary and regular health check-ups to pregnant women to prevent pregnancy and childbirth related health complications during the entire course of pregnancy and delivery and promote health in both mothers and their children. However, antenatal care has been simply measured here through four aspects and they are TT injection, three medical check-ups, healthy and nutritious food and consumption of 100 IFA tablets during gestation period. To ascertain the role of ANC on neonatal mortality among the PTG, two levels of measurements, namely correlation matrix and step-wise regression analysis have been carried out here. It is observed that all three components of infant deaths, namely NMR, PNMR and IMR are negatively associated with antenatal care and the values of correlation coefficients are -.34, -.26 and -.39, which are significant at 1 per cent level of confidence. The result through step-wise regression analysis is not satisfactory as there is problem of multicollinearity in the explanatory variables. The relationship between the above variables through step-wise regression analysis reveals that 1.6 per cent variation in NMR, 3.3 per cent variation in PNMR and 2.4 per cent variation in IMR are explained by antenatal care of PTG in the state.

As a matter of fact, only negligible number of pregnant women among the PTGs is taken care of the above concerns during the gestation period but the result is very much promising and all three components of child deaths get weakened through proper care of mothers. The result clearly adds up to the fact that there will be a dramatic decline in child deaths if the primitive tribal females are properly taken care of during their gestation period. The women who enjoyed superior physical conditions and good diets during pregnancy brought forth babies in excellent health condition. The above finding clearly approves the seventh hypothesis that antenatal care of mother creates a healthy environment for her offspring whereby there is reduction in neonate deaths. Thus, proper antenatal care of primitive mothers will thwart the alarming high rate of infant deaths. Nonetheless, the state government has launched Mukhbir Yojna for ANC in 2017 but that scheme is a complete failure in the localities of primitive tribes.

The hypothesis regarding importance of safe drinking water in lowering mortality rate of children among the PTG has been evaluated through the application of statistical techniques. It is noticed that the value of correlation coefficient between safe drinking water and IMR is -.25, which is significant at 5 per cent level of confidence. The negative relationship between the above variables illustrates that the provision of safe drinking water is accountable for reduction in child deaths of the PTG in the state. When the relationship between the above variables is sought through logistic regression analysis, it is perceived that the IMR is 1.2 times higher in case of those households, who use water of well as means of drinking in place of handpump and running tap. The situation is further deteriorated in case of those households, who use water of pond, stream and *chua* for drinking purposes and the IMR is as high as 1.6 times as safe drinking water of handpump and running tap. The relationship between the above variables is also examined with the application of stepwise regression analysis. It is found that there is 1 per cent decline in NMR, when the primitive tribal people use safe water for drinking purposes and the above relationship is also noticed between PNMR and safe drinking water, when there is reduction of 0.5 per cent of child deaths in those families, which are using water of handpump and tap for drinking purposes. Lastly, the benefit of safe drinking water is also reflected in infant mortality, while there is reduction of 1.6 per cent of child deaths in those families, where the inhabitants drink safe water of handpump and running tap. Safe drinking water is a burning problem of primitive tribes and even several new-born babies are given contaminated water of either ponds or streams. That is why, there will be drastic change in all components of infant deaths, when the primitive tribal people are provided with safe drinking water. As long as they drink contaminated water, there would not be any decline in IMR.

The ninth hypothesis regarding the longer distance of medical centre from the villages, the larger the share of infant mortality rate among the PTG stands true in Jharkhand through proper evaluation by various statistical techniques. It is noticed that the values of correlation coefficients are .26 and .21 for the villages situated at the distance beyond 5 km in context of NMR and IMR. The above relationship clearly indicates the importance of spatial distance and availability of transport facility for the survival of new-born babies among the PTGs in the state. Since almost all villages have dispersed patterns of settlement and they are all devoid of transport facility, they can not reach the medical centres during delivery period. Finally, it results into high child deaths. The above relationship is also endorsed by step-wise regression analysis whereby 2.5 per cent variation in NMR is explained by those medical centres having the distance of above 5 km from their localities. The above relationship is also vindicated for the correlation between PNMR and medical centre wherein the longer distance of medical centre account for 1.1 per cent of enhancement in PNMR. Lastly, 0.1 per cent acceleration in IMR is also noticed through the longer distance of medical centre. Unfortunately, majority of medical professionals are reluctant to stay in the areas of primitive tribes. That is why, efforts must be made to train local people and dais so that they can help them in time of health emergency. Besides this, the use of Ayurvedic and tribal herbal medicines ought to be encouraged because of the fact that the primitive tribal people are already accustomed to herbal remedies and hence there will be little problems in acceptability.

In order to reduce infant mortality among the primitive tribes in Jharkhand, the assessment of unwanted pregnancy and higher order of birth is of vital consideration for the overall development of the society. In this context, the hypothesis relating to the risk of very high infant death for fourth and higher order of child birth has been examined with the application of statistical techniques of correlation matrix and step-wise regression analysis. It is surprising to note that there is positive relationship of higher order of births with all components of infant deaths, viz. NMR, PNMR and IMR but the values of correlation coefficients are significant only for PNMR and IMR. It vividly points out that the later order of child births is not properly taken care of in later stage infancy by the tribal society due to severe economic hardships faced by them. That kind of relationship is also observed through step-wise regression analysis in which neonatal mortality is not explained by high order of child births. On the contrary, fourth and higher order of child births diminishes 2.5 per cent in PNMR. Overall, it curtails 1.3 per cent in infant mortality rate. The similar result is produced through logistic regression analysis, which explicitly manifests that there are 4 per cent reduction in the first order of birth, 68 per cent decline in second order of birth and 86 per cent decrease in third order of birth in comparison to fourth and high order of child birth. It is a universal phenomenon that there are high infant deaths in first order of births but in case of the PTG in Jharkhand the high incidences of child deaths are witnessed in fourth and higher order of births, which vividly point out towards their abject poverty. It clearly indicates that non-exposure of contraceptive methods, family planning, and early age of marriage are mainly responsible for unmet need of the family, which ultimately results into high infant deaths in the fourth and higher order of child births among the PTGs in the state of Jharkhand.

According to the WHO guidelines, children are considered fully immunized when they have received vaccination against tuberculosis, three doses of DPT, three doses of polio and one dose of tetanus. Unfortunately, only one-tenth children are immunized against the above diseases among the primitive tribes in Jharkhand. It is further observed that that small proportion of children, who had been immunized against the above diseases, the chances of their survival got increased and finally the administered immunized babies had negligible chances of their demises. This is evident from the values of correlation coefficients for immunization with NMR, PNMR and IMR are -.34, -.23 and -.30 respectively. That kind of association between immunization and infant death is also manifested through step-wise regression analysis. It is found that there is a decline of 11.4 per cent in NMR, when the children are immunized against the prevailing diseases among the PTGs in the state. It is also true for the association between child immunization and PNMR, when there is 5.5 per cent decline in PNMR, which is explained with proper immunization of child. Finally, 1.2 per cent decline in IMR is observed through the immunization of children.

Thus, from the above relationship, it becomes established fact that if there is higher share of immunization among the children of PTG, there will be lower proportion of infant deaths. In fact, extreme level of infant deaths among the primitive tribes is due to very low level of immunization among children. This is mainly because of the fact that there is complete dearth of the Sahiyas and health workers in inaccessible areas of their localities. Simultaneously, neither sub-centre nor primary health centre is found on the ground in any 100 villages of primitive tribes. Again, no doctor attends their duties regularly even in distance located primary health centre. As long as immunization of children is not done on a large scale in the above localities, there would not be any decline in infant death.

In order to reduce infant mortality among the primitive tribes in Jharkhand, there is an urgent need to connect their villages through road network so that in time of medical emergency they along with their sick children can reach medical centres and urban areas for their treatment. It is already discussed earlier that there is an extreme crisis of medical facilities within their localities. Consequently, all weather road and bus-stand facilities are the basic necessities for the all-round development of village and catering of patients. It is derived through correlation matrix that the villages lying beyond 5 km distance from bus-stand and *pucca* road have high share of infant deaths, which is verified by the positive correlation coefficients with NMR, PNMR and IMR. That kind of positive relationship is also substantiated by logistic regression analysis in which far located villages from bus-stand accelerate 0.4 per cent in NMR among the PTG. Altogether, the above variable add up to 0.4 per cent changes in IMR.

Thus, the credibility of thirteenth hypothesis is verified here through correlation matrix and stepwise regression that the inaccessibility from *pucca* road always enhances the IMR among the PTGs in the state. The primitive villages located away from bus-stand amenity increase infant deaths in general and neonate deaths in particular among the PTGs. Finally, it can be said that the inaccessibility of villages from *pucca* road and bus-stand facilities enhances the number in child deaths. Lack of adequate transportation facilities in inaccessible villages have been one of the major causes of infant deaths.

Now it can be easily summarized that the dogmas and superstitions of the primitive tribal groups enhance infant mortality. The traditions namely delayed start of breastfeeding by the mothers to the new-borns after throwing away colostrum, immediate bath to the new-borns, delivery of children in ill ventilated dark room with the use of unclean clothes by the untrained local old lady, addiction of drinking and smoking, inculcation of unhygienic habits and insanitation, complete faith for remedy of diseases upon traditional diviner through evil spirits and witches etc. enhance the infant mortality rate. Thus, the poor health with the unhygienic habits and unscientific sanitations lead to victims of various kinds of diseases among the children and finally take a heavy loss of infant lives. Around three-fourth of mothers are addicted to alcohol and narcotics. A majority of houses have the provision of animals residing within the houses, which naturally create unhygienic condition for the small children. They still today use contaminated stream and spring water for drinking purpose by their habit and tradition. Further more than 87 per cent of households do not use any kind of filter for purification of water. More than 91 per cent of primitive tribal people inhabit in a small *kutcha* house, which are generally made up of one room with ill ventilated and dark even during day time and one can enter into these houses through crawling only.

Policy Implications

The programmes and policies chalked out by the government and societies produce results of an action-oriented research programme on 'Infant Mortality Rate among the Primitive Tribal Groups in Jharkhand' through innovative methods for the development of primitive tribes. The children are considered to be the future of a state. Therefore, their health and proper development are of utmost importance to a state's well-being and needs urgent attention so that there would not be any further decline in their population. In order to reduce infant mortality among the primitive tribes, the following strategies are suggested on the basis of minute observation and analysis:

(A) Infrastructural Needs

1. The Health Sub-Centres (HSC) should be established in either those primary schools or Panchayat Bhavans situated in the localities of primitive tribes and these health centres should remain open in morning time, where local educated health

workers endowed with indigenous system of medicine and allopathic medicine along with local trained *dais* and health workers ought to be available everyday to administer first aid, impart training about health, hygiene and sanitation and bring up cases to Primary Health Centre and dispensary. The indigenous medicine would have the advantage of being cheap as it would use locally available herbs and better understood as the people have been using that kind of medicine since ages. All these health workers should be equipped with motor cycle facilities so that they can reach the patient's house on time in the difficult terrain. The dais should be given delivery kit and proper monetary incentive after every successful delivery at home.

2. It would be proper to take the primitive educated tribal youth as Para Medical Staff, Sahiyas and Anganwadi workers as far as possible; there would be no language and custom barrier for them as they would be talking to the patient in their own language. They still depend on the primitive treatment of their diseases by Ojhas and village quacks. They still feel shy in coming to the urban hospitals and health centres for the treatment of their diseases.
3. The Mobile Medical Unit (MMU) must visit the weekly market on a fixed day and time in the afternoon. It should consist of one doctor and one nurse besides the local health worker, anganwadi worker and mid-wife. The MMU must be equipped with medicines and medical equipment so that these local health workers and anganwadi workers will help the patients in taking medicine in proper quantity and time after the departure of MMU.
4. The health workers must be recruited from the local primitive tribal community since they would be aware of the local traditions, beliefs and superstitions of the community and will be entrusted a job of preventive and promotive health services in his community. These health workers will be fully provided with first aid medicine so that for minor treatment, people have not to go to PHCs, which are generally situated far away from their villages.

5. The responsibility of anganwadis workers should be fixed for nutrition care for the children and pregnant women through signatory of beneficiaries as no health worker had ever visited in their assigned villages during the survey year of 2017through the application of bottom to top approach for health amenities. In fact, she should be present in the schools along with health workers and indigenous trained *dais*. More or less, the similar pathetic approach was adopted by the Sahiyas, who had not assisted the primitive pregnant women for institutional deliveries in their localities.
6. The disposable sterile delivery kits consisting of blade, cotton, towel, dress of neonates, antiseptic lotion, soap, bed sheet and plastic sheet should be distributed to all pregnant women of the PTG.
7. Efforts should be made from the government side for supplying of 20 kg grains to every mother during gestation and lactation period so that the primitive mothers could improve their diet so that their siblings would not be underweight and stunted.
8. Setting up of referral hospital on an extensive scale is needed in the primitive tribal belt with dedicated medical staff and local workers.

(B) Health Awareness

1. The strategies of kangaroo mother care are essential for the survival of neonates among the PTGs in Jharkhand. They include skin-to-skin positioning of a baby on the mother's breast, adequate nutrition through immediate breastfeeding, ambulatory care in case of sickness among the neonates and emotional and dietary support for the mother in caring for the baby.
2. Every pregnant woman of PTG should be aware about three different aspects of maternal health care such as (i) at least two tetanus toxoid injection to pregnant women, (ii) at least three check-ups of antenatal mother, and (iii) consumption of at least 100 IFA and calcium tablets during pregnancy. The above precaution will not only reduce infant mortality but maternal mortality as well.

3. Immunization drive for the children of PTG against seven preventable childhood disease should be launched on a war footing. All children must be immunized against tuberculosis by BCG vaccination, diphtheria, pertussis and tetanus by three doses of DPT, polio by three doses of polio drops, measle by measle vaccination and HBV by hepatitis B vaccine.
4. The concept of immediate and exclusive breastfeeding during first six months of life should be popularized. As exclusive breastfeeding eliminates the risk infection and is associated with better weight gain because baby drinks more milk when he feels thirsty.
5. Pregnant women and lactating mother need extra food of all types especially protein and protective food through locally available leguminous, fishes, banana and guava so that malnutrition among the children and mothers can be wiped out in their areas.

(C) Social Awareness

1. In order to curtail IMR the primitive tribal mother ought to be encouraged to avoid child bearing before 20 years and after 35 years of age; birth interval should not be less than 2 years and higher birth order of child above 4th order should be avoided. The PTG should adopt family planning method for unmet need and higher order of births can also be addressed as well though the application of the above method.
2. There is an urgent need to encourage female education among the PTGs in Jharkhand as the result has shown negative relationship between female education and IMR. Female education has particularly suffered due to the lack of hostel facilities, very meagre amount of scholarship and the distance at which the middle and higher schools are located. It is usually said that female education brings prosperity, health awareness, raising living standard and enrichment in education to the families whereas male education is concerned with individual enhancement. In fact, the literacy levels among the females in the primitive tribal communities continue to be abysmally low, which has added to IMR at unprecedented level in the state.

3. It is recommended that gentle social persuasion among the PTGs in the state should be generated to still raise the age at marriage so that unwanted pregnancy of high order of births can be minimized, which ultimately escalate high LNMR and PNMR.
4. Total prohibition of liquor consumption and addiction of smoking should be strictly imposed upon the PTG. That kind of restriction in primitive tribal localities could be implemented with the involvement of tribal community and educated youth for saving the tribes from the scourge of drinking, which spoils health and leads to their children manifold of deaths. Due to excess drinking habit and ill health, they do not give proper care to their children. In fact, the PTG do not generally know how to save or how to plan for their future. They think of the present only, forget the past and do not care for the future, they are very easy-going people.
5. Awareness should be made to educate women of PTG for initiating breastfeeding immediately after birth as it contains colostrum and to depend upon it completely until the infant is about six months of age. Simultaneously women must be educated to introduce the infants with supplementary semi-solid smashed food after six months of age.
6. Social awareness also needs to be created among the females of PTG to ensure that no girl enters into nuptial relationship before 18 years of age.
7. There must be dissemination of information among the PTGs against the evils of fatalistic beliefs about pregnancy, death and diseases.
8. The popular witch-craft systems must be wiped out, which are practised by unscrupulous ojhas, who dupe and victimize the innocent children and their families.
9. Immediate bath after delivery of new-born is common among the PTG, which invites so many diseases to the children. That is why, that kind of practise must be stopped through social awareness.

(D) Improvement in Hygiene and Sanitation Practices

1. Motivating behavioural change among the PTGs is needed for the habit on key hygiene practices like washing hands with soap, washing the bowel with water and safe disposal of child and animal excreta.
2. Housing design of primitive tribes should have in built mechanisms for harvesting sun and wind through window and higher height of ceiling. Sewage treatment and waste disposal should form part of housing design. The kitchen must be separate and it should be made outside the bed room with proper ventilation. Again, animals must be kept outside the main house so that children can not play with animal excreta.
3. The primitive people in general and the children in particular should take bath daily and dressing clothes must be washed regularly with surf or soap. In absence of the above personal hygiene habits, they invite infections and skin diseases among them.
4. The primitive tribes should not throw away garbage, litter, child and animal excreta in their kitchen garden, where small children used to play during the investigation period.
5. There must be an approachable road to their houses, which should remain open even in the rainy season. Further these roads must be free from human and animal excreta.
6. There must be provision of safe drinking water through handpump and pipe water for every hamlet of primitive tribes. The above provision can be established through contractor with local participation for the maintenance of handpump and running tap. A significant portion of infant deaths is attributable to water-borne diseases and provision of potable water can bring down infant mortality to a noteworthy extent. Being totally ignorant about the need and importance of safe drinking water, the PTG themselves not only drink contaminated water but also give the same water to their siblings, leading to diarrhoeal disease.
7. The awareness campaign of hygiene and sanitation in the primitive villages ought to be imposed upon the anganwadis workers.

(E) Economic Improvements

1. The money lenders and middle men should be strictly prohibited to enter into the localities of primitive tribes. It is observed that whatever they produce is taken by the Mahajan at the time of harvesting. Generally, they return money to the Mahajan greater than the principal by way of interest, while the original amount remains due. A proper ban on such loan is absolutely necessary, which increases at least two times within four months.
2. The primitive tribes should be taught to produce enough vegetables in their kitchen gardens and fruit bearing trees in their fields. They should also be encouraged to keep milching cows and their surplus products ought to be purchased and marketed through agency like Megha. They should be given incentives for horticulture as their livelihood in place of primitive type of Kurwa and Beora shifting cultivation.
3. The primitive tribes should not be restricted from minor forest produces and the land grabbed by other people must be restored to them.
4. The local co-operative banks should be established in their localities with local participation so that the primitive tribal people can take loan in time of crisis and return back the loan in time of harvesting. Simultaneously, the dimension of grain stores (*golas*) should be widened so that the local people can participate in their functioning.
5. The primitive cottage industry with certain modifications through proper training should be encouraged so that they can alter their livelihood activities leading to more income generation and more saving to meet their livelihood challenges. Almost all eight primitive tribes are specialised in different kinds of occupation related to various cottage industries since ancient times. These environment friendly handicraft products should be procured by Jharkhand Emporium and to sell them into the open markets.

Appendices

Appendix 1.1

Village Schedule

Name of District (DIST)-	
Name of Block (BLOCK)-	
Name of Panchayat (PANCHA)-	
Name of Hamlet and Village (VILLAGE)-	
Educational facilities (within the village) (EDUINF)-	NO-0, P-1, PM-2, PMS-3, PMSH-4
(a) Primary School (b) Middle School (c) Secondary School (d) Higher Secondary School (e) Other (specify)	
Distance of Primary School in km (DISPRSC)-	
Distance of Middle School in km (DISMISC)-	
Distance of Secondary School in km (DISSESC)	
Distance of Higher Secondary School in km (DISHISS)-	
Distance of Medical facilities in km	
Dispensary (DISPEN)-	
Primary Health Centre (PHC)-	
Government Hospital (GH)-	
Private Hospital (PH)-	
Trust Hospital (TH)-	

Communication Facilities (COMUNIC)	
Post Office-1, Internet-2, Telephone-3, Mobile-4, Whatsapp-5, All facilities using-6, Post Office and Mobile-7, Mobile and Internet-8	
Transportation facilities	Yes-1 No-2
Distance of railway station (DRS)-	
Distance of Bus-stand (DBS)-	
Pucca road within the village (PRV)-	
Railway track within the village (RTV)-	Yes-1 No-2
Footpath (FOOTPH)-	Yes-1 No-2
Distance of various service centres in km -	
Block head office (DBLOCK)-	
District head office (DDISTR)-	
City/Town (DTOWN)-	
Hat/periodic market (DHAT)-	
Area of Village (AREVIL)-	
No. of Households (NHOUSH)-	
Language and Dialect (LANGUA)-	
Hindi-1, Bengali-2, Asuri-3, Birjian-4, Birhori-5, Korwa and Sadri-6, Parhiyan-7, Savari and Bengali-8, Malto-9	
Name of slash and burn cultivation (JHUMING)-	
No Slash and Burn-1, Kurwa-2, Bevara-3, Viyoda-4, Bir Ondor/Beora-5, Beora and Dalkha-6, Beora-7, Kheti-8, Kurwa/Kheti-9	
Name of Tribe (PTRIBE)-	
Asur-1, Birjia-2, Birhor-3, Korwa-4, Parhaiya-5, Savar-6, Mal Paharia-7, Sauria Paharia-8	
Location of village (LOCVIL)-	
Separate settlement-1, Mixed settlement with other tribe-2, Mixed settlement with other-3, Little distance (within 2 km)-4	
Head of locality (HLOCAL)-	Sardar-1, Nayak-2
Head of Village (HVILAGE)-	NoHead-0, Manjhi-1, Mahto-2, Pradhan-3
PRIEST-	No Priest-0, Baiga-1, Laya-2, Guru-3, Pujari-4

Messenger (MESENG)-	No Messenger-0, Paramanik-1, Gaurat-2, Suueri-3, Baidgiri-4, Pahan-5, Deowar/Pujar-6, Pahan, Suueri and Deori-7

Appendix 1.2

Household Schedule

<table>
<tr><td>Household No (HN)-</td><td></td></tr>
<tr><td>Religion (RELIGION)-</td><td></td></tr>
<tr><td colspan="2">Hindu-1, Muslim-2, Christian-3, Sarna-4, Other-5, Atheist-6, Sarna and Hindu-7</td></tr>
<tr><td>CLAN-</td><td></td></tr>
<tr><td colspan="2">No Clan-0, Hembram-1, Kamar-2, Bhuia-3, Sandhwar-4, Kuiri-5, Saoriya-6, Lakur Chata-7, Latta-8, Gairua-9, Simpuria-10, Mahali-11, Aandi-12, Murum-13, Tao-14, Murmu-15, Pattidar-16, Tuti-17, Chutia-18, Magia-19, Berwar-20, Lungam-21, Murgi-22, Toppo-23, Beng-24, Iend-25, Barwa-26, Kerketa-27, Andhuar-28, Dhora-29, Sour-30, Khanda-31, Ghora-32, Do not know-33, Pandubasia-34, Sonwar-35, Kansi-36, Nangbangsi-37, Tiring-38, Pancha Gulgu-39, Katla-40, Sarisa Gulgu-41, Aalkushi-42, Kaori-43, Dup Bhuia-44, Khela kamar-45, Dorra Bhuia-46, Rann Bhuia-47, Dumoria Bhuia-48, Sal Gulgu-49, Bagda Bhuia-50, Lal Bhuia-51, Pat-52, Tiram-53, Sama-54, Palas-55, Badda-56, Dhar Bhuia-57, Gadni match-58, Sal bata-59, Rang Bhuia-60, Tika murmur-61, Raj Hansda-62, Angari-63, Soren-64, Sal-65, Pichlo Bhuia-66, Telra-67</td></tr>
<tr><td>Type of family (TFAMILY)-</td><td></td></tr>
<tr><td colspan="2">Joint-1, Nuclear-2, Extended-3, Singal-4</td></tr>
<tr><td>AGE-</td><td>Child Death- 0</td></tr>
<tr><td>SEX-</td><td></td></tr>
<tr><td colspan="2">Male-1, Female-2 and Eunuch-3</td></tr>
<tr><td>Marital Status (MS)</td><td></td></tr>
<tr><td colspan="2">Child Death- 0, Married-1, Unmarried-2, Widowed-3, Divorced-4, and Single-5</td></tr>
</table>

Educational Qualification (EQ)-	
Child Death- 0, 1-10- Various Classes, Matric-11, Inter-13, Graduation -16, Post-Graduation-18, Engineering-19, Nursing-20	
Primary Occupation (POCCUP)-	
Cultivator-1, Agriculture Labour-2, Peon-3, Clerk-4, Transport Worker-5, Transporter-6, Trade Worker-7, Trader-8, Artisan Worker-9, Factory Worker-10, Student-11, Unemployed-12, Child-13, Pensioner-14, Rentier-15, Food Gathering-16, Collection of herbs and flowers-17, Grazing-18, Bee keeping-19, Mat making-20, Weaving-21, Basketry-22, Pottery-23, Fishing-24, Rope Making-25, Leaf plate making-26, Carpenter-27, Blacksmith-28, Lac collection-29, Tsar cultivator-30, Unpaid F.W.-31, Beggar-32, Out migrated-33, Rope making and Agriculture labour-34, Rope making, Agriculture labour and Pensioner-35, Government Service-37, Private School Teacher-38, PTG (Jharkhand) Police-39, Bricks factory-40, Cultivator and Agriculture Labour (if the pensioner then add 600 Rs.)-41, Basketry, Cultivator and Agriculture labour-42, Disable-43, Broom making, Rope making, Cultivator and Agriculture labour (if the pensioner then add 600 Rs.)-44, Anganwadi Sebika-45, Sahiya-46, Social worker-47, Para teacher-48, Nurse-49, Rajmistri-50, Teacher-51	
Income (in rupees) (INCOME)-	No Income-0
Land statuses-	
Irrigated (IRRIGAT)-	
Method of Irrigation (METIRR)	
Dari-1, Well-2, Dam-3, Canal-4, Tank-5, Other (Specify)	
Un-irrigated (UIRIGAT)-	
Fallow land (FALLOW)-	
Total land (TLAND)-	NO LAND- 0
Rice Area per acres (RICAR)-	
Rice Production in monnes (RICPR)-	
Wheat Area per acres (WHETAR)-	
Wheat Production in monnes (WHETPR)-	
Arhar area per acres (ARHARAR)-	
Arhar production in monnes (ARHARPR)-	
Maize area per acres (MAZEAR)-	
Maize production in monnes (MAZEPR)-	

Oil seed area per acres (OILAR)-	
Oil seed production in monnes (OILPR)-	
Sugarcane area per acres (SUGARAR)-	
Sugarcane production in monnes (SUGARPR)-	
Marwa area per acres (MARUAR)-	
Marwa production in monnes (MARUPR)-	
Area in acres (ARAC)-	
Production in monnes (PRODM)-	
Price per monne (PRICM)-	
Total value in rupees (TVALUER)- Production in per acres (PERACRE)- Production in per person (PERPERS)-	
Household gadgets (HOGADG)-	
a. Radio, b. Television, c. Refrigerator, d. Fan, e. Mobile, f. Bike, g. Bicycle, h. Sewing machine.	
R-1, RT-2, RTR-3, RTRF-4, RTRFM-5, RTRFMB-6, RTRFMBBc-7, RTRFMBBcS-8, T-9, TR-10, TRF-11, TRFM-12, TRFMB-13, TRFMBBc-14, TRFMBBcS-15, R-16, RF-17, RFM-18, RFMB-19, RFMBBc-20, RFMBBcS-21, F-22, FM-23, FMB-24, FMBBc-25, FMBBcS-26, M-27, MB-28, MBBc-29, MBBcS-30, B-31, BBc-32, BBcS-33, Bc-34, BcS-35, S-36, MBc-37, TMBc-38, TMBBc-39	
Movable Property (MOVPRO)-	
a. Cow, b. Buffalo, c. Goat, d. Sheep, e. Farm Cattle, f. Hen, g. Duck, h. Pig	
C-1, CB-2, CBG-3, CBGS-4, CBGSCa-5, CBGSFH-6, CBGSFHD-7, CBGSFHDP-8, B-9, BG-10, BGS-11, BGSF-12, BGSFH-13, BGSFHD-14, BGSFHDP-15, G-16, GS-17, GSF-18, GSFH-19, GSFHD-20, GSFHDP-21, S-22, SF-23, SFH-24, SFHD-25, SFHDP-26, F-27, FH-28, FHD-29, FHDP-30, H-31, HD-32, HDP-33, D-34, DP-35, P-36, CFH-37, GF-38, GH-39, CG-40, GFH-41, FP-42, GFP-43, FHP-44, GP-45, HP-46, GHP-47, CGH-48, CGHF-49, CGHFP-50, CGD-51, CGFHD-52, BH-53, GHD-54, CGHD-55, CH-56, CHP-57, BF-58, CSF-59, CGSF-60	
Housing Structure-	
No. of kutcha rooms (KUTCHA)-	

No. of pucca rooms (PUCCA)-	
No. of Semi-pucca rooms (SEMPUCC)-	
House amenities-	
Sources of lighting (LIGHT)-	
Fully electrified-1, Partially electrified-2, Solar-3, Kerosene-4, Solar and Kerosene-5, Partially electrified and Solar-6	
Water connection (WATCON)-	
Hand pump-1, Well-2, Running tap-3, Pond-4, Stream-5, Chua/Dandi-6, Other-7, Running tap and Stream-8, Hand pump and Stream-9	
Treatment of water (TRETWAT)-	
No-1, Add bleach/chlorine-2, Alum-3, Cloth-4, Water Filter-5, Electronic purifier-6, Boil-7	
Bath room (BATROM)-	Yes-1 No-2
Toilet facility (TOILET)-	
Flush-1, Pit-2, Community-3, Open defecation with water-4, Open defecation with dry leaves, stone and soil-5, Yes-6, No-7	
Kitchen (KITCHEN)-	
Inside house-1, Outside house-2, No kitchen-3	
Use of fuel for cooking (FUEL)-	
Wood-1, Coal-2, Gas-3, Heater-4, Cowdung-5	
Source of loan (LOAN)-	
Moneylender-1, Trader-2, Graingola-3, Bank-4, Government-5, Another (specify)-6	
Household utensil (UTENSIL)-	
Steel, bronze and brass-1, Aluminum-2, Earthen ware-3, Wooden-4, Leaf-5, Aluminum, Earthen ware and Leaf-6	
Storage of grain (STORAGE)-	
Earthen pot-1, Gunny bag-2, Basket-3, Metal container-4	
Use of forest (USEFOR)-	
a. Edible produce, b. Grazing cattle, c. Shelter and articles, d. Selling of wood, e. Selling of fruit.	
E-1, EG-2, EGS-3, EGSSw-4, EGSSwSf-5, G-6, GS-7, GSSw-8, GSSwSf-9, S-10, SSw-11, SSwSf-12, Sw-13, SwSf-14, Sf-15	

BATH-	
Daily-1, 2 and 3 times in a week-2, Weekly-3, Occasional-4	
Sanitation of house (SANITAT)-	
Spreading of animal waste-1, Lack of drainage system-2, Animals residing within the house-3, Separate house for animals-4, Neat and clean-5, Another (specify)-6	
Death rituals (DEATRIT)-	
Buried in graveyard-1, Cremation-2, Throwing in the forest-3, Other (specify)-4	
Liquor consumption (LIQUOR)-	
a. Teetotaler, b. Mahua wine, c. Rice beer, d. Toddy T-1, TM-2, TMR-3, TMRT-4, M-5, MR-6, MRT-7, R-8, RT-9, T-10	
Use of narcotic (NARCOT)-	
a. Biri and Cigarette, b. Tobacco (khaini), c. Chutti, d. Ganja, e. Hukka, f. Gutka B-1, BT-2, BTC-3, BTCG-4, BTCGH-5, T-6, TC-7, TCG-8, TCGH-9, C-10, CG-11, CGH-12, G-13, GH-14, H-15, Gt-16, NO-0	
Method of fishing (FISH)-	
Trap-1, Net-2, Hook-3, Line-4, Net, Hook and Line-5, No fishing-6, Other (specify)-7	
Name of hunting animals (ANIMAL)-	
a. Wild Pig, b. Rabbit, c. Mouse, d. Squirrel, e. Birds, f. Deer, g. No.	
W-1, WR-2, WRM-3, WRMS-4, WRMSB-5, WRMSBD-6, R-7, RM-8, RMS-9, RMSB-10, RMSBD-11, M-12, MS-13, MSB-14, MSBD-15, S-16, SB-17, SBD-18, B-19, BD-20, D-21, NO-22	

Appendix 1.3

Woman Schedule

Which of the family planning methods have used? (FAMPLAN)-	
Vasectomy-1, Copper-T-2, Pills-3, Condom-4, Herb-5, Rhythm abstinence-6, Withdrawal-7, No Family planning method-8	
The woman has no children (Acarpous/ Infructuous) (ACARPOU)	Yes-1 No-2
Live Birth (LIVBIRT)-	
Surviving-1, Not Surviving-2, Still Birth-3	
Cause of Abortion (CAABOR)-	
Unplanned pregnancy-1, Contraceptive failure-2, Complication in pregnancy-3, Health problem-4, Last child too young-5, No abortion-6	
Pregnancy no. (PREGNO)-	
Duration of pregnancy (in months) (DURPREG)-	
SEX-	
Male-1, Female-2	
Currently living or dead (CURLID)-	
Living-1, Dead-2	
Age of ANC in month (AGEANC)-	
AGE-	
Care of pregnancy in ANC (CARANC)-	
Abdominal examination-1, Pressure-2, Weight-3, Urine-4, Bloood-5, Ultrasound-6, TT injection-7, Iron and Folic Acid Tablets (IFA)-8, Both-9, None-10	

Cause of not care in ANC (CNCANC)-	
Cost too much-1, Far away-2, Not customary-3, Lack of knowledge-4, Poor quality service-5, Lack of knowledge and Poor-quality service-6, Care-0	
Place of delivery (PLDEL)-	
Government Dispensary-1, Government Hospital-2, Private Dispensary-3, Private Hospital-4, Trust Hospital-5, Ayush Hospital-6, Home-7	
Source of arrangement for transportation for institutional delivery (SATIDEL)-	
Family-1, Asha-2, Panchayat-3, Not required-4, Not provided-5	
How long did you stay in the institution after delivery? (STIND)-	
No. of hours for less than 24 hours-1, No. of days-2, No stay-3	
In case of delivery at home who conducted to delivery (HOMCOD)-	
Doctor-1, Nurse-2, Dai-3, Family member-4, None-5	
When were the new born baby and mother checked up after birth? (BMCHBIR)-	
Within 24 hours-1, 1 to 3 day-2, 4 to 7 day-3, After 7 day-4, Not Checkup-5	
Was birth weight of the baby taken? (WEIGHB)-	Yes-1 No-2
What was the birth weight of the baby (in kg)?-	
Was the baby ever received any vaccination (BBC, Polio, Diphtheria, Measles, Hepatitis B)? – VACINE-	Yes-1 No-2
What was the main reason of no vaccination? (RENVAC)-	
Not aware-1, Place of immunization not known-2, Far away-3, Fear of side effect-4, Not customary-5,Yes vaccination-6	
When did you start first breast feed your baby? (BREASTF)-	
Within 1 hour -1, 1-24 hour -2, 2-3 days -3, After 3 days -4, Never -5	
What was the first food given to child? (FFCH)-	
Colostrum milk of mother-1, Honey-2, Gutty-3, Ghee-4, Sugar and glucose-5, Boiled water-6, Another (specify)-7	

How many months did you breast feed your baby? (MBREF)-	
Below 6 months -1, 6 months to 1 year -2, 1-2 years -3, Above 2 years -4, No -5	
When did you start supplementary food to the baby?	
a. Water (WATSFO)- Below 6 months-1, 6 months to 1 year-2, Above 1 year-3	
b. Animal Milk (AMSFO)- Below 6 months-1, 6 months to 1 year-2, Above 1 year-3	
c. Semi Solid mashed (SSMSFO)- Below 6 months-1, 6 months to 1 year-2, Above 1 year-3	
d. Solid (SOLSFO)- Below 6 months-1, 6 months to 1 year-2, Above 1 year-3	
e. Fruit (FRSFO)- Below 6 months-1, 6 months to 1 year-2, Above 1 year-3	
Type of Delivery (TYPDEL)-	
Normal-1, Caesarean-2, Assisted-3	
Did you avail any maternity financial assistance? (FINAST)-	
Janani Suraksha Yojana-1, Other Government schemes-2, Not availed-3	
Food eaten by Mother during pregnancy (FEMPR)-	
Sufficient-1, Insufficient-2, Moderate-3	
Addictedness of mother (ADDICT)-	
Alcohol-1, Narcotic-2, Both-3, None-4	
Did you receive birth certificate for your baby (BIRCERT)-	
Yes-1 No-2	

Appendix 1.4

Infant Death Enquiry Schedule

Details of deceased infant-	
SEX-	
Male-1, Female-2	
Date of birth-	
Date of death-	
Age of ANC (AGEANC)-	
Age of Death (AGDEAT)-	
Type of Child Death (TCD)-	
Miscarriage-1, Foetal Death-2, Early Neonatal Death-3, Peri-natal Death-4, Late Neonatal Death-5, Neonatal Death-6, Post-Neonatal Death-7, Infant Death-8 and Child Death-9	
Medical Treatment (TRETME)-	
Government Dispensary-1, Government Hospital-2, Private Dispensary-3, Private Hospital-4, Trust Hospital-5, Ayush Hospital-6, Quack-7, No Medical Attention-8, First treatment quack, then Hospital-9	
Place of Death (PLDEA)-	
Home-1, In-transit-2, Hospital-3, Other-4	
Registration of death (REGDEA)-	
Yes-1, No-2, Do not Know-3	
Order of Birth (ORDBIRT)-	
Cause of Death (CAUDEA)-	

Respiratory infection-1, Diarrhoea/Dysentery-2, Fever with rash-3, Fever with convulsion-4, Low Weight-5, Bleeding from umbilicus-6, Prematuarity-7, Respiratory-8, Jaundice-9, Birth Injury-10, Congenital abnormality-11, Death of Mother-12, Obesity-13, Neonatal tetanus-14, Introduction to tobacco and Salt to girl child-15, Do not know-17, Malaria-18, Typhoid-19, Brain malaria-20, Snake bite-21, Rangbaj-22, Thunder-23, Pneumonia-24, TB-25, Infaction-26, Sink in water-27, Kala fever-28, Chor danth-29, Mirgi-30, Accident-31	
Immunization (IMMUNIZ)-	Yes-1, No-2
Delivery (DELVER)-	
Doctor-1, Nurse-2, Dai-3, Family member-4, Villager-5, No-6	
Characteristics of Deceased (CHARDEC)-	
Immunization status (IMMUST)-	
Timing of initiation of breast feeding (days/months) (INIBRFE)-	
Throwing away colostrum from the beast after childbirth (THCOLOS)-	Yes-1, No-2
Duration of Lactation (Month/year) (DURLACT)-	
Timing of introduction of Supplementary semi-solid food (Month/year) (SUPFOD)-	
Pre-lacteal feed (PLACFED)	
Gutty-1, Ghee-2, Honey-3, Sugar-4, Glucose-5, Boiled water-6, Another (Specify)-7	
Baby cried after birth (BABYCRY)-	Yes-1, No-2
Instrument used for cutting cord (INSTCOR)-	
Antiseptic razor-1, Shaving blade-2, Kitchen knife-3, Domestic scissor-4, Bamboo knife-5, Another (Specify)-6	
Cord care (CORDCAR)-	
Ash of cow dung-1, Butte ghee with or without turmeric-2, Talcum Powder-3, Antiseptic lotion-4, Pest of Cow urine and dry mushroom-5 Another (specify)-6	
Post-neonatal causes of death (PNCDETH)-	Yes-1, No-2
Disease-	

Tetanus-1, Diphtheria-2, Diarrhoea-3, Measles-4, Poliomyelitis-5, Acute respiratory infection-6, Convulsion-7, Jaundice-8, Accident-9, Burn-10, High Fever-11, Low weight-12, Influenza-13, Dysentery-14, Typhoid-15, Malaria-16, Bronchitis-17, Whooping cough-18, Malnutrition-19, Anaemia-20, HB-21, Evil eye-22, Do not know-23, Prematurity-24, Brain malaria-25, Snake bite-26, Rangbaj-27, Thunder-28, Pneumonia-29, TB-30, Infaction-31, Sink in water-32, Death of mother-33, Kala fever-34, Chor danth-35, Mirgi-36, Accident-37	
Place of treatment (PLTREAT)-	
Private Doctor-1, Dispensary-2, Primary health centre-3, Hospital-4	
Treatment by a Private Doctor (TRETDOC)-	
Ayurvedic-1, Unani-2, Allopathic-3, Homeopathic-4, Quack-5	
Nature of Treatment (NATTREA)-	
Injection and Medicine-1, Ointment-2, Operation-3	
Amount spent on treatment (AMSPTRE)-	
Discrimination against girl (DISAGIR)-	
Breast feeding-1, Food-2, Medical care-3, Identification of sex and abortion-4, No-5	

Appendix 1.5

Infant Mortality Rate in the World

Sl. No.	Country	1950/ 55	1975/ 80	2000/ 05	2005/ 10	2010/ 15	2015/ 20
	World	139.57	84.9	49.22	40.98	33.91	29.26
1	Iceland	21.57	8.94	2.54	1.99	1.57	1.25
2	Hong Kong (China)	61.89	12.91	2.52	1.86	1.59	1.32
3	Singapore	60.96	12.85	2.5	2.15	2.07	1.63
4	Finland	33.08	8.54	3.21	2.72	2.1	1.71
5	Japan	47.67	8.48	2.98	2.55	2.18	1.76
6	Slovenia	22.78	13.75	4.03	3.2	2.23	1.87
7	Sweden	19.37	7.75	3.23	2.57	2.4	2.04
8	Norway	21.69	8.77	3.46	3	2.45	2.07
9	Czech Republic	42.18	17.45	3.96	3.08	2.53	2.27
10	South Korea	159.09	33.6	5.01	3.51	2.97	2.11
11	Estonia	85.29	21.85	7.27	4.75	3.2	1.99
12	Spain	62.73	15.38	4.03	3.37	2.88	2.35
13	Italy	59.07	17.16	4.14	3.43	3.04	2.6
14	Macao (China)	65.86	19.52	4.92	3.8	3.06	2.62
15	Portugal	91.99	29.82	4.5	3.32	2.95	2.96
16	Netherlands	23	9.25	4.86	4.11	3.46	2.51

(*Contd.*)

Sl. No.	Country	1950/ 55	1975/ 80	2000/ 05	2005/ 10	2010/ 15	2015/ 20
17	Ireland	40.56	14.61	5.25	3.71	3.39	2.7
18	Greece	45.8	20.82	4.55	3.48	3.28	2.82
19	Israel	38.92	17.09	5.03	3.97	3.43	2.73
20	Belgium	44.74	13.68	4.22	3.83	3.46	2.83
21	Luxembourg	43.93	13.17	4.96	2.33	3.41	2.87
22	Belarus	95.38	21.89	9.59	6.27	3.43	2.97
23	Austria	53.14	16.24	4.47	3.76	3.33	3.15
24	France	44.22	11.54	4.19	3.72	3.49	3.03
25	Germany	46.36	15.52	4.15	3.66	3.36	3.19
26	Denmark	27.71	8.91	4.55	3.73	3.51	3.13
27	Australia	23.68	12.27	4.94	4.41	3.63	3.11
28	Réunion (France)	141.65	34.02	7.62	5.63	4.2	2.67
29	Montenegro	120.01	28.5	11.57	10.9	4.27	2.76
30	Switzerland	29.04	9.7	4.55	4.21	3.89	3.37
31	Poland	78.85	27.31	7.11	5.66	4.4	3.28
32	Cyprus	64.95	19.3	5.59	4.35	4.19	3.54
33	United Kingdom	28.24	13.83	5.3	4.83	4.06	3.76
34	Taiwan	78.79	11.15	6.05	5.16	4.23	3.71
35	New Zealand	26.56	13.6	5.4	4.95	4.37	3.8
36	Croatia	95.51	21.89	6.52	5.75	4.26	4
37	Mayotte (France)	142.6	34.01	7.62	5.63	4.2	4.2
38	Lithuania	107.49	22.44	7.66	5.97	4.36	4.04
39	Latvia	76.66	22.83	9.94	7.8	5.15	3.34
40	Hungary	71.87	25.8	7.44	5.65	4.96	4.05
41	Canada	37.82	12.23	5.27	5.11	4.65	4.51
42	Cuba	80.59	22.35	6.13	5.34	4.8	4.49
43	Slovakia	74.09	22.17	7.27	6.2	5.42	4.76

(*Contd.*)

Sl. No.	Country	1950/ 55	1975/ 80	2000/ 05	2005/ 10	2010/ 15	2015/ 20
44	Guadeloupe (France)	80.24	26.82	8.77	7	5.81	4.64
45	Malta	68.24	15.17	5.71	5.59	5.49	4.97
46	Serbia	117.49	40.15	9.52	7.07	6.07	4.9
47	United States	30.16	14.07	6.99	6.78	5.96	5.82
48	Puerto Rico (US)	63.35	19.66	8.01	7.19	6.37	5.45
49	Antigua and Barbuda	77.56	36.78	11.48	8.95	6.79	5.2
50	Martinique (France)	80.83	27.87	8.5	7.57	6.43	5.57
51	United Arab Emirates	180.61	37.01	9	7.71	6.5	5.52
52	Malaysia	101.52	29.45	7.62	6.99	6.42	5.9
53	Jersey Channel Islands (UK)	32.49	21.31	8.78	7.58	6.75	6.12
54	Bahrain	172	31.94	9.76	7.95	6.91	5.97
55	Bosnia and Herzegovina	188.58	34.03	9.83	9.03	6.91	6
56	French Polynesia (France)	129.51	58.64	9.4	8.78	6.91	6.66
57	Qatar	105.82	33.46	9.8	8.3	7.32	6.29
58	Bahamas	36.77	25.52	13.05	11.28	8.02	5.88
59	Chile	122.54	44.06	8.33	7.74	7.2	6.72
60	Russia	100.45	28.77	16.16	10.68	8.34	5.76
61	Bulgaria	90.16	21.83	12.75	9.55	8.32	6.29
62	Saudi Arabia	201.63	79.57	16.32	12.2	8.69	6.31
63	Romania	90.75	30.85	16.94	11.96	8.35	6.68
64	Kuwait	123.97	33.93	10.41	9.74	8.16	7.12
65	Maldives	268.25	121.31	26.62	14.76	8.95	6.77
66	Ukraine	78.52	22.91	14.8	12.64	8.75	7.2

(*Contd.*)

Sl. No.	Country	1950/ 55	1975/ 80	2000/ 05	2005/ 10	2010/ 15	2015/ 20
67	Sri Lanka	89.03	35.78	11.79	10.17	8.78	7.57
68	Costa Rica	103.26	35.1	10.89	10.02	9.33	7.32
69	Brunei	108.44	22.5	9.71	9.26	8.78	7.92
70	Oman	210.94	82.62	14.64	9.77	9.6	7.27
71	U.S. Virgin Islands (US)	58.2	24.92	11.63	10.66	8.96	8.16
72	Albania	144.77	46.84	21.15	16.78	9.21	8.03
73	French Guiana (France)	102.69	42.28	13.19	10.55	9.12	8.7
74	Thailand	127.16	50.85	16.7	13.4	10.08	7.75
75	Uruguay	57.31	42.42	14.53	11.28	10.05	8.7
76	Guam (US)	82.2	34.23	13.58	11.37	10.07	8.69
77	Lebanon	68.53	38.02	13.81	10.59	9.6	9.42
78	Curaçao (Netherlands)	66.27	21.55	14.67	12.98	10.27	9.05
79	North Macedonia	136.29	62.23	12.94	10.75	8.93	10.69
80	Turkey	217.18	120.07	24.7	16.37	11.84	8.9
81	Barbados	121.51	26.18	12.96	12.58	11.46	10.04
82	Kazakhstan	110.24	68.59	32.01	23.86	14.12	7.67
83	China	128.88	55	27.08	18.11	12.28	9.89
84	Argentina	63.89	39.04	16.75	14.21	12.06	10.23
85	Georgia	79.86	49.29	26.52	18.19	12.92	9.37
86	Mauritius	102.97	37.69	13.35	13.21	11.96	11.22
87	Seychelles	80.91	32.16	11.86	12.15	12.37	10.87
88	Libya	253.75	67.09	21.46	17.58	12.96	10.53
89	Armenia	82.72	57.97	27.05	20.99	13.23	10.78
90	New Caledonia (France)	116.57	44.14	17.29	15.1	13.01	11.51
91	Moldova	81.14	45.91	18.82	15.59	14.17	12.37

(*Contd.*)

Sl. No.	Country	1950/ 55	1975/ 80	2000/ 05	2005/ 10	2010/ 15	2015/ 20
92	Jamaica	82.66	35.28	18.03	16.7	14.94	11.78
93	Peru	158.53	94.94	24.92	18.13	14.09	12.79
94	Colombia	116.6	49.81	19.51	16.95	14.44	12.64
95	Tunisia	232.24	97.26	22.99	18.01	14.56	12.68
96	Tonga	80.03	27.06	14.38	14.38	14.74	12.54
97	Belize	100.17	50.49	20.15	17.3	14.98	12.81
98	Iran	220.32	95.47	24.82	19.13	15.16	12.82
99	Aruba (Netherlands)	68.97	24.51	17.77	16.18	14.78	13.61
100	Saint Lucia	118	29.67	15.69	16.26	16	12.49
101	Samoa	93.75	47.08	17	16.64	15.09	13.45
102	Grenada	76.72	29.46	12.66	12.34	13.67	14.99
103	Mexico	120.97	56.77	20.12	17.14	15.16	13.51
104	Ecuador	138.14	77.36	23.64	19.13	15.07	13.6
105	Brazil	136.25	83.46	28.16	20.34	15.79	13.02
106	Panama	85.64	36.08	20.62	17.78	16	14.13
107	Jordan	146.59	54.01	22.39	19.68	17.06	14.63
108	Saint Vincent	115.56	49.55	19.64	19.48	17.36	14.65
109	El Salvador	143.05	92.65	23.59	21.55	17.71	14.57
110	North Korea	121.32	36.31	28.5	27.27	18.54	13.9
111	Syria	141.55	55.31	17.74	14.96	17.87	15.54
112	Honduras	169.3	80.95	28.36	23.32	18.39	15.04
113	Egypt	248.64	133.16	29.35	23.47	18.92	15.61
114	Nicaragua	172.41	90.08	26.43	23.08	17.83	16.78
115	Vietnam	103.38	45.61	23.58	18.97	17.9	16.71
116	Kyrgyzstan	138.69	89.91	37.18	30.23	19.54	15.51
117	Solomon Islands	171.3	47.52	24.58	22.97	20.16	15.46
118	Palestinian territories	140.84	67.55	23.72	21.05	19.3	17.46

(*Contd.*)

Sl. No.	Country	1950/ 55	1975/ 80	2000/ 05	2005/ 10	2010/ 15	2015/ 20
119	Cape Verde	130.98	70.46	24.46	22.92	20.58	16.89
120	Suriname	77.43	50.19	27.97	23.72	20.26	17.49
121	Paraguay	73.45	52.59	27.06	24.05	20.78	19.02
122	Fiji	86.99	39.37	18.8	19.58	19.95	20.32
123	Venezuela	100.62	38.73	17.16	14.79	15.01	25.7
124	Mongolia	182.7	104.4	40.77	30.51	22.79	18.09
125	Philippines	85.13	53.99	27.9	25.46	23.72	19.66
126	Indonesia	183.96	90.76	37.25	30.39	25.03	18.91
127	Morocco	151.31	101.97	36.61	26.6	24.17	19.86
128	Algeria	163.01	105.46	33.62	29.4	24.94	21.24
129	Vanuatu	121.97	58.41	23.71	24.03	24.3	22.38
130	Guatemala	168.39	96.48	37.25	31.26	26.94	20.74
131	Trinidad and Tobago	69.64	37.01	28.81	28.47	26.09	21.98
132	Uzbekistan	124.37	77.78	49.4	40.73	27.68	20.83
133	Azerbaijan	119.87	94.97	54.17	40.7	31.39	20.83
134	Iraq	225.39	56.96	34.49	31.73	28.49	24.11
135	Dominican Republic	153.07	85.91	34.91	29.54	27.49	25.85
136	Cambodia	142.35	319.24	65.8	44.81	29.97	23.72
137	Micronesia	95.48	47.73	39.81	34.9 5	30.28	23.49
138	Bhutan	246.27	130.91	51.91	39.49	30.47	24.06
139	Guyana	72.06	54.41	35.29	31.95	31.66	26.76
140	Sao Tome and Principe	138.17	74.4	56.13	42.05	32.08	26.42
141	Bangladesh	210.9	138.48	55.48	43.32	33.15	26.85
142	South Africa	134.21	70.64	53.93	48.08	32.94	27.24
143	Nepal	224.16	148.88	53.66	42.62	33.78	27.93
144	Bolivia	177.71	128.19	51.97	42.12	32.4	29.71

(*Contd.*)

Sl. No.	Country	1950/ 55	1975/ 80	2000/ 05	2005/ 10	2010/ 15	2015/ 20
145	Western Sahara (disputed)	216.58	133.75	52.92	43.04	34.13	28.78
146	Tajikistan	140.82	96.63	57.25	39	34.05	29.26
147	Botswana	127.89	56.4	57.04	44.15	35.47	30.15
148	Madagascar	182.66	122.39	57.97	45.49	36.77	29.04
149	Rwanda	150.34	130.03	94.28	62.68	39.41	29.18
150	Senegal	127.55	97.32	61.13	47.48	38.27	32.75
151	India	180.95	120.8	59.95	49.46	39.08	32
152	Namibia	143.99	75.9	51.13	43.46	38.56	33.38
153	Republic of Congo	134.2	76.27	72.23	52.48	41.42	35.29
154	Gabon	159.91	100.5	59.72	49.93	41.91	35.28
155	Kenya	142.46	85.95	62.76	51.12	41.56	36.34
156	Eritrea	199.33	132.04	59.38	51.65	45.01	34.72
157	Ghana	147.44	99.16	60.9	53.72	44.83	35.63
158	Myanmar	213.03	100.3	57.82	51.98	43.66	38.4
159	East Timor	264.27	253.22	69.02	53.27	44.89	37.34
160	Ethiopia	199.25	136.49	77.9	59.82	45.79	37
161	Laos	175.86	130.25	69.95	57.53	46.97	38.76
162	Yemen	287.97	159.02	61.56	48.64	43.28	43.23
163	Tanzania	148.42	116.5	70.96	55.48	46.86	41.21
164	Djibouti	154.16	96.34	68.1	63.42	55.67	33.36
165	Zimbabwe	113.74	74.73	65.01	62.69	51.22	38.74
166	Turkmenistan	149.99	100.63	61.98	54.14	46.88	43.28
167	Papua New Guinea	158.09	82.44	58.19	54.48	48.31	41.95
168	Sudan	134.53	89.04	61.79	53.18	47.83	42.86
169	Kiribati	146.77	88.3	52.29	51.44	47.93	42.98
170	Eswatini (Swaziland)	144.8	89.05	86.32	74.23	51.61	41.36

(*Contd.*)

Sl. No.	Country	1950/55	1975/80	2000/05	2005/10	2010/15	2015/20
171	Malawi	178.42	155.29	86.94	68.43	52.55	41.33
172	Gambia	156.28	100.93	59.36	52.36	49.82	44.83
173	Burundi	166.26	131.53	87.54	69.99	52.33	42.44
174	Zambia	137.92	100.41	88.4	64.72	53.31	45.61
175	Niger	160.86	138.69	85.23	67.59	55.9	46.31
176	Uganda	150.34	115.92	79.51	70.73	58.96	46.15
177	Togo	185.96	100.61	77.31	64.16	55.67	49.68
178	Comoros	192.39	126.56	72.53	66.63	58.06	53.1
179	Afghanistan	275.87	171.52	84.65	72.19	60.1	51.71
180	Mauritania	147.77	96.63	69.2	65.57	58.86	53.44
181	Liberia	165.36	144.21	100.28	72.88	60.13	54.06
182	Haiti	221.29	131.73	68.94	63.82	60.96	54.3
183	Mozambique	164.47	152.11	98.79	78.68	62.78	53.91
184	Guinea	206.75	171.27	95.16	77.65	65.7	51.64
185	Burkina Faso	228.11	132.94	89.98	77.53	64.74	54.21
186	Guinea-Bissau	162.52	140.57	103.87	85.25	68.1	57.12
187	Lesotho	128.02	90.89	78.96	74.94	65.37	62.25
188	Côte d'Ivoire	189.17	115.11	87.92	77.2	67.46	60.42
189	Benin	207.82	135.25	84.03	74.51	67.66	61.15
190	Pakistan	250.03	127.31	82.92	75.64	68.1	61.33
191	South Sudan	248.1	168.71	101.32	78.57	65.81	64.36
192	Cameroon	154.96	112.4	92.17	80.45	70.66	61.18
193	Nigeria	200.29	134.06	103.96	89.33	74.97	62.14
194	Democratic Republic of Congo	166.33	129.04	99.47	83.83	73.15	64.92
195	Angola	192.8	154.58	128.76	104.21	78.25	61.46

(*Contd.*)

Sl. No.	Country	1950/55	1975/80	2000/05	2005/10	2010/15	2015/20
196	Equatorial Guinea	167.05	143.43	95.42	84.63	73.79	66.13
197	Mali	241.92	162.69	106.53	89.06	78.47	65.8
198	Somalia	199.81	136.58	96.96	89.76	79.44	69.31
199	Chad	186.05	137.63	108.34	97.53	84.06	74.5
200	Central African Republic	169.91	122.55	105.11	99.65	90.29	81.9
201	Sierra Leone	237.16	179.68	141.88	122.09	97.13	80.77

Appendix 1.6

Distribution and Composition of Scheduled Tribes in Jharkhand, 2011

S.T.	Total	Per cent of S.T.	Male	Female	Sex Ratio
Santhal	2754723	31.86	1371168	1383555	1009
Oraon	1716618	19.86	855210	861408	1007
Munda	1229221	14.22	614199	615022	1001
Ho	928289	10.74	459209	469080	1021
Kharwar	248974	2.88	126763	122211	964
Lohra	216226	2.50	109383	106843	977
Bhumij	209448	2.42	104910	104538	996
Kharia	196135	2.27	97139	98996	1019
Generic Tribe	173746	2.01	87388	86358	988
Mahli	152663	1.77	76631	76032	992
Mal Paharia	135797	1.57	67791	68006	1003
Bedia	100161	1.16	50207	49954	995
Chero	95575	1.10	48860	46715	956
Karmali	64154	0.74	33203	30951	932
Chick-Baraik	54163	0.63	27126	27037	997
Gond	53676	0.62	26925	26751	994
Kol	53584	0.62	27037	26547	982

(*Contd.*)

S.T.	Total	Per cent of S.T.	Male	Female	Sex Ratio
Sauria Paharia	46222	0.53	22970	23252	1012
Kisan	37265	0.43	18880	18385	974
Korwa	35606	0.41	18000	17606	978
Kora	32786	0.38	16487	16299	989
Parhaiya	25585	0.30	13070	12515	958
Asur	22459	0.26	11473	10986	958
Binjhia	14404	0.17	7320	7084	968
Birhor	10726	0.12	5472	5254	960
Savar	9688	0.11	4864	4824	992
Kawar	8145	0.09	4082	4063	995
Birjia	6276	0.07	3174	3102	977
Gorait	4973	0.06	2527	2446	968
Baiga	3582	0.04	1829	1753	958
Bathudi	3464	0.04	1754	1710	975
Banjara	487	0.01	242	245	1012
Khond	221	0.01	114	107	939
Jharkhand	8645042	100.00	4315407	4329635	1003

Source: Census of India 2001, Series 1, Social and Cultural Tables, Table A-II, District-wise Scheduled tribe Population for Each Tribe Separately, Delhi: Controller of Publications.

Appendix 1.7

District-wise percentage and share of S.T. Population in Jharkhand, 2011

	District	Persons	ST POP	% of ST	% of Gen	Share of ST
1	Bokaro	2061918	255626	12.40	87.60	2.96
2	Chatra	1042304	45563	4.37	95.63	0.53
3	Deoghar	1491879	180962	12.13	87.87	2.09
4	Dhanbad	2682662	233119	8.69	91.31	2.70
5	Dumka	1321096	571077	43.23	56.77	6.61
6	Garhwa	1322387	205874	15.57	84.43	2.38
7	Giridih	2445203	238188	9.74	90.26	2.76
8	Godda	1311382	279208	21.29	78.71	3.23
9	Gumla	1025656	706754	68.91	31.09	8.17
10	Hazaribagh	1734005	121768	7.02	92.98	1.41
11	Jamtara	790207	240489	30.43	69.57	2.78
12	Khunti	530299	389626	73.47	26.53	4.51
13	Kodarma	717169	6903	0.96	99.04	0.08
14	Latehar	725673	331096	45.63	54.37	3.83
15	Lohardaga	461738	262734	56.90	43.10	3.04
16	Pakur	899200	379054	42.15	57.85	4.38
17	Palamu	1936319	181208	9.36	90.64	2.10

(Contd.)

	District	Persons	ST POP	% of ST	% of Gen	Share of ST
18	Pashchimi Singhbhum	1501619	1011296	67.35	32.65	11.70
19	Purbi Singhbhum	2291032	653923	28.54	71.46	7.56
20	Ramgarh	949159	201166	21.19	78.81	2.33
21	Ranchi	2912022	1042016	35.78	64.22	12.05
22	Sahibganj	1150038	308343	26.81	73.19	3.57
23	Seraikella Kharsawan	1063458	374642	35.23	64.77	4.32
24	Simdega	599813	424407	70.76	29.24	4.91
	Total	**32966238**	**8645042**	**26.22**	**73.78**	**100.00**

Source: Census of India, 2011, Series-21, Paper-1, Jharkhand, Final Data of Population.

Appendix 2.1

District-wise Distribution of Primitive Tribes in Jharkhand, 2001

District	Asur	Birhor	Birjia	Korwa	Mal Paharia	Parhaiya	Savar	Sauria Paharia	Total	% of PTG
Garhwa	0	159	0	18144	0	3264	0	0	21567	11.21
Chatra	0	1256	0	0	0	1322	0	0	2578	1.34
Kodarma	0	766	0	0	0	0	0	0	766	0.4
Giridih	0	258	0	0	0	0	0	0	258	0.13
Deoghar	0	0	0	0	6368	47	0	0	6415	3.33
Godda	0	0	0	0	1451	0	27	14624	16102	8.37
Sahibganj	0	0	0	0	442	0	0	34687	35129	18.26
Pakur	0	0	0	0	16902	0	0	10530	27432	14.26
Dhanbad	0	137	0	0	0	0	0	0	137	0.07
Bokaro	0	297	0	0	0	0	0	0	297	0.15
Lohardaga	1170	58	396	0	0	29	0	0	1653	0.86

(*Contd.*)

District	Asur	Birhor	Birjia	Korwa	Mal Paharia	Parhaiya	Savar	Sauria Paharia	Total	% of PTG
Purbi Singhbhum	0	58	0	0	626	0	10736	320	11740	6.1
Palamu	0	0	0	2126	100	5175	45	0	7446	3.87
Latehar	226	94	3731	1518	0	3945	0	0	9514	4.94
Hazaribagh	0	1873	0	0	0	0	0	0	1873	0.97
Dumka	4	0	0	0	31546	0	0	0	31550	16.4
Jamtara	0	0	0	0	3339	0	0	0	3339	1.74
Ranchi	0	636	0	0	9	0	0	107	752	0.39
Gumla	7700	141	1266	1636	0	66	71	0	10880	5.65
Simdega	0	174	0	603	0	0	0	0	777	0.4
Pashchimi Singhbhum	0	585	0	0	0	0	0	0	585	0.3
Seraikella Kharsawan	0	87	0	0	0	0	695	853	1635	0.85
Total	**9100**	**6579**	**5393**	**24027**	**60783**	**13848**	**11574**	**61121**	**192425**	**100**

Source: Census of India 2001, Series 1, Social and Cultural Tables, Table A-II, District-wise Scheduled Tribe Population for Each Tribe Separately, Delhi: Controller of Publications.

Appendix 2.2

District-wise Distribution of Primitive Tribes in Jharkhand, 2011

District	Asur	Birhor	Birjia	Korwa	Mal Paharia	Parhaiya	Sauria Paharia	Savar	Total	% of PTG
Garhwa	1584	0	115	25268	420	6489	0	4	33880	11.59
Chatra	33	2337	1	0	8	590	0	1	2970	1.02
Kodarma	145	1321	8	0	4	2	7	10	1497	0.51
Giridih	59	554	1	6	173	2	21	17	833	0.29
Deoghar	19	40	0	0	12269	63	121	13	12525	4.29
Godda	2	0	0	1	16183	138	13688	63	30075	10.29
Sahibganj	17	1	0	17	21409	219	21004	58	42725	14.62
Pakur	3	1	0	5	38120	125	10875	104	49233	16.84
Dhanbad	48	310	3	30	214	7	13	111	736	0.25
Bokaro	1194	305	3	16	58	28	40	79	1723	0.59
Lohardaga	2004	117	584	1	19	402	0	3	3130	1.07
Purbi Singhbhum	22	343	41	176	566	25	136	8117	9426	3.22

(Contd.)

District	Asur	Birhor	Birjia	Korwa	Mal Paharia	Parhaiya	Sauria Paharia	Savar	Total	% of PTG
Palamu	447	4	16	3397	247	10330	1	3	14445	4.94
Latehar	2096	192	4124	2733	69	6954	0	5	16173	5.53
Hazaribagh	1640	2049	6	4	93	0	4	6	3802	1.3
Ramgarh	1412	590	17	1	24	13	20	40	2117	0.72
Dumka	51	3	0	0	39534	66	57	210	39921	13.65
Jamtara	8	18	0	0	5014	30	82	56	5208	1.78
Ranchi	109	791	49	32	177	17	44	33	1252	0.43
Khunti	55	56	13	12	13	0	82	7	238	0.08
Gumla	11396	696	1267	2930	87	71	0	104	16551	5.66
Simdega	38	314	18	564	22	0	2	3	961	0.33
Pashchimi Singhbhum	65	553	2	65	77	3	6	140	911	0.31
Seraikella Kharsawan	12	131	8	348	997	11	19	501	2027	0.69
Total	22459	10726	6276	35606	135797	25585	46222	9688	292359	100

Source: Census of India 2011, Series 1, Social and Cultural Tables, Table A-II, District-wise Scheduled Tribe Population for Each Tribe Separately, Delhi: Controller of Publications.

Appendix 2.3

District-wise Decennial Growth of Primitive Tribes in Jharkhand, 2001-2011

District	PTG in 2001	PTG in 2011	GT01-11	G Rate in 2011
Garhwa	21567	33880	12313	57.09
Chatra	2578	2970	392	15.21
Kodarma	766	1497	731	95.43
Giridih	258	833	575	222.87
Deoghar	6415	12525	6110	95.25
Godda	16102	30075	13973	86.78
Sahibganj	35129	42725	7596	21.62
Pakur	27432	49233	21801	79.47
Dhanbad	137	736	599	437.23
Bokaro	297	1723	1426	480.13
Lohardaga	1653	3130	1477	89.35
Purbi Singhbhum	11740	9426	-2314	-19.71
Palamu	7446	14445	6999	94.00
Latehar	9514	16173	6659	69.99
Hazaribagh	1873	5919	4046	216.02
Dumka	31550	39921	8371	26.53
Jamtara	3339	5208	1869	55.97
Ranchi	752	1490	738	98.14

(*Contd.*)

District	PTG in 2001	PTG in 2011	GT01-11	G Rate in 2011
Gumla	10880	16551	5671	52.12
Simdega	777	961	184	23.68
Pashchimi Singhbhum	585	911	326	55.73
Seraikella Kharsawan	1635	2027	392	23.98
Total	**192425**	**292359**	**99934**	**51.93**

Source: Census of India 2001 & 2011, Social and Cultural Tables, District-wise Scheduled Tribe Population for Each Tribe Separately, Delhi: Controller of Publications.

Appendix 2.4

District-wise Percentage of Separate of Primitive Tribal Groups in Jharkhand, 2011

Name of District	% of Asur	% of Birhor	% of Birjia	% of Korwa	% of Mal P.	% of Parhaiya	% of Saur. P.	% of Savar	% of PTG
Garhwa	7.05	0.00	1.83	70.97	0.31	25.36	0.00	0.04	11.59
Chatra	0.15	21.79	0.02	0.00	0.01	2.31	0.00	0.01	1.02
Kodarma	0.65	12.32	0.13	0.00	0.00	0.01	0.02	0.10	0.51
Giridih	0.26	5.17	0.02	0.02	0.13	0.01	0.05	0.18	0.28
Deoghar	0.08	0.37	0.00	0.00	9.03	0.25	0.26	0.13	4.28
Godda	0.01	0.00	0.00	0.00	11.92	0.54	29.61	0.65	10.29
Sahibganj	0.08	0.01	0.00	0.05	15.77	0.86	45.44	0.60	14.61
Pakur	0.01	0.01	0.00	0.01	28.07	0.49	23.53	1.07	16.84
Dhanbad	0.21	2.89	0.05	0.08	0.16	0.03	0.03	1.15	0.25
Bokaro	5.32	2.84	0.05	0.04	0.04	0.11	0.09	0.82	0.59
Lohardaga	8.92	1.09	9.31	0.00	0.01	1.57	0.00	0.03	1.07

(*Contd.*)

Name of District	% of Asur	% of Birhor	% of Birjia	% of Korwa	% of Mal P.	% of Parhaiya	% of Saur. P.	% of Savar	% of PTG
Purbi Singhbhum	0.10	3.20	0.65	0.49	0.42	0.10	0.29	83.78	3.22
Palamu	1.99	0.04	0.25	9.54	0.18	40.38	0.00	0.03	4.94
Latehar	9.33	1.79	65.71	7.68	0.05	27.18	0.00	0.05	5.53
Hazaribagh	7.30	19.10	0.10	0.01	0.07	0.00	0.01	0.06	1.3
Ramgarh	6.29	5.50	0.27	0.00	0.02	0.05	0.04	0.41	0.72
Dumka	0.23	0.03	0.00	0.00	29.11	0.26	0.12	2.17	13.65
Jamtara	0.04	0.17	0.00	0.00	3.69	0.12	0.18	0.58	1.78
Ranchi	0.49	7.37	0.78	0.09	0.13	0.07	0.10	0.34	0.43
Khunti	0.24	0.52	0.21	0.03	0.01	0.00	0.18	0.07	0.08
Gumla	50.74	6.49	20.19	8.23	0.06	0.28	0.00	1.07	5.66
Simdega	0.17	2.93	0.29	1.58	0.02	0.00	0.00	0.03	0.33
Pashchimi Singhbhum	0.29	5.16	0.03	0.18	0.06	0.01	0.01	1.45	0.31
Seraikella Kharsawan	0.05	1.22	0.13	0.98	0.73	0.04	0.04	5.17	0.69

Appendix 2.5

Decennial Growth of PTGs in Jharkhand (1872-2011)

Year	Asur	Birjia	Birhor	Korwa	Mal P.	Parhaiya	Savar	Sauria P.	Total
Pop.1872	1578	976	2139	5214	18000	5487	768	68335	102497
Pop.1881	1204	1021	2278	7561	21873	5789	892	89653	130271
G.R.1881	-23.70	4.61	6.5	45.01	21.52	5.5	16.15	31.2	27.1
Pop.1891	2303	1165	1833	9710	24905	6140	913	111592	158561
G.R.1891	91.28	14.1	-19.53	28.42	13.86	6.06	2.35	24.47	21.72
Pop.1901	2784	1243	848	11105	41048	6549	984	47066	111627
G.R. 1901	20.89	6.7	-53.74	14.37	6.66	6.66	7.78	-57.82	-29.6
Pop.1911	3716	1567	2026	13720	38553	7891	1045	62734	131252
G.R. 1911	33.48	26.07	138.92	23.55	-6.08	20.49	6.2	33.29	17.58
Pop.1921	2245	1684	1363	11387	39972	8762	1178	55600	122191
G.R. 1921	-39.59	7.47	-32.72	-17	3.68	11.04	12.73	-11.37	-6.9
Pop.1931	2024	1842	1870	13021	37437	9672	762	59891	126519
G.R. !931	-9.84	9.38	37.2	14.35	-6.34	10.39	-35.31	7.72	3.54

(Contd.)

Year	Asur	Birjia	Birhor	Korwa	Mal P.	Parhaiya	Savar	Sauria P.	Total
Pop.1941	4388	2075	2530	13472	40148	10134	1645	58654	133046
G.R. 1941	116.80	12.65	35.29	3.46	7.24	4.78	115.88	-2.07	5.16
Pop.1961	5819	4029	2438	21168	45423	12268	1561	55606	148312
G.R. 1961	32.61	94.17	-3.64	57.13	13.014	21.06	-5.11	-5.2	11.47
Pop.1971	7026	3628	3464	18717	48636	14651	3548	59047	158717
G.R. 1971	20.74	-9.95	42.08	-11.58	7.07	19.42	127.29	6.19	7.02
Pop.1981	7783	4057	4377	21940	79322	24012	3014	39269	183774
G.R. 1981	10.77	11.82	26.36	17.22	63.09	63.89	-15.05	-33.5	15.79
Pop.1991	9122	4029	8032	24146	79154	29256	4203	47826	205774
G.R. 1991	17.20	-0.69	83.64	10.05	-0.21	21.84	39.45	21.79	11.97
Pop.2001	10347	5365	7514	27177	115093	20786	6004	31050	223336
G.R. 2001	13.43	33.16	-6.52	12.55	45.4	-28.95	42.85	-35.08	8.53
Pop.2011	22459	6276	10726	354606	135797	25585	9688	46222	292359
G.R. 2011	117.06	16.98	42.75	31.02	17.99	23.09	61.36	48.86	30.91

Source: Various Census Reports, Gazetteers and District Census Handbooks.

Appendix 2.6

Regional Concentration of Primitive Tribes through Location Quotient in Jharkhand (2011)

District	Total PTG	Total ST	Tot Pop	% of PTG to ST	% of PTG to TP	LQ of PTG	% of ST	LQ of ST
Garhwa	33880	205874	1322387	16.46	2.56	2.88	15.57	0.59
Chatra	2970	45563	1042304	6.52	0.28	0.32	4.37	0.17
Kodarma	1497	6903	717169	21.69	0.21	0.23	0.96	0.04
Giridih	833	238188	2445203	0.35	0.03	0.04	9.74	0.37
Deoghar	12525	180962	1491879	6.92	0.84	0.94	12.13	0.46
Godda	30075	279208	1311382	10.77	2.29	2.58	21.29	0.81
Sahibganj	42725	308343	1150038	13.86	3.72	4.17	26.81	1.02
Pakur	49233	379054	899200	12.99	5.48	6.15	42.15	1.61
Dhanbad	736	233119	2682662	0.32	0.03	0.03	8.69	0.33
Bokaro	1723	255626	2061918	0.67	0.08	0.09	12.40	0.47
Lohardaga	3130	262734	461738	1.19	0.68	0.76	56.90	2.17

(*Contd.*)

District	Total PTG	Total ST	Tot Pop	% of PTG to ST	% of PTG to TP	LQ of PTG	% of ST	LQ of ST
Purbi Singhbhum	9426	653923	2291032	1.44	0.41	0.46	28.54	1.09
Palamu	14445	181208	1936319	7.97	0.75	0.84	9.36	0.36
Latehar	16173	331096	725673	4.88	2.23	2.50	45.63	1.74
Hazaribagh	3802	121768	1734005	3.12	0.22	0.25	7.02	0.27
Ramgarh	2117	201166	949159	1.05	0.22	0.25	21.19	0.81
Dumka	39921	571077	1321096	6.99	3.02	3.40	43.23	1.65
Jamtara	5208	240489	790207	2.17	0.66	0.74	30.43	1.16
Ranchi	1252	1042016	2912022	0.12	0.04	0.05	35.78	1.36
Khunti	238	389626	530299	0.06	0.04	0.05	73.47	2.80
Gumla	16551	706754	1025656	2.34	1.61	1.81	68.91	2.63
Simdega	961	424407	599813	0.23	0.16	0.18	70.76	2.70
Pashchimi Singhbhum	911	1011296	1501619	0.09	0.06	0.07	67.35	2.57
Seraikella Kharsawan	2027	374642	1063458	0.54	0.19	0.21	35.23	1.34
Total	**292359**	**8645042**	**32966238**	**3.38**	**0.89**	**1.00**	**26.22**	**1.00**

Source: Census of India 2011, Series 1, Jharkhand, Social and Cultural Tables, Table A-II, District-wise Scheduled Tribe Population for Each Tribe Separately, Delhi: Controller of Publications.

Appendix 3.1

Average Distance of Medical Facilities in Primitive Tribal Villages

Primitive Tribe	Primary Health Centre in km	Govt. Hospital in km	Private Hospital in km	Trust Hospital in km
Asur	12.8	41.5	65	88
Birjia	10	10	75	75
Birhor	8.7	15.8	29.1	25.6
Korwa	14.08	17.77	76.69	76.69
Parhaiya	3.53	16.87	34.2	34.2
Savar	6.07	9.47	15.93	15.93
Mal Paharia	2.45	7	22.73	22.73
Sauria Paharia	9.07	24.43	37.29	37.29
Total	**8.16**	**17.38**	**43.62**	**45.57**

Appendix 3.2

Percentage Distribution of Communication Facilities in PTG Villages

Primitive Tribe	Mobile	Mobile with Internet	Post Office
Asur	100	0	0
Birjia	75	0	25
Birhor	100	0	0
Korwa	100	0	0
Parhaiya	80	0	20
Savar	66.7	20	13.3
Mal Paharia	81.9	9.1	0
Sauria Paharia	92.9	0	7.1
Total	87	4	9

Appendix 3.3

Average Distance of Transportation Facilities in PTG Villages

Primitive Tribe	Railway Station in km	Bus Stand in km
Asur	87.50	14.20
Birjia	58.67	9.92
Birhor	35.30	14.80
Korwa	76.69	16.31
Parhaiya	19.47	16.53
Savar	14.73	12.53
Mal Paharia	22.73	7.00
Sauria Paharia	90.21	24.36
Total	49.55	14.75

Appendix 3.4

Average Distance of Market Centres in PTG Villages

Primitive Tribe	Distance of Town in km
Asur	8.00
Birjia	9.08
Birhor	12.20
Korwa	13.77
Parhaiya	6.33
Savar	7.20
Mal Paharia	4.82
Sauria Paharia	9.50
Total	**8.79**

Appendix 3.5

Distribution and Distance of Educational Facilities in PTG Villages

Primitive Tribe	No School	Primary School		Middle School		Secondary School		Higher Secondary School	
	Percentage	Percentage	Distance in km	Percentage	Distance in km	Percentage	Distance in km	Percentage	Distance in km
Asur	20	50	0.5	20	3.6	10	7.4	0	36.5
Birjia	41.7	41.7	1.1	16.7	6.6	0	9.9	0	9.9
Birhor	40	20	1.1	30	4.2	10	10.4	0	16
Korwa	15.4	53.8	0.2	30.8	3.6	0	12.2	0	17.9
Parhaiya	13.3	33.3	0.2	53.3	2	0	6	0	16.9
Savar	26.7	26.7	0.5	40	2.4	6.7	6.5	0	9.7
Mal Paharia	9.1	36.4	0.2	45.5	1.7	0	4.8	9.1	4.8
Sauria Paharia	21.4	57.1	0.4	14.3	6.2	0	11.9	7.1	22.6
Total	**23**	**40**	**0.5**	**32**	**3.8**	**3**	**8.6**	**2**	**16.4**

Bibliography

Books

Adhikari, R. (2003). "Early Marriage and Childbearing: Risks and Consequences", pp. 62-66, in S. Bott, S. Jejeebhoy, I. Shah and C. Puri (eds.), *Towards Adulthood: Exploring the Sexual and Reproductive Health of Adolescents in South Asia*, Geneva: World Health Organization.

Ahmad, A. (1983). "Regional Development Process and Redistribution of Tribal Population in Mid-India", in L.A. Kosinskiand K.M. Elahi (eds.), *Population Redistribution and Development in South Asia*, Dordrecht: D. Redial Publishing Company, pp. 65-78.

Ahuja, Ram (2007), *Indian Social System*, New Delhi: Rawat Publication.

Ambastha, N.K. (1969). *A critical Study of the Tribal Education*, Delhi: S. Chand and Co.

Balakrishnan, R. (2004). *Jharkhand Matters: Essays on Ethnicity, Regionalism and Development*, New Delhi: Konark Publishers Pvt Ltd.

Basu, S.K. (1990). *Tribal Health in Rural Area*, New Delhi: National Institute of Health and Family Welfare.

Bhowmick, P.K. (1973). *Dynamics of Tribal Development*, New Delhi: Inter India Publication.

Bogue, D.J. (1969). *Principles of Demography*, New York: John Wiley and Sons.

Bose, N.K. (1971). *Tribal Life in India*, New Delhi: National Book Trust.

Chandrasekhar, S. (1950). *India's Population: Fact and Policy*, Indian Institute of Population Studies, Annamalai University.

Chandrasekhar, S. (1959). *Infant Mortality in India, 1901-51*, London: George Allen and Unwin Ltd.

Chandrasekhar, S. (1974). "Abortion in a Crowded World", London: George Allen and Unwin Ltd.

Chandrasekharan, C. (1961). *Physiological Factors Affecting Fertility in India*, (mimeographed), Bombay: Demographic Training and Research Centre.

Chatterjee, P.K. (1979). *Aspect of Human Fertility: A Socio-economic Study*, University of Kalyani, Kalyani, West Bengal.

Daradhiyar, S.K. and P.K. Verma (1991). *Ecological Survey of Paharia Community in Santhal Paragana*, Final Technical Report submitted to submitted to Department of forest and Environment, Government of India.

Das, A.N. (1992). *The Republic of Bihar*, New Delhi: Penguin.

Das, N.C. (1997). *Tribal Demography*, Bhubaneswar: Sagar Purblication.

Fuchs, Stephen (1973). *The Aboriginal Tribe of India*, Delhi: McMillan Co. of India.

Gales, R.R. (1962). *The Asur and the Birhor of Chotanagpur in Indian Anthropology*, New Delhi: Asia Publishing House.

Ghurye, G.S. (1963). *Scheduled tribes*, London: Luzac and Co.

Gupta, R. (1977): *Planning for Tribal Development*, New Delhi: Ankur Publishing House.

Hasnain, Nadeem (1983). *Tribal India Today*, New Delhi: Harmam Publications.

Jain, S.P. (1955). "Mortality Trends in India", *Proceedings of the World Population Conference, 1954*, New York: United Nations.

Kanitkar, T. and R.K. Sinha (1989), "Antenatal Care Services in Five States of India, in S.N. Singh (ed.), *Population Transition in India*, Vol. 2, Delhi: B.R. Publishing Corporation, pp. 201-11.

Khan, M.F. and C.V.S. Prasad (1982). "Family Planning Practices in India-Second All India Family Planning Survey", *Monograph*, New Delhi: ORG-MARG.

Kohli, K.L. (1977). *Mortality in India: A State-wise Study*, New Delhi: Sterling Publishers Pvt. Ltd.

Kulkarni, M.G. (1974). *Problems of Tribal Development*, Delhi: Parimal Prakashan.

Kumar, A. (1986). *Tribal Culture and Economy: The Mal Paharia of Santhal Pargana*, New Delhi: Inter India Publication.

Kumar, R. (1998). *Child Development in India: Health, Welfare and Management*, Vol. 1, New Delhi: Ashish Publishing House.

Leridon, H. (1977). *Human Fertility: The Basic Components*, Chicago: University of Chicago Press.

Leuva, K.K. (1964). *The Asur, A Study of Primitive Iron Smelters*, New Delhi: Bharatiya Adimjati Sevak Sangh.

Majumdar, D.N. (1937). *A Tribe in Transition—A Study in Cultural Pattern*, London: Longmans Green and Co.

Majumdar, D.N. (1973). *The Tribal Village in Bihar*, Delhi: Munshi and Manohar Lal Oriental Publishers and Book Sellers.

Mitra, S.C. (1937). *A Note on Curious Customs of the Santal Pargmans*, London Green and Co.

Mukerji S. (1977). "Estimation of Infant Mortality from Fertility Data—A Linear Programming Approach", International Conference on Optimization in Statistics, December 20-22,1977, IIT, Bombay.

Mukherjee, R. (1987). *The Quality of Life: Valuation in Social Research*, New Delhi: Sage Publication.

Natrajan, N. (1986). *Tribal India, Some Dimensions of Development*, New Delhi: Indian Institute of Public Administration.

O'Malley, L.S.S. (1910). Bengal District Gazetteers: Singhbhum, Logos Press, New Delhi.

O'Malley, L.S.S. (1926). Bihar and Orissa District Gazetteers: Palamu, Logos Press, New Delhi.

O'Malley, L.S.S. (1938). Bihar District Gazetteers: Santhal Parganas, Logos Press, New Delhi.

Pandey, A., M. Kim Choe, N.Y. Luther, D. Sahu and J. Chand (1998). *Infant and Child Mortality in India*, Mumbai: International Institute for Population Sciences.

Prasad, A. (1966). "Sequent Occupancy and Peopling of Chotanagpur", *Proceedings of the Indian Science Congress*, Part III.

Prasad, N. (1962). *Tribal Bihar*, Ranchi: Tribal Research Institute.

Roy, S.C. (1925). "The Birhor, A Little-Known Jungle Tribe of Chotanagpur", *Man in India Office.*

Roy, S.C. (1925). "The Birhor, A Little-Known Jungle Tribe of Chotanagpur", *Man in India Office.*

Ruzicka, L.T. and T. Kanitkar (1972). "Infant Mortality in an Urban Setting: The Case of Greater Bombay", in K.E. Vaidyanathan (ed.), *Studies on Mortality in India,* Madras: The Gandhigram Institute of Rural Health and Family Planning, pp. 186-204.

Saha, C. (1999). "A Geographical Analysis of Health Education and Work of Female Child in Rajasthan", Unpublished Ph.D. Thesis, CSRD, SSS, JNU, New Delhi.

Satur, D.M. and S. Bhatia (1957). "A Review of Work Done on Infant Mortality", New Delhi: Indian Council of Medical Research.

Singh, J. (1964). *Transport Geography of South Bihar,* Varanasi: B.H.U. Press.

Singh, R.L. ed. (1971). *India: A Regional Geography,* Varanasi: National Geographical Society of India.

Sinha, V.N.P. (1976). *Chotanagpur: A Study in Settlement Geography,* New Delhi: K.B. Publication.

Srinivas, M.N. and E.A. Ramaswamy (1977). *Culture and Human Fertility in India,* Delhi: Oxford University Press.

Srinivasan, K. (1995). *Regulating Reproduction in India's Population: Efforts, Results and Recommendations,* New Delhi: Sage Publications.

Thompson, C.J. (1931). *Stillbirths and Neonatal Deaths in India: A Preliminary Inquiry,* London: Lewis.

Tiwari, P.D. (1989). *Nutritional Problems in Rural India,* New Delhi: Northern Book Centre.

Vidyarthi, L.P. (1963). *The Maler,* Calcutta: Brookland Ltd.

Vidyarthi, L.P. (1969). *Cultural Configuration of Ranchi: Survey of an Emerging Industrial City of Tribal India (1960-62),* Calcutta: J.N. Basu and Co.

Vidyarthi, L.P. and B.K. Roy (1976). *The Tribal Culture of India,* New Delhi: Concept Publishing Co.

Articles

Adayar, A.R. (1946). "The Kumarbhag Paharia", *Man in India,* Vol-26, No. 224, pp. 24-30.

Agarwal, V.K. *et al.* (1982). "Some Observations on Perinatal Mortality", *Indian Pediatrics*, 19(3), pp. 233-38.

Alhaji, M.A., M.A. Bello, H.A. Elechi, Akuhwa, R.T. Bukar, and H.A. Ibrahim (2013). "A review of neonatal tetanus in University of Maiduguri Teaching Hospital, North-eastern Nigeria", *Nigerian Medical Journal, 54*(6), 398-401, doi:10.4103/0300-1652.126294.

Ambastha, M.P. (1963). "Mal Paharia: Material Culture", *Bulletin of the Bihar Tribal Research Institute*, Vol. 5, No. 1, pp. 17-36.

Ansari, M., M.M. Ibrahim, and P.R. Shankar (2012). "Mothers" Knowledge, Attitude and Practice regarding Diarrhoea and its Management in Morang Nepal: An Interventional Study", *Tropical Journal of Pharmaceutical Research, 11*(5), 847-854. doi:10.4314/ tjpr. v11i5.19

Azad, Md. H. (1977). "Where do Our Tribals Live?", *Geographical Bulletin of India*, Patna University, Vol. 1, No. 1, pp. 1-4.

Bainbridge, R.B. (1907). "The Saorias of the Rajmahal Hills", *Memoirs of the Asiatic Society of Bengal*, Vol. 2, No. 4, pp. 42-75.

Bhargava, V. *et al.* (1969). "Survival Rate, Growth and Development Pattern of Low-Birth-Weight in First Year of Life", *Indian Pediatrics*, No. 6, pp. 224-233.

Chen, X.K. *et al.* (2007). "Teenage Pregnancy and Adverse Birth Outcomes: A Large Population Based Retrospective Cohort Study", *International Journal of Epidemiology*, 36 (2), pp. 368-373.

Chhapola, V. and R. Brar (2015). "Impact of an Educational Intervention on Hand Hygiene Compliance and Infection Rate in a Developing Country Neonatal Intensive Care Unit", *International Journal of Nursing Practice, 21*(5), 486-492. doi:10.1111/ ijn.122

Choulagai, B., S. Onta, N. Subedi, S. Mehata, G.P. Bhandari, A. Poudyal, and A. Krettek (2013). "Barriers to using skilled birth attendants" services in mid- and far-western Nepal: A cross-sectional study", *Bio Med Central International Health and Human Rights, 13*(1), 49-67. doi:10.1186/1472-698X-13-49

Chowdhury, A.K.M. *et al.* (1976). "The Effect of Child Mortality Experience on Subsequent Fertility in Pakistan and Bangladesh", *Population Studies, 30*, pp. 249-62.

Dalfulani, A. (1991). "Environment and Development Policy", *Journal of Rural Development*, Vol. II, No. 2, pp.127-139.

Dolo, O., A. Clack, H. Gibson, N. Lewis, and D.P. Southall, (2016). "Training of Midwives in Advanced Obstetrics in Liberia", *Bulletin of the World Health Organization, 94*(5), pp. 383-387, doi:10.2471/BLT.15.160473

Dube, S.C. (1960). "Approaches to Tribal Problems in India", *Anthropology in Action,* Council of Social and Cultural Research, pp. 87-91.

Flegg, A.T. (1982). "Inequality of Income, Illiteracy and Medical Care as Determinants of Infant Mortality in Underdeveloped Countries", *Population Studies, 36*(3), pp. 441-58.

Fraser, A.M. (1995). "Association of Young Maternal Age with Adverse Reproductive Outcomes", *New England Journal of Medicine, 332*(17), pp. 1113-17.

Frenzen, D.P. and D.P. Hogan (1982). "The Impact of Class, Education, and Health Care on Infant Mortality in a Developing Society: The Case of Rural Thailand", *Demography*, Vol. 19, No. 3, pp. 391-408.

Ghosh, S. *et al.* (1971). "Perinatal Mortality: A Preliminary Report on a Hospital Based Study", *Indian Pediatrics, 8*(9), pp. 421-26.

Gibbs, C.M. (2012). "The Impact of Early Age at First Childbirth on Maternal and Infant Health", *Pediatric and Perinatal Epidemiology*", *26*(1), pp. 259-284.

Greenwood, B.M. *et al.* (1987). "Deaths in Infancy and Early Childhood in a Well-Vaccinated Rural West African Population", *Annals of Tropical Paediatrics, 7*, pp. 91-99.

Gulati, P.N. (August, 1967). "Mortality Rate and Causes of Deaths among Children below Five Years", *Indian Journal of Pediatrics*, 2(3), pp. 40-48.

Gupta, S.D. *et al.* (1981). "Infant Mortality in Rajasthan Villages", *Indian Pediatrics*, 18, pp. 87-101.

Gupta, S.P. (1964). "An Appraisal of the Food Habits and Nutritional State among the Asur, the Korwa and the Sauria Pahariya of Chotanagpur Plateau", *Bulletin of the Bihar Tribal Welfare Research Institute*, Vol. VI, No. 1, pp. 127-79.

Gupta, S.P. (1975). "Utility of Medicinal Herbs in Relation to Reproductive Life of Asur and Oraon Women", *Bulletin of the Bihar Tribal Welfare Research Institute*, Vol. XVII, No. 2, pp. 121-32.

Howlader, A.A. and M.U. Bhuiyan (1999), "Mothers" Health-Seeking Behaviour and Infant and Child Mortality in Bangladesh (Demographers' Notebook)", *Asia-Pacific Population Journal*, Vol. 14, No. 1, pp. 59-75.

Hussain, S. (2018). "Livelihood Practices among the Birhor Tribes of Jharkhand State", *The Journal of Jharkhand Tribal Welfare Research Institute*, Vol. 45, pp. 25-30.

Jain, A.K. (1976). "Revising the Role and Responsibility of the Welfare Programme in India", *Economic and Political Weekly*, Vol. 21, pp. 2729-37.

Jain, A.K. and M. Nag (1986). "The Importance of Female Primary Education for Fertility Reduction in India", *Economic and Political Weekly*, Vol. 21, pp. 1602-08.

Jain, V.C. (1968). "Some Social Components of Infant Mortality in India", *Indian Journal of Pediatrics*, 3(5), pp. 60-69.

Jaiswal, D.P. *et al.* (1981). "Study of Feeding Practices and Morbidity Pattern During First Year of Life", *Indian Pediatrics*, 18(10), pp. 735-41.

Jayaswal, M. (1985). "Health Modernity and its Correlate in Women of South Bihar", *Social Change*, 19, pp.13-29.

Kabir, M. and A. A. Howlander (1980). "Socio-economic determinants of Mortality in Bangladesh", *Rural Demography*, 7(1-2), pp. 1-13.

Kayastha, S.L. and Mishra, S.N. (1968). "Growth of Tribal Economic Development on Tribal Economy and Society in Sonepur Region", *National Geographical Journal of India*, Vol. XIV, Part 2-3, pp. 238-47.

Khan, M.E. (1990). "Contraceptive Use Dynamics of Couples Availing of Services from Government Family Planning Clinics—A Case Study of Orissa, *Journal of Family Welfare*, 36 (3), pp. 18-30.

Khan, M.E. *et al.* (1986). "Nutrition and Health Practices among the Rural Women-A Case Study of Uttar Pradesh, India", *The Journal of Family Welfare*, *33*(1), pp. 3-20.

Kumar, A. (1977). "Ecological Study of Tribal Village: Eco System of Santhal Pargana", *Journal of Environmental Population*, Vol. 4, pp. 271-79.

Kumari, K. *et al.* (2018). "A Study on the Livelihood Patterns of Sabar Primitive Tribes", *The Journal of Jharkhand Tribal Welfare Research Institute*, Vol. 45, pp. 13-24.

Lal, S.B. (1954). "Changes in Dietary Habits and Physique of Aboriginals in Santhal Pargana", *Indian Journal of Medical Research*, Vol. 42, No. 2, pp. 167-79.

Leuva, K.K. (1956). "Paharias and their Welfare—Some Glimpses", *Vanyajati*, Vol. 4, No. 1, pp. 10-17.

Manchanda, S.S. and K.K. Sachdev (1962). "Morbidity and Mortality in Children in Northern India", *Indian Journal of Paediatrics, 2*(5), pp. 62-71.

Matijasevich, A., C.G. Victora, A.J.D. Borross, I.S. Santos, P.I. Marco and F.C. Barros (2008). "Widening Ethnic Disparities in Infant Mortality in Southern Brazil: Comparison of 3 Birth Cohorts", *American Journal of Public Health*, Vol. 98, No. 4, pp. 1-7.

Mitra, S.C. (1937). "A Note on Curious Customs of the Santal Parganas", *Journal of Bihar and Orissa Research Society*, Vol. 23, pp. 324-429.

Mohan, H. (1961). "Socio-Economic Organization and Religion among the Hill Kharias of Dhalbhum", *Bulletin of Bihar Tribal Welfare Research Institute*, Vol. III, No. I, pp. 180-212.

Mohan, H. (1959). "Economic Organization of the Sauria Pahariyas", *Bulletin of Bihar Tribal Research Institute*, Vol. 2, No. 2, pp. 33-66.

Mohan, H. (1960). "Economic Organization of the Mal Paharia and the Kumarbagh of Santal Pargana", *Bulletin of Bihar Tribal Research Institute*, Vol. 2, No. 2, pp. 33-66.

Mohan, H. (1962). "The Cultural Perspective of a Paharia Colony: Purrkola, A Case Study", *Bulletin of Bihar Tribal Research Institute*, Vol. IV, No. 1, pp. 143-52.

Mohan, H. (1979). "The Korwa: A Study in Culture Change", *Bulletin of Bihar Tribal Welfare Research Institute*, Vol. XXI, Nos. I and 2, pp. 79-104.

Mohan, H. (1981). "The Changing Korwa Scene: A Micro Study of a Korwa Village", *Bulletin of Bihar Tribal Welfare Research Institute*, Vol. XXIII, Nos. I and 2, pp. 120-28.

Mohan, H. (1982). "Customary Laws of the Korwa Tribe", *Bulletin of Bihar Tribal Welfare Research Institute*, Vol. XXIV, Nos. 1 and 2, pp. 39-44.

Mohan, H. (1993). "The Korwa: A Tribe in Transition", *Bulletin of Bihar Tribal Welfare Research Institute*, Vol. XXXII, No. I, pp. 12-22.

Mudgal, S., V.J. Rajput, M. Chansoria, and K.K. Kaul (1979). "Tribals of Madhya Pradesh—A Knowledge, Attitudes and Practice Survey of Infant Feeding Practices", *Indian Pediatrics, 16* (7), pp. 617-22.

Oraon, P.C. (1994). "Government Strategies for Tribal Development", *Bulletin of Bihar Tribal Welfare Research Institute*, Vol. XXXIV, No. 1, pp. 1-18.

Oraon, P.C. ed. (2001). Health, Disease and Modern Treatment of Paharias, *Bulletin of Jharkhand Tribal Welfare Research Institute*, Vol. XXXIX, pp. 1-46.

Oraon, P.C. *et al.* (2015). "Indebtedness among the Paharias of Santhal Parganas of Jharkhand State: A Review", *The Journal of Jharkhand Tribal Welfare Research Institute*, Vol. 44, pp. 8-13.

Oraon, P.C. *et al.* (2015). "Nutritional, Assessment among the Primitive Tribes of Jharkhand", *The Journal of Jharkhand Tribal Welfare Research Institute*, Vol. 44, pp. 1-7.

Padhi, S. (2001). "Infant and child survival in Orissa: An Analysis with NFHS Data", *Economic and Political Weekly*, Vol. 36, pp. 3316-25.

Pandey, G. (2018). "Continuity and Change in Livelihood of Asur in Jharkhand: An Anthropological Enquiry", *The Journal of Jharkhand Tribal Welfare Research Institute*, Vol. 45, pp. 5-12.

Pathak, K.B. *et al.* (1988). "A New Method of Estimating Infant and Child Mortality from Data on Children Ever Born and Children Surviving", *Jansankhya*, *6*(2), pp. 159-68.

Phadke, M.V. (1962). "Causes of Infant Mortality and Morbidity", *Journal of Indian Paediatric Society*, *3*(2), pp. 34-51.

Qureshi, S. *et al.* (1973). "Effect of Maternal Nutrition Supplementation on the Birth Weight of the Newborn", *Indian Journal of Pediatrics*, *10*(7), pp. 541-44.

Raman, M.V. (1968). "A Study of Some Aspect of Mortality and Medical Facilities in India", *Indian Journal of Public Health*, No. 12, pp. 1-15.

Roy, B. (1993). "Tribal Development in World System Perspective", *Social Change*, *23*(2-3), pp. 27-32.

Roy, S.C. (1965). "The Asur: Ancient and Modern", *Journal of Bihar and Orissa Research Society*, Vol. 12, pp. 147-52.

Sarkar, S.S. (1944). "The Reproductive Life of Maler Women", *Man-in-India*, Vol. 24, pp. 29-32.

Saxena, G.B. (March, 1962). "Analysis of Inequalities in Infantile Mortality: A Sample Survey of Rural Uttar Pradesh", *Medical Digest*, *2*(4), pp. 70-78.

Saxena, K.B. (1983). "Tribal Development in Bihar: An Appraisal", *Bulletin of the Bihar Tribal Welfare Research Institute*, Vol. XXV, Nos. 1 and 2, pp. 1-108.

Saxena, K.B. (1983). "Tribal Development in Bihar", *Bulletin of the Bihar Tribal Welfare Research Institute*, Vol. XXV, Nos. 1 and 2, pp. 140-47.

Sengupta, P.N. (1979). "Malnutrition, Fertility and Family Planning", *Journal of the Indian Medical Association*, 72: 194-99.

Sharma, P.V. and P.V.S. Prabhavati (2000). "Disparity and Determinants of Quality of Life: An Empirical Study", *IASSI Quarterly*, Vol. 18, No. 4, pp.13-24.

Sheth, S.C. (July, 1961). "Perinatal Morbidity and Mortality", *Indian Journal of Child Health*, 3(6), pp. 38-45.

Simmons, G.B. (1982). "Post-neonatal Mortality in Rural India: Implications of an Economic Model", *Demography*, *19*(3), pp. 371-89.

Singh, S.K. *et al.* (1998). "Socio-Economic Differentials in Child Mortality in Three Selected States of India", *Indian Association of Social Science Institutions (IASSI) Quarterly*, Vol. 16, pp. 53-73.

Singh, A.K. and M. Jayaswal and A. Has (1991b). "Cleanliness Education in the Tribals of South Bihar", *Social Change*, *21*(2), pp. 3-17.

Singh, A.K. *et al.* (1987b). "Family Planning and Child Care in Rural Tribals of Chotanagpur", *Social Change*, *17*(3), pp. 85-86.

Singh, K.P. (1974). "Child Mortality, Social Status and Fertility in India", *Social Biology*, *21*: 385-88.

Singh, R. (1963). "Reproductive Life of Birhor Women", *Bulletin of the Bihar Tribal Welfare Research Institute*, Vol. V, No. 1, pp. 124-42.

Stockwell, E. (1962). "Infant Mortality and Socio-Economic Status: A Changing Relationship, *Miliband Memorial Fund Quarterly*, *40*: 101-11.

Vidyarthi, L.P. (1969). "Cultural Configuration of Ranchi: Survey of an Emerging Industrial City of Tribal India (1960-62)", Calcutta: J.N. Basu and Co.

Visaria, L. (1997). "Unmet Need for Family Planning in Gujarat: A Qualitative Exploration", *Economic and Political Weekly*, Vol. XXXII, pp. WS-29-36.

Viswanathan, T.K. and V.B. Athvale (1969). "Morbidity and Motility in the Neonates", *Indian Paediatrics*, 2(3), pp. 45-63.

Vyas, K.J. (1962). "Morbidity and Mortality in Children", *Indian Journal of Child Health*, 3(7), pp. 11-19.

Yankaur, A. (1959). "An Approach to the Cultural Base of Infant Mortality in India", *Population Review*, 3(1), pp. 39-51.

You, D., L. Hug, S. Ejdemyr *et al.* (2017). "Global, regional, and national levels and trends in under-5 mortality between 1990 and 2015, with scenario-based projections to 2030: a systematic analysis by the un-Inter-agency group for child mortality estimation", *The Lancet*, Vol. 386, pp. 2275-86, 2015.

Zachariah, K.C. and S. Patel (1983). "Trends and Determinants of Infant and Child Mortality in Kerala", *Janasamkhya*, *1*(2), pp. 125-41.

Government Publications and Reports

Annual Health Survey 2010-11 Factsheet, Jharkhand, Office of the Registrar General and Census Commissioner, Ministry of Home Affairs, Government of India, New Delhi.

Census of India (1961-1991). Bihar District Census Handbook, Santhal Pargana, Census Operations, Government of Bihar, Patna

Census of India (1961-1991). Bihar District Census Handbook, Santhal Pargana, Census Operations, Government of Bihar, Patna.

Census of India (2011). Jharkhand, Village Directory and Town Directory, District Census Handbook, Series-21, Part XII-A and B, Latehar.

Census of India (2011). Jharkhand, Village Directory and Town

Directory, District Census Handbook, Series-21, Part XII-A and B, Ranchi.

Census of India (2011). Jharkhand, Village Directory and Town Directory, District Census Handbook, Series-21, Part XII-A and B, Gumla.

Census of India (2011). Jharkhand, Village Directory and Town Directory, District Census Handbook, Series-21, Part XII-A and B, Palamu.

Census of India (2011). Jharkhand, Village Directory and Town Directory, District Census Handbook, Series-21, Part XII-A and B, Garhwa.

Census of India (2011). Jharkhand, Village Directory and Town Directory, District Census Handbook, Series-21, Part XII-A and B, Dumka.

Census of India (2011). Jharkhand, Village Directory and Town Directory, District Census Handbook, Series-21, Part XII-A and B, Pakur.

Census of India (2011). Jharkhand, Village Directory and Town Directory, District Census Handbook, Series-21, Part XII-A and B, Godda.

Census of India (2011). Jharkhand, Village Directory and Town Directory, District Census Handbook, Series-21, Part XII-A and B, Sahibganj.

Census of India (2011). Jharkhand, Village Directory and Town Directory, District Census Handbook, Series-21, Part XII-A and B, Purbi Singhbhum.

Census of India (2011). Jharkhand, Village Directory and Town Directory, District Census Handbook, Series-21, Part XII-A and B, Seraikella Kharsawan.

Census of India (2011). Jharkhand, Village Directory and Town Directory, District Census Handbook, Series-21, Part XII-A and B, Latehar.

Department of Family Welfare, Government of India (1992). "Family Welfare Programme in India, Year Book (1990-91)", New Delhi: Ministry of Health and Family Welfare.

Dhebar, U. N. (1961). "Report of the Scheduled Areas and Scheduled Tribes Commission", New Delhi: Government of India, Vol. I, pp. 1-245.

GOI (2000). "The National Population Policy, 2000", Government of India, http: //india.unfpa.org/drive/ National Population-Policy2000.pdf.

GOI (2011). "Report of the Working Group on National Rural Health Mission (NRHM) for the Twelfth Five Year Plan (2012-17)", New Delhi: Planning Commission.

Government of India (2017): Mission Indradhanush, Available from: *http://www. missionindradhanush.in.* Accessed July 27, 2017.

Government of India (2017): National Health Policy 2017, 2017; 1-31. Available from: *http://www.mohfw.nic.in/showfile. php? lid=4275.* Accessed July 27, 2017.

Indian Council of Medical Research (2009). "Study on Causes of Death by Verbal Autopsy in India", New Delhi: ICMR, India.

International Institute for Population Science (IIPS) and ORC Macro, (2000b). "National Family Health Survey (NFHS-2), 1998-99, Jharkhand" Mumbai: IIPS.

International Institute for Population Science (IIPS) and ORC Macro, (2000a). "National Family Health Survey (NFHS-2)", 1998-99, India", Mumbai: IIPS.

International Institute for Population Science (IIPS), (1995a). "National Family Health Survey (NFHS-1), 1992-93, India", Mumbai: IIPS.

International Institute for Population Sciences (1995), National Family Health Survey, 1992-93 (MCH and Family Planning), Mumbai: IIPS.

International Institute for Population Sciences (2000), National Family Health Survey, 1998-99 (NFHS-2: Preliminary Report), State-Level Reports, Mumbai: IIPS.

International Institute for Population Sciences (2006). Ranking and Mapping of Districts-Based on Socio-Economic and Demographic Indicators, Mumbai: IIPS.

International Institute for Population Sciences (IIPS) and Macro International, (2000), "National Family Health Survey (NFHS II)", 1998-99, India: Vol. I, Mumbai: IIPS.

International Institute for Population Sciences (IIPS) and Macro International, (2007), "National Family Health Survey (NFHS III), 2005-06, India", Mumbai: IIPS.

International Institute for Population Sciences (IIPS) and Macro International, (2012), "National Family Health Survey (NFHS IV), 2010-11, India", Mumbai: IIPS.

International Institute for Population Sciences (IIPS) and Macro International, (2017), "National Family Health Survey (NFHS IV), 2015-16, Ministry of Health and Family Welfare, Government of India", Mumbai: IIPS.

International Institute for Population Sciences (IIPS), (1995), "National Family Health Survey (NFHS I), 1992-93, India", Mumbai: IIPS.

Jharkhand Economic Survey, 2018-19, Planning-cum-Finance Department, Centre for Fiscal Studies, Government of Jharkhand.

Kulkarni, S. and M.K. Choe (1998). "Wanted and Unwanted Fertility in Selected States of India", National Family Health Survey Reports, No. 6.

Ministry of Health and Family Welfare (1997). "Family Welfare Programme in India", *Year Book, 1995-96*, New Delhi: MKOHFW.

Ministry of Health and Family Welfare (1999), "Family Welfare Programme in India", Year Book, 1997-98, New Delhi: MKOHFW.

Ministry of Health and Family Welfare (2001). "Annual Report, 2000-01", New Delhi: MKOHFW.

Ministry of Health and Family Welfare (2007). "National Health Profile 2006", New Delhi: MKOHFW.

Ministry of Welfare, Government of India (1985). "Child in India: A Statistical Profile", New Delhi: Government of India.

Ministry of Welfare, Government of Jharkhand (2002-03). "Primitive Tribal Groups of Jharkhand Survey Report", Ranchi: Jharkhand Tribal Welfare Research Institute.

National Health Policy (2002). Ministry of Health and Family Welfare, Government of India, New Delhi.

Registrar General India, 2005: "Report No. 2 of 2005, Sample Registration System Statically Report 2003", New Delhi: Registrar General of India.

Registrar General of India (1988). *Child Mortality Estimates of India*, Occasional Paper No. 5 of 1988, Demography Division, Census of India, Ministry of Home Affairs, New Delhi.

Registrar General, India (2005). Census of India, 2001, Series 1, India, Primary Census Abstract, Scheduled Tribes: Table A-9", New Delhi: Registrar General of India.

Registrar General, India 2004a: "Report No.1 of 2004, Sample Registration System Statistical Report 2001", New Delhi: Registrar General of India.

Registrar General, India 2006: "Report No.1 of 2006, Sample Registration System Statistical Report 2004", New Delhi: Registrar General of India.

Registrar General, India, 2003: "SRS Analytical Studies Report No.4 of 2003, Below State Level Estimates of Vital Rates 1995-99", New Delhi: Registrar General of India.

Registrar General, India: 2007. "Report No.4 of 2007, Sample Registration System Statistical Report 2006", New Delhi: Registrar General of India.

Shihu Ao Team (1969). Report on Tribal Development Programmes.

U.N. (1994). International Conference on Population and Development (ICPD), Summary of the Programme of Action.

United Nations (1966). *Report on the Family Planning Program in India*, New York: United Nations.

United Nations (1969). *Evaluation of the Family Planning Programme in India,* New York: United Nations.

United Nations (1983). *Indirect Techniques for Demographic Estimation*, Manual X, Department of International Economic and Social Affairs, Population Studies, No. 81, New York.

United Nations Children Fund (2005). "The State of World's Children 2006; Excluded and Invisible", New York: UNICEF.

United Nations Children Fund (2006). "The State of World's Children 2007: Women and Children", New York: UNICEF.

United Nations Children's Fund (2007). *The State of the World's Children 2008*, New York: UNICEF.

United Nations Development Programme (2003). "Human Development Report 2003, Millennium Development Goals: A Compact among Nations to End Human Poverty", UNDP.

World Health Organization-UNICEF (1978). Alma-Ata 1978, Primary Health Care, Report of the International Conference on Primary Health Care, Alma-Ata, USSR, 6-12 September, 1978.

Index